RIGHT TO INFORMATION
VARIOUS DIMENSIONS

RIGHT TO INFORMATION

VARIOUS DIMENSIONS

DR. MANISH KUMAR CHAUBEY
LL.M, Ph.D. (LAW)

REGAL

REGAL PUBLICATIONS
New Delhi - 110 027

RIGHT TO INFORMATION
Various Dimensions

ISBN 978-81-8484-174-9

Typeset by
S.S. COMPOSERS
3190, Mohindra Park, Shakur Basti, Delhi-110034.

Printed in India at
MAYUR ENTERPRISES
WZ Plot No. 3, Gujjar Market, Tihar Village, New Delhi-110018.

Published by
REGAL PUBLICATIONS
F-159, Rajouri Garden, New Delhi-110 027.
Phone: +91-11-45546396
E-mail: regalbookspub@yahoo.com

समर्पित

''यह पुस्तक पूज्यनीय माता एवं पिता के चरण कमलों में सादर समर्पित।''

विजयदशमी

CONTENTS

PREFACE

The present book is designed for a broad audience. As a survey of textual materials about the Right to Information law, it will be useful to planners, reformers, policy makers, lawyers and people of wide range of interest. It will be useful to social scientists and scholars in other disciplines and general students too as a survey which includes references to numerous research studies. Hopefully, the numerous questions it implicitly raises and the resources it supplies will stimulate further research and thus contribute to the existent knowledge about the Right to Information.

It is a matter of great pleasure that **Prof. (Dr.) Jitendra Tiwari** who has been my teacher since I joined LL.B. agreed to supervise my Ph.D. and under his able direction I could complete my research work. He has been immensely helpful and generous in providing me study material and valuable thoughts, because of which this research could be done. For this support I feel really indebted and obliged.

I am sincerely thankful to my learned teachers of the Department of Law mainly Prof. Dr. G.S. Tewari, Prof. Amerendra Kumar Mishra (Head, Department of Law), Prof. Arvind Kumar Mishra, Dean Faculty of Law and Prof. Dr. R.K. Pathak who, too, have supported during my study.

I am also thankful to Prof. Jai Narayan Pandey, Prof. S.N. Mishra (Allahabad University), Prof. Dr. Anirudh Prashad and Dr. Mahendra Kumar Sharma (Reader), L.B.S. Degree College who assisted me with suggestions and materials from time to time. I am greatly indebted to them for their valuable and inspiring suggestions.

I am highly thankful to my parents **Shri Ram Awadh Chaubey** (Ex. DGC) and **Smt. Kamala Chaubey** for providing mental support during my study, they showered the blessings on me for my work. I must admit contributions of my wife Smt. Sunita Chaubey who has been a pillar of strength for me during my work and never entrusted any family responsibility to me.

I also address the support of my sister Bandita Chaturvedi her husband Shri D.N. Chaturvedi (*Dharmaguru Indian Army*) and my niece Pushpit Kashyap my younger sister Saumya Chaubey who is a LL.B. student and has helped me in sorting and compiling materials.

I am sincerely thankful to my friend Kanderpash Diwedi (*A.P.O.*), Vishnu Dev Singh, P.C.S (J), Pankaj Singh and Ashok Kumar who have helped me immensely at different levels. Moreover, I must admit the help of my Computer Operator Shri Santosh Kumar Tripathi who typed this work in this presentable manner.

Vijaya Dashmi DR. MANISH KUMAR CHAUBEY

ABBREVIATIONS

A.L.R.	Administrative Law Review
A.L.R.	Aligarh Law Review
A.I.R.	All India Reporter
A.C.	Appeal Cases
Art.	Article
A.P.I.O.	Assistant Public Information Officer
C.I.C.	Central Information Commission
C.P.I.O.	Central Public Information Officer
C.H.R.I.	Commonwealth Human Rights Initiative
C.E.R.C.	Consumer Education and Research Council
D.L.R.	Delhi Law Review
F.O.I.	Freedom of Information
I.J.P.A.	Indian Journal of Public Administration
I.L.R.	Indian Law Reporter
M.K.S.S.	Mazadoor Kisan Shakti Sangathan
N.C.P.R.I.	National Campaign for People's Right to Information
O.S.A.	Official Secrets Act
P.U.C.L.	People's Union for Civil Liberties
P.C.I.R.	Press Council of India Review
R.T.I.	Right to Information
S.C.	Supreme Court
S.C.C.	Supreme Court Cases
S.C.J.	Supreme Court Journal
i.e.	That is
U.O.I.	Union of India
U.N.D.P.	United Nations Development Programe
U.D.H.R.	Universal Declaration of Human Right
U.P.	Uttar Pradesh
V	Versus
VOL	Volume

TABLE OF CASES

S

T

U

CHAPTER

1

INTRODUCTION

The development and interrelation of Human being and social structure is closely associated with communication and information. Today we are precisely living in an information age and we are talking about Right to Information. This Right to Information has a long history of development. The position of this right has been different Ancient Indian holy literature shows that there was the recognition of right to information, though it was restricted. The information relating to governmental policies could not be obtained. On the other hand, there are certain instances in Buddhist literature showing that information was given to general public without being asked for that.

Literary personalities too have mentioned about Right to Information, Eminent literary personality. Ravindra Nath Tagore in his book "Gitanjalee" made an extensive reference to Right to Information.

Earlier our country was a colony of British empire. The British ruled here for a long time. So, it is required to know whether at the time of British rule there was Right to Information? By a thorough study of the then prevailing laws it is clear that Right to Information was almost absent at that time. Confidential information relating to government could not be obtained. There was an official secrets Act, which was a great barrier in the way of Right to Information. The press had played a significant role during the colonial rule. From Tilak to Gandhi, every leader who had mobilsed the people against colonial rule has used the press as a means of informing the people and educating them about liberal values. Tilak fought against the law of sedition, which as interpreted by the courts punished even an honest and non-violent criticism of the rulers in newspapers.[1] Gandhi insisted on the truth and ahimsa (non-violence) for India's struggle for independence and such struggle could succeed only if the people could speak freely and fearlessly. The entire Gandhian movement highlighted the value of freedom of speech.[2]

If we see the history of Right to Information in India we find that for the right a campaign was started under the leadership of **Aruna Roy**[3] in Rajasthan, which spread throughout India rapidly. Other than this our supreme Judiciary too gave recognition to this right as a fundamental right. This aspect also strengthened the campaign of Right to Information. Finally, we have before us an enactment named Right to Information Act, 2005.

Parliamentary democracy is a part of the basic structure of the constitution. Thus, such is the importance of the parliamentary democracy that it has been made immutable. At the same time fundamental right to receive information, which springs path from the right of freedom of speech and expression enshrined in Art. 19(1)(a), is also a part of the basic structure of the constitution. This right must be ensured to the citizens with reference to the elections as well. This right along with other fundamental rights constitute the core of our constitution, which will not acquire its full potential till the voter is posted with right information for making a right, choice which the **Vohra Committee**[4] *has brought out in its report.*

This is the new democrâtic culture of an open society towards every liberal democracy. Our country is no exception to this. The concept of a open government is the direct emanation guaranteed under Art. 19(1)(a), therefore, disclosure of information in regard to the functioning of government must be rule and secrecy on exception justified only where the strictest requirement of public interest so demands.[5] The approach of the court must be to attenuate the area of the secrecy as much as possible consistent with the requirement of public interest fearing in mind all the time that disclosure also serves an important aspect of public interest.[6]

This study traces developments regarding the Right to Information both in the social and legal spheres as well as demonstrating the relevance of the Right to Information to the entire spectrum of right. Development regarding the Right to Information has taken place at a number of levels and around many issues, all of which now complement each other in a forceful campaign of greater appears and transparency. Over the last five years in particular, move frequent interventions regarding transparency and access to information across a range of issues have brought it into sharp focus.

The phrase Freedom of information has itself become a subject to debate in India. Many local activities[7] and legal experts prefer to use the term 'Right to Information' as they see freedom as signifying more prohibition of government interference, whereas applying the term right imposes a positive duty on Government to disseminate information of the people.

Although 'information' in the current study refers primarily to information held by public authorities, strong arguments can be made to extent the scope of the term to certain kinds of information held by private parties. The Right to Information would then become a right to seek and recieved information from public authorities, as well as right to access certain kinds of information from private sectors.

The Right to Information has been derived from the democratic frame established by the Constitution and rests on the basic premise that since government is 'for the people', it should be open and accountable and should have nothing to conceal from the people it purports to represent. The importance of Right to Information lies in the functioning of administrating call for good governance and transparency in Administration.

The history of Right to Information law can be traced back to Sweden where in 1766, the parliament passed the Freedom of the Press Act, which required the disclosure of official documents upon request. Another country with a long history of Right to Information legislations is Columbia, whose 1988 Code of Political and Municipal Organization allowed individuals to request documents held by government agencies or in government archives. Recently many other European Countries have also passed law regarding openness of information. These Countries are Albania, Bosnia and Herzegovina and Bulgaria. The Czech

Republic, Georgia, Hungary having passed such laws recently in a number of other countries including Armenia, Macedonia, Montenegro, Poland, Romania and Serbia. There are moves to prepare or pass such legislation. In U.S.A. the Freedom of Information Act was enacted in 1966 followed by its statutory Cousin the Privacy Act in 1947 and the Sunshine Act, 1976.

In India Right to Information Act was passed in 12 May 2005. The State of Tamilnadu has become the flag bearer State to pass a Right to Information Act, 1997 and under the Act the Public has been provided a statutory right to know in details about the Schemes of the government. The Right to Information has been welcomed by the public and State government deserves a wide and profound appreciation. This legislation provides the right to the citizens to question and to known about the malfunction, irregularities in the system of governance.

Our Supreme Court recognized the concept of Right to Information.[8] A part from many Constitutional and legislative provisions regarding disclosure of information, the judiciary has also created many other provisions, which were not clearly stated in those provisions. For free and fair election of candidates, their back history and encouraged the citizen to cast their votes to their right choice.

NOTES AND REFERENCES

1. S.P. Sathe, 'Tilak's Philosophy of Law' in N.R. Inamdar (ed.) Political Thought and Leadership of Lokmanya Tilak, p. 119.
2. P.K. Tripathi, 'Free Speech in the Indian Constitution: Background and Prospect', 67, *Yale Law Journal*, p. 384 (1957-58).
3. Social Activists; related to M.K.S.S.
4. Vohra Committee Report, New Delhi.
5. Association for Democratic Reforms *v.* Union of India, AIR 2001 Delhi 126.
6. S.P. Gupta *v.* Union of India, AIR 1982 Supreme Court, p. 334.
7. Aruna Roy, Arvind Kejriwal, Subhash Chandra Agarwal, Anna Hazare.
8. State of U.P. *v.* Rajnarayan, AIR 1975 SC 865.

CHAPTER

2

GENERAL ASPECT AND HISTORICAL EVOLUTION OF RIGHT TO INFORMATION

I. INTRODUCTION

The development of mankind and society has been largely contributed by information achieved and delivered. Generation after generation there has been the chainwise flow of information which has resulted into the present structure of complex society. As we know that society is nothing but a complex net of human beings in a delivering certain set. This is a fact that the society revolves around information. The receiving and delivering of information give rise to strength in society and makes the bond stronger. For the purpose of clear understanding of the subject a chronological study is required.

So, the historical background of information can be traced back to the period of the evolution of mankind. In other words, it can be taken since time inamenouid. It is the information, whether in the form of knowledge or skill which paves the way for development. So, it is rightly understood that development and information go hand in hand.

Mere information cannot get transformed into wisdom unless certain intermediate processes are passed through. In that sense, information is a means, not the end. In short, freedom of information, challenging infallibility, had new applications and is relevant wherever the human search reaches. Therefore, we must affirm the writ of truth in every sphere of enquiry and from this age be hospitable to information without fear or favour.[1] The man, who finds truth, lights a torch. **Galileo's words are a concluding thought:**

> *"Since the Holy Writ is true, and all truth agrees with truth, the truth of Holy Writ cannot be contrary to the truth obtained by reason and experiment."*
>
> **—Galileo**

During the second half or the 20th century, the Right to Information globally became a powerful human rights movement. In most countries this right had been linked with the right to freedom and expression where only the press and media were enjoying the right. But the real value of this right was brought to the forefront by the civil society. What is the value of the right to information? To have an answer it requires understanding about the meaning of values. A clue is a belief that something is good and desirable differs from group to group, person to person, and society to society. It defines what is important, worthwhile and worth striving for. "A value is regarded as something that must be sustained and defended as an institution, a preferred course of action, or whatever" (International Encyclopedia of Sociology: 1473). The word "value" is developed from its original Latin root with its predominantly physical significance of strength, health efficiency to the more abstract concept of "merit" or "worth" (F.R. Cowel: 1970: 270). Hence the real value of the right to information signifies its worth, merit and strength in providing message, evidence and facts for the larger interest of the public. Its real value can be assessed after its successful implementation. This article will focus on the right to information movement in the backdrop of the major role played by civil society.[2]

The civil society's endeavour in ensuring good governance with the help of the right to information became a popular mass movement before it finally took shape as an Act by a historic legislation. It is expected that the Right to Information will herald a new era of governance, transparency and accountability. The

European Enlightenment and the French Revolution have left an indelible account on human thought, as the concept of right, liberty and equality became an instrument for the progress of modern society. The evolution of the human rights movement cannot ignore incidents like British Magna Carta (1215), French Declaration of Right of Man (1789), American Bill of Right (1789), and The Geneva Convention (1864). In the 17th century, the declarations of independence by all the North American countries from the British Empire have greatly influenced the concept of human rights. In recent years, there has been an unstoppable global trend towards recognition of the right to information by countries, inter-government organizations, civil society and the people. Good governance, free from corruption in public life and people's participation decision-making, etc. always have linkages with the involvement of civil society. The present form of Right to Information was not a product of several weeks or months; it took long struggles to finally have the Act. In ancient days very less information were saved which used to be of secret nature and directly affecting the war and foreign relation. Other information was shared with entire public. So that the man could be confident of the well being and show confidence in their ruler. The sharing of information was like confidence building measure between the rulers and the ruled. The logic is vided and easily understandable. So, the concept of right to information is very deep-rooted in our society by the way of religious and political practice.[3]

The right to know, to question, to dissent belong to every person whether the domain is political or religious, says Justice V.R. Krishna Iyer. Many other instruments, resolutions and learned reports like the Mac-Bride Report have integrated the trinity of freedom—of information, communication and expression—into the World Legal Order and Jurisprudence of Human Rights.

As discussed in earlier paragraph that information is the main stay of mankind and society, so there must be a right to gain access to information so it can be used favorably. Because if one is not aware of one's right, how can one's enjoy those rights and claim the compensation for the infringement of those rights. So it becomes very apt to have the right to information by which there can be profitable use of every information and skill.

2. MEANING OF RIGHT

There are many factors which contribute to the origin of right. In the field of law right is a fundamental concept. In the words of **B.A. Wortley,**[4] 'rights are recognized in any legal order. In a broad sense they originate in social life and aspirations, in daily living. Rights arise from the every nature of man as he is created, a social animal.' However, the concept of right, like many other concepts of law, does not carry one meaning and jurists differ about its exact connotation.[5] In its most general sense it means a reasonable expectation which in entertains. In its wider sense it is identified with the 'power', with 'privileges' and with 'immunity'.

According to **Roscoe Pound,**[6] 'as a noun right has been used in five senses. **One meaning** in interest-here it may mean (a) an interest one holds out to be recognised and secured or (b) it may mean the interest recognised, and delimited with respect to other recognised interests and secured. **A second meaning** is a recognised claim to acts or forbearances by another or all others in order to make the interest effective. **A third use** is to designate a capacity of creating, diverting or altering duties. In this sense right become power. **A fourth use** is to designate certain conditions of general or special non-interference with natural faculties of action. These are better called liberties and privileges. **In the fifth** sense the term 'right' is used as an adjective to mean that which accords with injustice or that which recognises and gives effect to moral right.'

In the 19th century various expressions were used for the word 'right'. Every right has two elements and definitions of right given by different jurists are mostly based on either one or the other element of rights. These two elements are viz., 'the material element of interest' like reputation, property, money, etc. and 'formal element' namely will, capacity, power to realise the interest, etc. Those who emphasis the formal element take the view that interest is not right, it is merely the object of a right. The will, capacity, power, faculty to realise the interest is in fact the right. Austin and Gray take the view that right is a faculty or power residing in a determinate party and parties.

Austin defines[7] right as 'a faculty which resides in a determinate party or parties by virtue of a given law and which availed against a party or parties, other than the party or parties in whom it resides'.

Gray observes that 'the right is not the interest itself; it is the means by which enjoyment of the interest is secured. It is the power to get the money from Balbus or the power to leave the room, not the payment of the money or the leaving of the room'.[8]

Professor Holland[9] had defined a right as follows:

> "When a man is said to have a right to as anything, or to be treated in a particular manner, what is meant is that public opinion would see him do the act, or make use of the thing, or be treated in that particular way, with approbation, or at least with acquiescence; but would reprobate the conduct of any one who would prevent him from doing the act or make use of the thing or should fail to treat him in this particular way."

Keeton defines[10] right as under:

> "A right, therefore, may be defined as the enjoyment of the interest which some individual or collection of individuals has in the performance of some act, or in some forbearance, either of himself or others based upon some factor other than the brute force of the individual or collection of individuals to perform or compel the performance of that act or forbearance towards the accomplishment of which the individual or collection of individuals has directed his or their mind."

An American realist Jurist **Oliver Wendell Holmes**[11] defines right as "nothing but a permission to exercise certain natural powers and upon certain conditions to obtain protection, restitution or compensation by the aid of public force." Thus, legal right is the power of removing or enforcing legal limitation on conduct.

In an important case ***Done* v. *State***[12] the Court has also realized the difficulty of explaining the concept of right Madras High Court has held that "The expression 'legal right' is a difficult concept." The Court further held that the 'legal right in its strict sense is one which is an ascertainable claim, unforeseeable before courts and administrative agencies; in its wider sense a legal right has to be understood as any advantage or benefit conferred upon a person by a rule of law'.

The Supreme Court has in ***State of Rajasthan v. Union of India***[13], observed: "In a strict sense, legal rights are correlative of legal duties and are defined as interests which the law protects by imposing corresponding duties on others. But in a generic sense, the word 'right' is used to mean an immunity from the legal power of another, immunity is exemption from the power of another. Immunity, is short, is no-subjection."

3. MEANING OF INFORMATION

'Information' as a term has been derived from the Latin words 'Formation' and 'Forma' which means giving shape to something and forming a pattern respectively? It adds something new to awareness. It enables one to assimilate on what we may

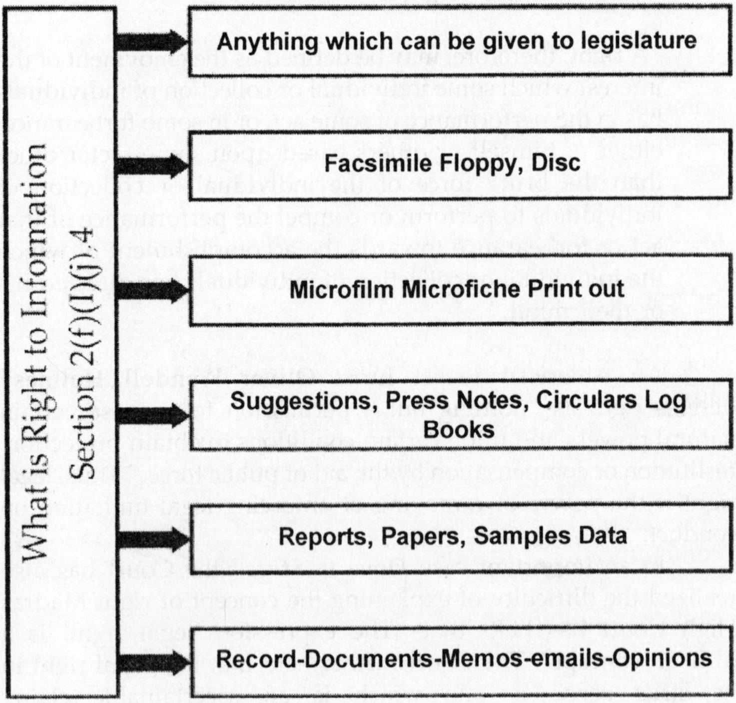

be conscious of but may not be aware of or to build on something new. Information is about 'democratization of communication'.

Literally 'information' means instruction or knowledge derived from an extended source concerning facts or particulars.

As per Oxford dictionary[14] 'information' means knowledge communicated or received concerning a particular fact or circumstance or knowledge gained through study communication research data, etc. It means information is knowledge communicated or received concerning a particular fact.

As per Webster's third new international and seven language dictionary,[15] "information means something received or obtained through informing as a (a) knowledge communicated by others or obtained from investigation, study or instruction or (b) knowledge of particular event or situation intelligence news, advices or (c) facts or figures or ready for communication or use as distinguished from those incorporated in a formally organized branch of knowledge. Here, information is a wider term, which includes knowledge from any source, other than those incorporated in formally organised branch of knowledge.

In the words of Corpus Juris Secondum,[16] Information is general means, "the acts of process of information, communication or reception of knowledge or intelligence, inspiration or animation, instruction intelligence's, also more specifically that which is received or obtained through information, training or discipline, knowledge communicated or received, knowledge of a special event situation or the like knowledge acquired, derived or inoculated as by observation or by reading or study or in conversation. Knowledge communicated by others or obtained by a personal study and investigation, knowledge derived from reading observation or instruction, hence advices, news, notice, particular, intelligence or report."

In law Lexicon[17] the term "information" means the acts or process of the informing communication, or reception of knowledge. It may be knowledge acquired directly as by observation or study or derived inferentially or from communication from others.

In the case of ***I.T. Commissioner* V. *Jagannath***[18] Apex Court said word 'information' is therefore synonymous with the knowledge or awareness in contradistinction to apprehension, suspicion or misgiving.

The Right to Information Act, (Act No. 22 of 2005) defines the term 'information'[19] as:

> "Information" means any material in any form, including records, documents, memos, e-mails, advices, press release, circulars, orders, logbooks, contracts, reports, papers, samples, models, data material held in any electronic form and information relating to any private body that can be accessed by a public authority under any other law for the time being in force.

The term 'information' here is broadly defined to include all kinds of information held by the state. The Act confers a right to "information" rather than just "records" or "documents." In keeping with best practice in some Indian States' Law, information has been broadly defined to permit the inspection of public works including taking samples of materials.

4. MEANING OF RIGHT TO INFORMATION

The phrase freedom of information has itself become a subject of debate in India. Many local activists and legal experts prefer to use the term right to information as they see freedom as signifying mere prohibition of Government interference, whereas applying the term right imposes a positive duty on the

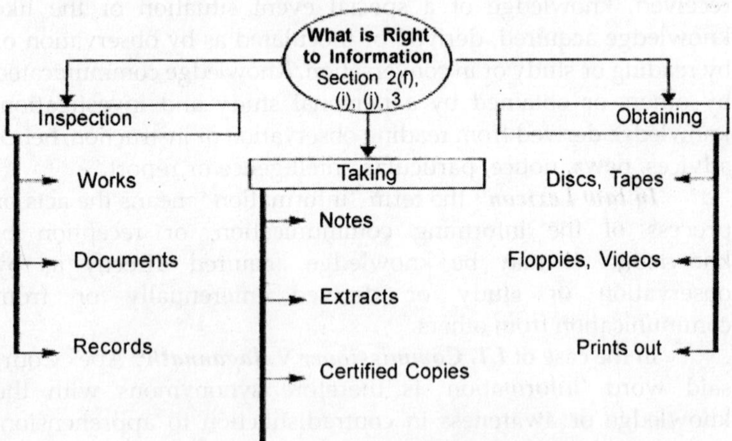

Government to disseminate information to the people. In the Indian Constitution, most of the freedoms enumerated in Article 19, which guarantees freedom of expression, require the State to refrain from interfering. A right, on the other hand, is understood in India as placing a positive duty on the State to take steps to ensure its fulfilment. **Modhav Godbole**, the erstwhile Union Home Secretary and Right to Information Activist, says in his critique on the Freedom of Information Bill, 2000, "Since the Bill makes it a point to talk only about freedom of information as opposed to right to information, it has lent itself to some clumsy construction ..... all citizens have a right to information."

Two aspects of the right to information are particularly important to the current debate:

(1) Information to which access must be given upon request; and
(2) Information which must be published and disseminated *suo motu* (operatively) by public authorities including information which would affect fundamental right such as food, environment and civil liberties. Particular emphasis is being paid to *suo motu* publication, given the background of illiteracy and poverty that prevails in most parts of the country.

The right to information derives from the democratic framework established by the Constitution and rests on the basic premise that since the Government is for the people, it should be open and accountable and should have nothing to conceal from the people it purports to represent. In this context, the following observation seems to sum up the philosophical basis of the right to information.

Right to Information as defined[20] under the Right to Information Act (Act No. 22 of 2005) means: "the right to information accessible this Act which is held by or under the control of any public authority and includes the right to—

(i) inspection of work, documents, records;
(ii) taking notes, extracts or certified copies of documents or records;
(iii) taking certified samples of materials; and

(iv) obtaining information in the form of diskettes, floppies, tapes, video cassettes or in any other electronic mode or through print outs where such information is stored in a computer or any other device.

According to this law, every citizen has a right to know how the Government is functioning. It empowers every citizen to seek any information from the Government, inspect any Government documents and seek certified photocopies thereof. This law also empowers citizens to inspect any Government work or to take sample of material used in any work. However, this right is not absolute. There are restrictions to this right as mentioned in Section 8(1), clauses (a) to (j) of the Right to Information Act, 2005. Further Section 9 lays down the grounds for rejection to access in certain basis.

5. WHY RIGHT TO INFORMATION IS RECOGNISED AS A RIGHT?

Right to Information is recognised as a right[21] because it:—

(1) Creates a duty-holder on the one hand and a beneficiary of a legal entitlement on the other. Non-disclosure of information is therefore a violation and the beneficiary can seek legal remedy.
(2) Distances it from being merely an administrative measure by which information is gifted by governments to their people at their discretion since a legally enforceable right cannot be narrowed or ignored at the whim of government.
(3) Sets a higher standard of accountability.
(4) Signal that information belongs to the public and not government. The idea that everything is secret unless there is a strong reason for releasing it is replaced by the idea that all information is available unless there are strong reasons for denying it. The onus is on the duty-holder to prove its case for refusing to disclose documents.
(5) Accords it sufficient importance, as being inherent to

democratic functioning and a pre-condition to good governance and the realisation of all other human rights.

(6) Becomes part of the accepted international obligations of the state. This means that the right to access information attracts the *guarantee of protection* by the state.

(7) Gives citizens the legal power to attack the legal and institutional impediments to openness and accountability that still dominate the operations of many governments. It moves the locus of control from the state to the citizen, reinstating the citizen as sovereign.

6. CONCEPTUAL HYPOTHESIS OF RIGHT TO INFORMATION

Underpinning the concept of Right to Information is the premise that information belongs to the people. The state has an obligation under international law to disclose information to them. Governments that ensure access to information for their citizens are simply fufiling that obligation and giving people their fundamental rights. Even though Right to Information should be given—it is not a voluntary matter in which governments decide whether or not to provide Right to Information—individual countries still need national Right to Information legislation to ensure their citizens can access information.

The design of Right to Information legislation greatly determines its impact. Over-restrictive laws, those with vague provisions, with lots of scope for exemptions, etc. will not deliver Right to Information in practice. There are a number of features which must be included in any Right to Information legislation if it is to be effective.[22]

(i) Right to Information legislation should spell out the goals it is trying to achieve, e.g. ensuring rights to citizens, promoting democracy, and so on. Spelling out these objectives will ensure Right to Information regimes are focused on ends rather than means: they serve as a reminder that Right to Information in place to help achieve something. A statement of principles lays out the underlying premise of Right to Information—that information belongs to the people and hence should be available to the maximum extent possible.

(ii) Right to Information legislation should stipulate that no justification or reason needs to be given when accessing information. Right to Information is a fundamental right and its use requires no explanations.

(iii) Right to Information legislation should be based on the premise that the maximum information relating to public bodies should be available to the citizens. That must be the starting point, and exceptions/restrictions reducing the amount of information available should be applied later. The sequence should not be *vice versa,* i.e. where governments start off with a blank sheet and add on information they are ready to make public.

(iv) Right to Information legislation should be applicable to all public bodies (including those providing public services, private bodies receiving public funds, any entity performing a public function...) and to all information held by them (organizational set-up and functions, reports, budgets...).

7. RIGHT TO INFORMATION AS A FUNDAMENTAL HUMAN RIGHT

Right to Information has been recognised as Fundamental Human Right. Lack of information denies people the opportunity to develop their potential to the fullest and realise the full range of their human rights. Individual personality, political and social identity and economic capability are all shaped by the information that is available to each person and to society at large. The practice of routinely holding information away from the public creates 'subjects' rather than 'citizens' and a violation of their rights. The right to access information underpins all other human rights. For example, Freedom of expression and thought inherently rely on the availability of adequate information to inform opinions. The realisation of the right to personal safety also requires that people have sufficient information to protect themselves.[23]

The right to food is also often reliant on the right to information. In India for example, people have used access laws to find out about their ration entitlements and to expose the fraudulent distribution of foodgrains.[24] The right to information is at the core of the human right system because it enables citizens to more meaningfully exercise their rights, assess when their rights are at risk and determine who is responsible for any violations.

8. PRINCIPLES OF RIGHT TO INFORMATION

The right of access to information is a fundamental human right crucial to the development of a democratic society. The Justice Initiative works with partner organization to promote implementation of these laws and to press for adoption of robust laws that entrench the Right to Information. To assist these efforts, the Justice Initiative has developed the following principles, in consultation with our partners, based on international law and standards and the comparative law and practice in these 68 countries. These principles represent evolving international standards on how governments should respect the Right to Know in law and practice.[25]

Principle-I

Access to information is a right of everyone.

Anyone may request information, regardless of nationality or profession. There should be no citizenship requirements and no need to justify why the information is being sought.

Principle-II

Access is the rule—secrecy is the exception!

All information held by government bodies is public in principle. Information can be withheld only for a narrow set of legitimate reasons set forth in international law and also codified in national law.

Principle-III

The right applies to all public bodies.

The public has a right to receive information in the possession of any institution funded by the public and private bodies performing public functions, such as water and electricity providers.

Principle-IV

Making requests should be simple, speedy, and free.

Making a request should be simple. The only requirement is to supply a name, address and description of the information sought. Requestors should be able to file requests in writing or orally. Information should be provided immediately or within a short timeframe. The cost should not be greater than the reproduction of documents.

Principle-V

Officials have a duty to assist requestors.

Public officials should assist requestors in making their requests. If a request is submitted to the wrong public body, officials should transfer the request to the appropriate body.

Principle-VI

Refusals must be justified.

Governments may only withhold information from public access if disclosure would cause demonstrable harm to legitimate interests, such as national security or privacy. These exceptions must be clearly and specifically defined by law. Any refusal must clearly state the reasons for withholding the information.

Principle-VII

The public interest takes precedence over secrecy.

Information must be released when the public interest outweighs any harm in releasing it. There is a strong presumption that information about threats to the environment, health, or human rights, and information revealing corruption, should be released, given the high public interest in such information.

Principle-VIII

Everyone has the right to appeal an adverse decision.

All requestors have the right to a prompt and effective judicial review of a public body's refusal or failure to disclose information.

Principle-IX

Public bodies should proactively publish core information.

Every public body should make readily available information about its functions and responsibilities, without need for a request. This information should be current, clear, and in plain language.

Principle-X

The right should be guaranteed by an independent body.

An independent agency, such as an ombudsperson or commissioner, should be established to review refusals, promote awareness, and advance the right to access information.

9. NEED OF RIGHT TO INFORMATION

Information is the currency that every citizen requires to participate in the life and governance of society. The greater the access of the citizen to information, the greater would be the responsiveness of the Government to community needs. Alternatively, the greater the restrictions that are placed or access, the greater the feelings of powerlessness and alienation. Without information, people cannot adequately exercise their rights and responsibilities as citizens or make informed choices. Government information is a national resource. Neither the particular Government of the day nor public officials create information for their own benefit. This information is generated for purpose related to the legitimate discharge of their duties of office, and for the service of the public for whose benefit the institutions of the Government exist, and who ultimately (through one kind of import or another) fund the institutions of the Government and the salaries of officials. It follows that the Government and officials are trustees of this information for the people. The net result of secrecy has been dismemberment of common people and their exclusion from processes which vitally affect their existence.[26]

Right to Information has four broad social purposes to serve:

(i) it helps an individual to attain self fulfilment,
(ii) it assists in the discovery of truth,
(iii) it strengthens the capacity of an individual in participating in decision-making, and
(iv) it provides a mechanism by which it would be possible to establish a reasonable balance between stability and social change. All members of society should be able to from their own beliefs and communicate them freely to others. In sum, the fundamental principle involved here is the peoples' right to know information. Freedom of speech and expression should, therefore received a generous support from all those who believed in the participation of people in the administration.[27] "The need for more openness as a aspect of democratic and effective governance has been accepted not only by International Organization like the World Bank, but also by private enterprise. A recent industry report on infrastructure development made a strong case for greater transparency."

In recent years, the historic lack of information on these and other matters has been mitigated by factors such as the growth of democratic values, the information revolution and the decentralization of governance through the Gram Panchayats, which are responsible for all of the issues.

Needs for the Right to Information can be discussed with regard to following topics.[28]

(i) Reduces Corruption

India has the dubious tag of being the eight-fifth most corrupt nations in a recently compiled list of 180 countries around the world. This is consistent with most people's everyday experiences; corruption in India is rampant, from the common clerk to the highest offices of the country. Big scams, for example, regarding defense deals, fodder procurement and sugar prices have frequently made the headlines. People even have to pay bribes to access basic information, such as their own electricity bills. The right to information is thus a potent tool for countering corruption and for exposing corrupt officials. Lack of transparency even when it is absent mining the government is unnecessary controversy and showing down reform.

(ii) Limiting Abuse of Discretion

Officials can abuse their discretion to suit various political or other vested interests, as well as to misappropriate funds. For instance, the power given to Collectors to allocate tribal land to non-tribal people or to convert agricultural land to non-agricultural land has been seriously misused all over the country. Since these are administrative matters, they tend to be hidden from disclosure, fostering abuse of power. While in theory it is possible to obtain a State High Court order to compel disclosure of this information, in practice, this is not possible for poor indigenous people or villagers, given the cost, distance and delays involved. The right to information is therefore important to check abuse of administrative discretion and to ensure fair process.

(iii) Protection of Civil Liberties

The right to information is also necessary for protecting civil liberties, for example, by making it easier for civil society groups to monitor wrongdoing such as encounter killings or the abuse of preventive detention legislation. The fact that the authorities regularly refuse to release information to civil society on such issues is indicative of the need for right to information legislation.

(iv) Knowledge of Various Dchemes

Food, shelter, livelihood and education, the most important aspects of a person's life, are provided in most rural areas through numerous schemes run by the Central or the State Government.

In most cases, people do not know about the existence of these schemes, or at least salient details, such as their entitlements under the scheme, paving the way for them to be tricked into accepting less than their allocation through forgery. Furthermore, records are often tampered with, a relatively simple practice because no one outside the tight-knit governmental circle has access to them.

(v) Participation

Participation in political and economic processes and the ability to make informed choices is restricted to small elite in India. Consultation on important policy matters, even when they directly concern the people, is rare. Even where consultation is mandatory, for example, under the Environment Protection Act, information sharing is limited, undermining the whole consultative process. Furthermore, reports pertaining to those consultations are difficult to access.

(vi) Knowledge of Laws and Policies

India has some very progressive legislations backed up by progressive court judgments, but these laws are often largely confined to the books and fail to be fully implemented they have not been effectively disseminated. For example, for years after the forest laws were put into place, few people understood the conditions they created on cutting down trees, leading to harassment and threats by local forest officials against villagers for cutting on their own land. In Madhya Pradesh, it was reported that any pink-coloured paper could be used to exploit indigenous people as they identify it as a penalty slip for violating forest laws.

(vii) Elixir for the Media

The need for the media to be able to access information is or crucial importance in India, as it is elsewhere in the world. The media provides a link between the people and their Government and acts as a vehicle of mobilization. This role is particularly important in India, where the media played a major role in the freedom struggle as well as during the period of internal emergency, when civil and political rights were suspended. The media's right to information is not a special privilege but rather an aspect of the public's right to know, which the media play a key role in ensuring. This view finds support in statements of the Supreme Court of India in cases involving claims of press freedom.

As rightly pointed out by Ralph Nader, "Information is the currency of democracy." We call this an age of information inevitable. India presents a mixed picture with much secrecy legislation still in place restricting the free flow of information, but at the same time some significant developments at State level in terms of promoting freedom of information laws, as well as draft national legislation. Unfortunately, the draft law presently being considered by the Central Government is woefully inadequate. It is essential that decision-makers fundamentally rework this draft, to ensure that legislation is passed which protects the public's right to know and promotes the free flow of information in India.[29]

(viii) Survival of Democracy

In a democracy, people are the masters. Government exists to serve them people have right to information how they being governed. Ours is a representative democracy. We elect our representatives who rule us. We, therefore, should have a Right to question them on what decisions they take on our behalf and why such decisions are being taken.[30]

10. IMPORTANCE OF RIGHT TO INFORMATION

'Without information, accountability will merely be the shadow of an idea lacking any substance.'[31]

Right to Information has many benefits. It facilitates public participation in public affairs by providing access to relevant information to the people who are them empowered to make inform choice and better exercise their democratic rights. Right to Information is a fundamental human right. As far back as 1946 the UN General Assembly passed a resolution recognizing this. It is guaranteed in Article 19 of the Universal Declaration of Human Rights.

The importance of information as an empowering tool is well explained by several traditional scripts and international associations. Information is basis for knowledge which provokes thought and without thinking process there is no expression. Freedom of expression is running theme of democratic governance. Information is oxygen for the democratic society. In a Foreword by the Director General of UNESCO to the Mac Bride Report titled "Many Voices, One World", the distinguished statement emphasizes that communication is at the heart of all social intercourse. Why, because in the words of the Director

General, *"It is essential that all men and women, in all social and cultural environments, should be given the opportunity of joining in the process of collective thinking thus initiated, for new ideas must be developed and more positive measures must be taken to shake off the prevailing inertia. With the coming of a new world communication order, each people must be able to learn from the others, while at the same time conveying to them its own understanding of its own condition and its own view of world affairs. Mankind will then have made a decisive step forward on the path to freedom democracy and fellowship."*[32]

Right to Information is important because it is fundamentally related to citizen empowerment, good governance and development. **Hursh Mander**[33] a government official and advocate of the Right to Information, has described the importance of this right as follows:

> *'Information is the currency of that every citizen requires to participate in the life and government of society. The greater the access of the citizen to information, the greater would be responsiveness of government to community needs. Alternatively, the greater the restrictions that are placed on access, the greater the feelings of 'powerlessness' and 'alienation.' Without information, people cannot adequately exercise their rights and responsibilities as citizens or make informed choice. Governmental information is a national resource. Neither the particular government of the day nor public officials creates information's for their own benefit, this information is generated for purposes related to the legitimate discharge of their duties of office, and for the service of the public for whose benefit the institutions of government exists, and who ultimately (through one kind of import or another) found the institutions of government and the salaries of officials. If follows that government and officials are 'trustees' of this information for the people.*

Right to Information is important because of following principles.[34]

(i) Promotes Transparency and Good Governance

Right to Information enables citizens to see how governments, those in public offices, are working. There is a presumption that all that the government does is for the well-being of the people—which means it is done to further the objective of public well-being, and is done honestly optimizing benefits of the funds being used. This presumption has however eroded to a great extent in the recent times to the misuse, misappropriation and careless use of public funds. Only making all public dealings transparent can check such things.

(ii) Promotes Accountability

Once citizens know what their government is doing they are in a position to hold those in office accountable for their decisions and actions. The same applies for designated oversight bodies such as parliamentary committees: they need information to be able to fufil their mandate.

In a democracy, those who manage the affair of the Society are supposed to be the trustees of the people and have to be accountable for their acts and omissions. The basic postulate of accountability is that the people should have information about the functions of government. It cannot be over emphasized that even from a conceptual standpoint, the public Right to Information is an indispensable prerequisite of democracy. To ensure such accountability, the people must have Right to Know about the policies, programmers, doing or misdoings of their representatives in the legislative and executive branches of administration.

(iii) Reduces Corruption

Secrecy and lack of information create a breeding ground for corruption and abuses of power. By promoting transparency and accountability Right to Information curbs such abuses.

(iv) Improves Service Delivery and Government Functioning

By making those in office accountable for their actions and by giving citizens a voice, Right to Information helps ensure the former work for the benefit of the latter. It thus promotes better planning and service delivery, i.e. improved education, health care....

(v) Promotes Access to Services/Entitlements

When citizens have access to information about service

delivery and other government functions, they know *what* they are entitled to and they know *how* and *where* to demand their right to those services and other benefits.

(vi) Promotes Political Participation

Citizens who understand public affairs and what government is doing can voice their opinion on issues that affect their lives: they can *participate* in the business of government. Right to Information facilitates citizens in making political and economic choices and thus strengthens democracy.

(vii) Strengthens Press Freedom

The media are sometimes referred to as the 'fourth pillar of the state'. They have an important role to play in keeping citizens informed, keeping those in office 'on their toes', highlighting issues of public interest, and so on. In order to be able to perform this role properly the media need access to information. Right to Information strengthens the media, and thus democracy;

(viii) Promotes Economic Growth

By promoting transparency and reducing corruption, Right to Information creates a rule-based environment in which, for example, information about business opportunities is equally accessible to everyone, contracts are awarded in an open and transparent manner, investor confidence is high....... Right to Information thus creates an environment conducive to investment and business.

In sum, Right to Information is an essential requisite for democracy, good governance development and poverty reduction.

11. HISTORICAL EVOLUTION OF RIGHT TO INFORMATION

(i) Right to Information in Ancient Indian Society

When we talk about Right to Information in ancient Indian society after the detailed study of different ancient mythological text we find that the scope and ambit of right to information was very restricted. Information regarding administration and governance could not be achieved. The ruler was told to conceal his policies. It was told that the king must do consultation at solitary place. Koutilya, an eminent ancient political thinker wrote that the king should commence his administrative work after consulting his ministers and the consultation must be made at such place which is solitary. So that even birds and animals could not hear because it was supposed that parrot and dogs could disclose the secret. The text in this regard is as under:

मन्त्रपूर्वा: सर्वारम्भा:।
तदुद्देश संवत: कथानामानेस्रावी पक्षिभिरनालोक्य: स्यात् ।
श्रूयते हि शुकसारिकाभिन्त्रो भिन्न: श्वभिरन्यैश्च तिर्यग्योनिभि: ।[35]

And conveying the same sense and meaning:

'नागकुलजन्मन: सारिकाश्रावित – मन्त्रस्यासीन्नाशो नागसेनस्य पद्मावत्याम् ।
शुकश्रुतरहस्यस्य च श्रीरशीर्यत श्रतवर्मण: श्रावस्त्याम्।'[36]

Manu,[37] Yagyawalkya,[38] Kamandak,[39] Agnipuran,[40] etc. have references of the fact that "No outsider could know the policies of the king but only those who had to enforce it and that too at an appropriate time only." We can have the reference of Manu[41] at this point:-

नास्य छिद्रं पर: पश्येच्छिद्रेषु परमन्वियात्।
गूहेत्कूर्म इवाङ्गानि रक्षेद्विवरमात्मन: ॥

There is a statement of Yagyawalkya[42] in this regard that "the state is dependent on mantra. So the king must keep his policy secret in such a way that the people may not be able to know about that unless the outcome of work is not conspicuous by itself."

Kautilya[43] has told the importance of Mantra "A stretched arrow can kill anyone or cannot kill any one but a plan by a learned person can mar that also which has just been sown.

एकं हन्यान्न वा हन्यादिणु: क्षिप्तो धानुष्मता ।
प्राज्ञेन तु मति: क्षिप्ता हन्याद् गर्भगतानपि ॥

Likewise in Ayodhya Kand,[44] we can find one thing that Mantra is the basis of victory.

मन्त्रो विजय मूलं हि राज्ञां भवति राघव ।

On the other hand when we glean through our ancient Indian texts as Vedas, Upanishad, Ramayana, Puranas, etc., regarding right to information, we find that there was the existence of Right to Information but in limited sense and in restricted aspect. In those days this right was confined to elete class of society as saints and hermits.

However, in certain texts of Buddha religion we find the evidence of the fact that the king used to disclose the information to his ruled or citizens. A learned thinker ***Shri Karpatriji Maharaj*** in his book **Vichar Piyush** : ***"Bharatiya Rajneete me Mahabharat"*** has given a useful example of this fact. Where the kings themselves explain and declare before their subjects different points relating to their policies and administration. The text is as under :

न मे स्तेनो जनपदे न कदर्यो न मद्यपः।
नाऽनाहिताग्निर्नाऽयज्वा मामकान्तरमाविण:।।
न च में ब्राह्मणो विद्वात्रावती नाप्यसोमपः।। (77.8 - 9)
न याचन्ते प्रयच्छन्ति सत्यधार्मविशारदाः।
नाध्यापयन्त्यधीयन्ते यजन्ते याजयन्ति न।।
ब्राह्मणान् परिरक्षन्ति संग्रामेण्वपलायिनः।
क्षत्रिया में स्वकर्मस्या मामकान्तरमाविशः।। (77.13 - 14)
न मे राण्ट्रे विधवा ब्रह्मबन्धुर्न ब्राह्मण: कितवो नोत चौरः।
अयाज्ययाणी न च पाककर्मा न मे भयं विद्यते राक्षसेभ्यः।। (77.26)

Same another text is as under Chandogupnishad[45]

न मे स्तेनो जनपदे न कदर्यो न मद्यपः।
नानाहिताग्निर्नाविद्वान्न स्वैरी स्वैरिणी कुत: (4/11/5)

So, generally it can be told that there existed the right to information though in defferent context.

(ii) Right to Information in Various Texts and Literature

We can find the origin of Right to Information in different ancient texts and literature of ancient poets. Famous Judge of the Supreme Court, V.R. Krishna Iyer very aptly finds the source of 'right to information' from Rig Veda, Bible and Rabindranath Tagore's famous poem.[46]

(a) Rig Veda on Right to Information

From the Rig Veda downwards the Indian heritage has been an eclectic university and cultural hospitality for creative ideas and educative information.

"Let noble thoughts come to us from every side."

(Rigveda, 1-891)

By this way The Ancient Indian epic Rig Veda also talk about Right to Information.

(b) Mahabharat on Right to Information

We can find the apt example of this in different slokas of Vth chapter of Mahabharta.

In these texts Naradji asked Information in different types of Government activities. He even asked about the Administration, defence and security matters. In detail[47] we can see these informations in the following way :

तुतोष च यथावच्च पूजां प्राप्य युधिष्ठिरात्।
सोऽचिंतः पाण्डवैः सर्वैर्महर्षिर्वेदपारगः।
धर्मकामार्थसंयुक्तं पप्रच्छेदं युधिष्ठिरम्।। 16।।
कच्चिदर्थाश्र कल्पन्ते धर्मे च रमते मनः।
सुखानि चानुभूयन्ते मन श्च न विहन्यते।। 17।।
कच्चिदाचरितं पूर्वैर्नरदेव पितामहैः।
वर्तसे वृत्तिमक्षुद्रां धर्मार्थसहितां त्रिषु ।। 18।।
कच्चित्रोग्रेण दण्डेन भृशमुद्विजसे प्रजाः।
राष्ट्रं तवानुशासन्ति मन्त्रिणो भरतर्षभ।। 45।।
कच्चित् पुरुषकारेण पुरुषः कर्म शोभयन्।
लभते मानमधिकं भूयो वा भक्तवेतनम्।। 53।।
कच्चिद् दारन्मनुष्याणां तवार्थे मृत्युमीयुषाम्।
व्यसनं चाभ्युपेतानां बिभर्षि भरतर्षभ।। 55।।
कच्चिच्चायव्यये युक्ताः सर्वे गणकलेखकाः।
अनुतिष्ठिन्ति पूर्वोन्हे नित्यमायं व्ययं तव ।। 73।।
कच्चिद् विदित्वा पुरुषानुत्तमाधममध्यमान्।
त्वं कर्मस्वनुरूपेषु नियोजयसि भारत ।। 75।।

कच्चिन्न चौरैर्लुब्धैर्वा कुमारैः स्त्रीबलेन वा।
त्वया वापीडयते राष्ट्रं कच्चित् तुष्टाः कृषीबलाः।। 77।।
कच्चिच्छूराः कृतप्रज्ञाः पञ्च पञ्च स्वनुष्ठिताः।
क्षेमं कुर्वन्ति संहत्य राज ञ्जनपदे तव ।। 81।।
कच्चिद् बलेनानुगताः समानि विषमाणि च।
पुराणि चौरान् निघ्नन्त श्चरन्ति विषये तव।। 83।।
कच्चित् ते सपफला वेदाः कच्चित् ते सपफलं धनम्।
कच्चित् ते सपफला दाराः कच्चित् ते सपफलं श्रुतम्।।
कच्चिदभ्यागता दूराद् वणिजो लाभकारणात्।
यथोक्तमवहार्यन्ते शुल्कं शुल्कोपजीविभिः ।। 115।।
कच्चित् ते पुरुषा राजन् पुरे राष्ट्रे च मानिताः।
उपानयन्ति पण्यानि उपधाभिरव ञ्चिताः।। 116।।
कच्चिदभ्यस्यते सम्यग् गृहे ते भरतर्षभ।
धनुर्वेदस्य सूत्रं वै यन्त्रसूत्रं च नागरम्।। 122।।
कच्चिदन्धां श्च मूकांश्च पङ्गान् व्यङ्गानवान्धवान्।
पितेव पासि धर्मज्ञ तथा प्रव्रजितानपि।। 125।।
षडनर्था महाराज कच्चित् ते पृष्ठतः कृताः।
निद्राऽऽलस्यं भयं क्रोधोऽमार्दवं दीर्घसूत्रता ।। 126।।

(c) Bible on Right to Information

We can find the glimps of Right to Information in these words of Bible.

> "And ye shall know the truth,
> *And the truth shall make you free."* ***(John-8:32)***

(d) Gitanjali on Right to Information

The philosophy which inspires the Indian people's hunger for freedom of information is best expressed in Verse XXXV of the ***Gitanjali*** by Rabindra Nath Tagore, who won noble prize for this poetry.

> *"Where the mind is without fear and the head is held high;*
> **Where knowledge is free;**
> Where the world has not been broken up into fragments by narrow domestic walls;

Where words come out from the depth of truth;
Where tireless striving stretches its arms towards perfection;
Where the clear stream of reason has not lost its way into the dreary desert sand of dead habit;
Where the mind is led forward by thee into ever-widening thought and action;
Into that Heaven of Freedom My Father, Let My Country Awake."

(e) *Famous poet Eliot on Right to Information*

In the following poem of Eliot there is seen the Right to Information:

"Where is the Life, we have lost in living?
Where is the Wisdom, we have lost in knowledge?
Where is the Knowledge, we have lost in information?

(iii) Right to Information in British Period

In Indian context the Right to Information is more or less new and contemporary in its present form. Certain old Indian literatures and epics directly or indirectly point towards this right, but today in complex society the Right to Information is more relevant and a mighty weapon for healthy functioning of democracy.

India became free after a long struggle for independence. Actually Indian independence struggle was against atrocities and oppressive laws of Englishmen and to keep them out of India. The Englishmen exploited the Indians with their heinious laws, which were there only for their convenience In those days freedom of speech and expression was very restricted. Though many Indian leaders made objection on the situation but in vain. There was censorship on press also and earlier permission was required to print any news. There was a vernacular press act which imposed censorship. In those days no common man could know the internal day-to-day happening of government and administration. The Englishmen had enacted an Official Secret Act by virtue of which they used to deny to give any information.

The Official Secrets Act, 1923

The Indian official Secrets Bill having been passed by the legislature received its assent on 2nd April, 1923. It came on the statute book as the Indian Official Secrets Act, 1923. Earlier in regard to the protection of official secrets in India the Indian Official Secrets Act, 1889 was enacted and it was amended by the Indian Official Secrets (Amendment) Act, 1904. Later, the Official Secrets Act, 1911, a British Act was brought into force in India. The provisions of the British Statute had, as a result of experience gained during the War, been considerably modified by the enactment of the Official Secrets Act, 1920, but the later Statute did not apply to British India. It had been recognised that it was unsatisfactory to have two separate laws in force simultaneously in India. Further, although the British Act, 1911 was in force in India, difficulties arose in applying it because of the use in it of English common law terms and so on. For these reasons it was felt desirable to enact a single consolidated Act applicable to Indian conditions. To achieve this objective the Official Secrets Bill was introduced in the Legislature. The position in regard to the protection of official secrets in India is briefly as follows: The provisions of the law which are now in force are : (a) An Act of the Legislature in India—The Indian Official Secrets Act, 1889, as amended by the Indian Official Secrets Act, 1911. The provisions the British Statute have, as a result of experience gained during the War, been considerably modified by the enactment of the Official Secrets Act, 1920, but the latter Statute does not apply to British India.[48]

In India, official secrets legislation is wide ranging. **Section 3** of the Act prohibits approaching, inspecting, passing over or entering in the vicinity of a prohibited place. Further, under the Act, it is also an offence to obtain, collect record, publish or communicate to any other person these items or any *"other document or information which calculated to be or might be or is interned to be, directly, useful to an enemy or which is likely to affect the sovereignty and integrity of Indian, the security of the State or friendly relations with Foreign State."* The basic premise of the Section is that even if the case against the accuse is not proved, *"his conduct or his known character as proved"* could create a presumption that his action was prejudicial to the safety or interest or the state. As in British courts, *"enemy"* has been interpreted to include *"potential enemy."* However, **Section 5** is the catch all provision. It relates to the wilful communication, uses, retention or failure to take reasonable care of all information which has been entrusted in confidence to him by any person which has been entrusted in confidence to him by any person holding office, or which he has obtained or which he has had access to owing to his position. Further, the voluntary reception, possession or control of any such information is also an offence, if there is knowledge or reasonable cause to believe that such information is communicated in contravention of the Act under Section 5(2) of the Act. Hence, this Section has been interpreted widely to cover, for example, budget leaks as was held in the landmark case of Nand Lal More. The most intriguing aspect of the Official Secrets Act is that there is very little case law reported on this statue. The efficacy of the status rests on its presence as a symbolic statement and a warning. The case of R.K. Karanjia was concerned with the legality of a forfeiture deposit on a newspaper, which asked information to leak official information to it. The legitimacy of the forfeiture deposit system was reinforced by references to the broad sweep of the Official Secrets Act. This approach was again affirmed in the *Budget Proposals* case, which held that a pre-publication leak of budget details to fall within the general *"catch all"* provisions of the Act.[49]

(iv) Right to Information After Independence

(I) Contribution of Government and Non-government Organisations in Right to Information Campaign

The Right to Information movement in India is basically an out come of gradual development. There has always been a demand for transparency and accountability in Indian context. Infact the demand became more frequent after independence and every section of society started taking about transparency in the works of governance and administration. Different Non-governmental organisations also started raising their voices at different times. These organisations have played a major role in right to information campaign. Precisely it were these groups who stated Right to Information movement. But as we must not forget that this movement has been given the tangible form by our governmental organisation. So, it is apt to say that the success of this movement is a collective effort of different governmental and non-governmental organisations a brief discussion of which is as under:

(A) Contribution of Governmental Organisation

Different government organisations made various attempts to achieve the right to information. Some important effort has also been undertaken by 'activist' bureaucrats. A key example is the initiative of the then Commissioner of Bilaspur Division[50] **Harsh Mander** who introduced a records maintenance and disclosed system, including through on the spot photocopying in key departments such as the Public Distribution System[51]. The impact of these simple steps soon become apparent when the ration shops, whose normal response has been 'no stocks available' started showing excesses because it was now difficult to siphon-off stocks. Pollution levels, which were required to be published daily, come down drastically in an area that is one of the most polluted in the country due to the multiple polluting industries.[52] The Right to Information is now a regular part of the training given to new civil servants at the Lal Bahadur Shastri National Academy of Administration, Mussorie. At the academic level the Right to Information has been supported by several civil servants, whose advocacy has lent credence to the issues raised by civil society groups and has helped to counter some of the standard challenges raised by bureaucrats. Regular and thorough analysis of draft laws by Dr. Madhava Godbole for instance has helped to refine and define the issues for civil society advocates as well as public at large.[53]

(i) The Press Council Draft

The Press Council of India headed by **Justice P.P. Sawant** presented a draft model law on Right to Information to the Government of India. This draft Bill was named Right to Information Bill, 1996. This draft was derived from an earlier one, which had been prepared in October 1995,[54] at a meeting of social activities, civil servants and lawyers at the Lal Bahadur Shastri National Academy of Administration, Mussorie.[55]

Importantly, the Press Council Draft affirmed in its preamble that the Right to Information is already protected under the Constitution as an aspect of the fundamental right to free speech and expression in line with a number of superior Court rulings, noted earlier. The Draft affirmed the right of every citizen to information from any public bodies. Significantly, the term 'publicbody' included not only the State, as defined in the Constitution[56], but also all privately owned undertakings, non-statutory authorities, companies and other non-state bodies whose activities affect the public interest.

(ii) Shourie Committee Draft

A working group on Right to Information and promotion of and open and Transparent government was set-up in January 1997 by the Minister of Personnel and Pensions Affairs to examine the feasibility and need either of a full-fledged Right to Information Act or its introduction in a phased manner to meet the need of open and responsive government. The group was also asked to consider amendments to various other relevant legislations, including the Official Secrets Act and to examine the framework of rules with particular references to the existing conduct Rules and Manual of Office Procedure. The working group was chaired by H.D. Shourie and included former Attorney General Soli J. Sorabjee and other officers of the concerned ministries and public undertakings with large public interface.[57] The working group submitted its report in May 1997 and it was circulated in the Conference of Chief Ministers held on May 25 1997. There were broad consensus in support of a legislation for Freedom of Information in the Conference. The decision taken in the Conference is reflected in para 7.2 of the Conference which read as follows:[58]

> "The Government of India would take immediate necessary steps, in consultation with State Governments, for examining the report of the working group on Right to Information, and for introducing in Parliament before the end of 1997 a legislation for Freedom of Information and amendments to the relevant provisions of the Official Secrets Act 1923 and the Indian Evidence Act. Endorsing the proposals made in the Action Plan, some of the State Governments indicated the need to include provisions which would ensure that the misuse of provisions do not lead to embarrassment of the governments, while, some of

the State have already initiated steps to provide the Right to Information, others would also undertake a similar exercise."

In pursuance of this decision, the Government of India have invited the State Governments on the report of the Working Group and the Freedom of Information drafted by the Working Group.

(B) Contribution of Non-governmental Organisations

The newspapermen have been agitating for the right of access to official information from the very birth of the modern Press in India. That was a little over 200-year age when the British East India Company was struggling to establish its supremacy over our country. The company regime resisted the journalist's demand by every means possible. Communication of information to the general public being newspaperman's their main business, they had to seek and obtain information from the authorities. They had little opinion but to wage a battle against secrecy at great suffusing and sacrifice to themselves occasionally at the cost of many a valuable life.[59]

The fact remains that the demand of Press for free flow of information form the government and other public authorities to the general public through the medium of the news papers has gone on ever since, but official resistance to it continued even after 50 years of independence. Successive government in Independent India has fought against the demand for free flow of official information as doggedly as the colonial rulers did. It is only during the last decade or so that some light was visible at the end of the tunnel. This time around other social groups notably the jurists Non-Governmental Organizations, intelligentia, and some parliamentarians—joined hands with the Press. All of them have started demanding the outright repeal of the Official Secrets Act and its replacement by the legislation making a duty to disclose the norm and secrecy the exception. But the Official resistance to these demands has only highlighted the need for legal enforcement of the Right to Information.

(i) Consumer Education Research Council Draft

To propose a law at national level, a draft Right to

Information law was proposed by the Consumer Education and research Council, Ahmedabad in 1993. This draft, in link with international standards gives the Right to Information to anyone except "alien enemies" whether or not they are citizen. It requires public agencies at the federal and State levels to maintain their records in good order, to provide a directory of all records under their control, to promote the computerization of records in interconnected networks, and to publish all laws, regulations, guidelines, circulars related to or issued by government department and any information concerning welfare schemes.

Requests are liable only for the cost of supplying copies of records, with fees being waived for journalists, newspapers' organistions and public interest groups. The Consumer Education Research Committee draft contains a class exception for Cabinet document but documents relating to security, defense, international relations and economic and commercial affairs are subject to a "grave and significant damage test." There are also exceptions for personal information in the interest of privacy and the research activities of voluntary organizations if disclosure would undermine their functioning or result in "grave and significant damage" to another person, Records relation to the international deliberative processes of government—the one exception being the Cabinet documents and Centre-State relations are not excepted under the Consumer Education Research Committee draft. The draft also provides for the outright repeal of the Official Secret Act, but does not provide specific protection for whistleblowers. Finally, the CERC draft provides for an appeal against refusals to disclose information first to a network of independent information, commissioners at the national state and districts levels and then to and information tribunal.[60] The draft was introduced as a private member's Bill in Parliament, but was never taken up for discussion.

(ii) Role of People in National Campaign of Right to Information

Right to Information began to receive attention only when people's group began to work in rural India. Through grassroots mobilization, building coalitions and strong advocacy, it exerted pressure on government to bring about Right to Information legislation. The national campaign for a people's Right to Information was formed as a support group for the MKSS and also to carry out advocacy on the Right to Information at the national level. The presence in the NCPRI of senior and respected medial persons, serving and retired bureaucrats and members of the Bar and Bench make it an important nodal body. Members like ***Prabhash Joshi,*** one of the India's most senior journalists have been publicising the issue through their writing and travelling around the country.

The National Campaign also brought out a journal, 'Transparency' which was very useful for campaigning and networking purposes, but which has been discontinued for the time being of want of funds. Member of the National Campaign on People's Right to Information have also made submissions on the Freedom of Information Bill, 2000 to the Standing Committee.

(iii) Progressive Politicians and Right to Information

For the first time, among the politicians of India, in 1990, Mr. V.P. Singh, the then Prime Minister of the Country headed by National Front Government stressed on the importance of Right to Information Act as a legislated right. Due to lack of political supports and will the right to information Act was not materialized during V.P. Singh period. The freedom movement, the Constitution of India, Supreme Court and some of the politicians supported for the right to information, but not materialized due to various reasons like policy support, institutional arrangements, etc.

(iv) Role of National Campaign for People's Right to Information (NCPRI)

The National Campaign for people's Right to Information (NCPRI) was founded in 1996. The NCPRI is a non-registered group that is managed according to a constitution. Its funding members included social activists, Journalists, lawyers, retired civil servants and academics and one of its primary objectives was to campaign for a national law faculties the exercise of the fundamental Right to Information. As a first step the NCPRI and the Press Council of India formulated an initial draft of a Right to Information law. This draft after extensive discussions, was send to the government of India in 1966. The government finally introduced the Freedom of Information Bill in parliament, in 2002. This was a very watered down version of the Bill first drafted by the NCPRI and others in 1996. In August 2004 the NCPRI forwarded to the National Advisory Council a set of suggested amendments to the Freedom of Information Act, 2002. These amendments, designed to strengthen and make more effective the 2002 Act, were bused on extensive discussions with Civil Society groups working on transparency and other related issues and were in response to the undertaking given by the UPA government, in their Common Minimum Programme, that the "Right to Information Act will be made more progressive, participatory and meaningful."

The NCA included most of the suggested amendments and recommended them to the Prime Minister of India for further action. These formed the basis of the subsequent Right to Information Bill, introduced in Parliament on 22 December 2004.

However, this bill, as introduced in Parliament, had many weaknesses. Most significantly, unlike the NCPRI suggestion, it did not apply to the whole country but only to the Union Government. The consequent outrage from civil society groups, including the NCPRI, forced the government to review the changes. The Bill was referred to Standing Committee of the Parliament and to a Group of Ministers. The standing committee asked several of the NCPRI members to give evidence before it, and ultimately endorsed the stand taken by the NCPRI in most matters. In the next session of Parliament, the bill was passed after over a hundred amendments introduced by the government to accommodate the recommendations of the Parliamentary Committee and the Group of Ministers. Most important, the jurisdiction of the Bill has been extended to cover the whole of India. The Right to Information Act has come into effect all over India from 13 October 2005.

Only 11 of 54 Commonwealth Nations—Australia, Belize, Canada, India, Jamaica, New Zealand, Pakistan, South Africa, Trinidad and Tabago, the United Kingdom and Zimbabwe—have passed legislation guaranteeing the Right to Information.

(v) Commonwealth Human Right Initiative Campaign

The Commonwealth Human Right Initiative Campaign views the Right to Information as providing a basic links between various human rights and promotes that perspective in its advocacy work. It has also conducted a number of workshops and other smaller meetings, mostly at the regional level but also nationally[61] and internationally[62].

Commonwealth Human Right Initiative has also been involved in governmental initiatives on the Right to Information in the State of Madhya Pradesh, Delhi, Rajasthan as well as with the central government. Commonwealth Human Right Initiative has brought together people doing advocacy work at all levels and has forged links between areas working at different levels both within civil society as well as within government.

(vi) *Mazdoor Kisan Shakti Sangathan Movement (MKSS)*

This perspective of the right to information demand formulated initially by members of the Mazdoor Kisan Shakti Sangathan (MKSS) is indeed a story of the extraordinary efforts of ordinary people. A combination of their clarity of thought and purpose and their instinctive understanding of the problems they faced in their lives has led to simple and straightforward translations of their ideas into practice. The MKSS is a non-party political organization of poor farmers and workers, men and women alike, many of whom have never been to school. Yet, their efforts have not only raised the issue of RTI in such a potent manner, it has also changed the discourse on what had been seen for many years as a largely academic issue. It was also in the course of a battle for the payment of the statutory minimum wage under government-sponsored public works programmes that the group first understood the significance of transparency and the right to information.[63]

Every time the workers asked to be paid the minimum wage, they were told that they had not done the work, a claim that, they were also told, was based on records. When the MKSS demanded to see the records, the reply was that these were government accounts and therefore secret. And so it was that a simple demand for minimum wages which became a fight for the right to information. Those who descended upon Beawar in April 1996 were even astute enough to time the dharna with the campaign period of that year's national parliamentary election. Citizens were offered a small glimmer of hope to break out of the vicious cycle that was Indian politics, which forced them to choose among undeserving candidates. For a change, during that election campaign in Beawar, democracy was being debated and redefined. Those taking part in the dharna began to drive home the point that by using the right collectively and individually to ask questions and demand answers, citizens could begin to shift the control from the ruling elite to the people. It was a first step towards participatory governance, where the disadvantaged and the dispossessed could establish their right to livelihood and, in a democracy, effectively to govern themselves. The poor started to see that they had to be involved in the Right to Information campaign because it was an issue connected intrinsically to their livelihood and survival. One of the slogans born during the struggle is self-explanatory: *'The Right to Know, The Right to Live.*

Journalist Nikhil Chakravarty, who came to beware during the dharna, said in a speech that the struggle was like a second battle for independence. Leaders of the independence movement, he said, exposed how the riches of the people were looted by foreign rulers. This struggle, said Chakravarty, showed the way to uncover how the people's own homegrown rulers were now robbing them. These were dramatic words, especially for a small struggle in such a huge country. But what had apparently drawn Chakravarty's attention was the movement's potential to allow ordinary citizens to address many of the fundamental shortcomings of parliamentary democracy as practiced in India. The demand was not to do away with democracy but to create opportunities for more meaningful and appropriate democratic practice.[64]

It is clear to many activists and citizens that democracy itself is being hijacked in India. Most critical to this development has been the continued separation of the rulers from the people. Internal accountability in India, is only of the rules to each other. For decades, regular sops have been handed out in the form of half-hearted land reform, 'poverty alleviation', public distribution measures, reservations, statehood, lip service to education and health—the list is endless. The present demands of India's citizens, however, are no longer for a particular concession, but for a share of governance itself. The right to information movement has grown to be an important part of this demand.[65]

But there has been another aspect to the Right to Information struggle that has allowed for its organic growth. To be sure, the right to access government records was an assertion of many democratic principles and a claim on a share of governance.

Public Hearing is the Genesis of Right to Information Movement

Public Hearing or *Jan Sunwais* is the origin point of the Right to Information Movement in India. The instrument of public hearing was initiated by the MKSS in some parts of rural areas of Rajasthan. In order to check the corruption with the involvement of the people the public hearing was begun. The public hearing is nothing but an open and democratic debate about the public issues. In this type of public hearings Elected Representatives, Government Officials, People, Local Intelligentsia such as lawyers, media persons, Non-Governmental Organisations, Community Based Organisations, External Observers, etc. will participate. The public hearings are being conducted in Panchayati Raj Institutions, Government Offices and Non-Governmental Organisations, which are receiving the substantial financial support from the public authorities. In these public hearings in front of the public it is proved that a great deal of corruption and misuse is taking place. It was happened due to secrecy in the maintenance of records and registers and lock of accessibility to the public information for the citizens.

(vii) Parivarthan (N.G.O.) in Delhi State

Parivarthan a NGO working in the urban slums of Delhi on awareness building on Right to Information Act and using RTI as the potential instrument for transparent delivery of services like Public Distribution System, infrastructure such as public roads and buildings and electoral reforms. The Parivarthan also used the right to information in conducting the social audit in the urban areas on spending or the public investment. Parivarthan being a part of the National Campaign for People's Right to Information put consistent effort for the National Right to Information.

(v) Role of Legislative Institutions in Right to Information Campaign

The campaign for Right to Information, which was being run by the people of civilized society for the protection of their right and interest; was at last accepted by legislature after a long struggle and gap. The legislature could not oversee the mass movement regarding Right to Information. The legislature tried to give an arranged and tangible from time to the Right to Information movement due to mounting pressure of society for the building of healthy democracy. And because of this act different times the legislature made numerous attempts and finally we have before us an enactment which is Right to Infirmation Act, 2005.

Earlier in the Chief Ministers' **Conference on Effective and Responsive Government** held on May 24, 1997, it was realized that the citizens' freedom to access information is an important means to achieve accountable, transparent and participatory government. The Conference adopted an Action Plan to take initiatives in the following three areas:

(i) Making administration accountable and citizen-friendly.
(ii) Ensuring transparency and right to information.
(iii) Taking measures to motivate civil services.

Thus the Action Plan included, among others, ensuring right to information. It called for amending laws that stipulate unnecessary restrictions on the free access of the public to information. Following the adoption of an Action Plan, efforts to legislate for the right to information, at both the State and National level, quickened. Even before the Government of India drafted its Bill, a significant pro-active step was taken in 1999 by the then Union Minister for Urban Development. He issued an administrative order empowering citizens to inspect and receive photocopies of any file in his ministry. Disappointingly, the Cabinet Secretary did not permit this order to come into effect. This prompted the Centre for Public Interest Litigation and Common Cause to file a writ petition in the Supreme Court seeking relief that: (1) that the Cabinet Secretary's restraint on order be declared unconstitutional and violative of the citizens' right to information; (2) that section 5 of the Official Secrets Act, which makes it an offence for a public servant to disclose any information that has come to his knowledge in his official capacity, be declared unconstitutional; 3) that the Government of India be directed to frame and issue suitable administrative instructions on the subject.[66]

Eventually, the Shourie Committee draft law was reworked into the Freedom of Information Bill, 2000. This was less satisfactory Bill than what was given by the Shourie Committee.

The Freedom of Information Bill was finally introduced in the Parliament in 2000. The Bill remained pending for about two years. During this time it was referred to a Parliamentary Standing Committee. The report of the Committee was presented to both houses in July 2001. It recommended that the Government should address the flaws in the draft Bill. Unfortunately, the Government did not implement the recommendation, to the detriment of the final content of the Bill. However, the ***Freedom of Information law was passed in 2002*** (in Lok Sabha on December 3, 2002 and in Rajya Sabha on December 16, 2002) after a long debate. But even before the Central Act was passed some of the States introduced their own RTI legislation. The first amongst these was **Tamil Nadu** (1997), **Delhi** (2001), **Maharashtra** (2002), **Assam** (2002), **Madhya Pradesh** (2003) and **Jammu and Kashmir** (2004). It is only with constant efforts that the revised Bill on Right to Information was reintroduced and was passed on 11th May, 2005 in Rajya Sabha on 12th May, 2005 in Lok Sabha. It received assent of the President on 15th June, 2005 and was published in the Gazette of India on 21st June, 2005. This new Act applies uniformly to all the States except the State of Jammu and Kashmir and makes all other state laws redundant. ***The Right to Information Act, 2005*** is a milestone in India's progress as the biggest democracy in the world.[67]

(vi) Contribution of Indian Judiciary

Our Indian Judiciary has hugely contributed to the movement of Right to Information be it directly or indirectly. Infact, it is the judiciary which works as an enforcement mechanism for Right to Information. After Independence our apex court has immussely helped this movement by giving various landmark judgements in favour of Right to Information. Right to Information is implicit in the constitution of India, which establishes a representative democracy with inalienable right for the citizens of the country, which have been reinforced time and again by judiciary. Right to Information in India has significantly sought to expand democratic space and empower the citizens to exercise more control on the corrupt practices under the power of the state.

The movement for Right to Information can be traced back to the grassroots struggle of the rural poor, who have sought to fight against corruption in their areas affecting their livelihood and justice around them. The Right to Information got the legal support for the first time in 1975 in Supreme Court case of ***State of U.P. v. Raj Narain***[68] (1975) in which **Mr. Justice Mathew** gave a landmark judgment, "In a government of responsibility like ours, where all the agents of public must be responsible for their conduct, there can be but few secrets. The people of this country have a right to know, every public act, every thing that is done in a public way by the public functionaries. They are entitled to know, the particulars of every public transaction in all its bearing. Their right to know, which is derived from the concept of freedom of speech, though not absolute, is a factor, which should make one wary when secrecy is claimed for transactions which can at any rate have no repercussion on public security."[69]

In the year of 1981 Right to Information matured to the status of a constitutional Right in the famous case of Supreme Court of ***S.P. Gupta* v. *Union of India.***[70] In this case our Supreme Court applied the Rule of generous interpretation of the guarantee of freedom of speech and expression elevated the Right to know and Right to access to Information to the status of fundamental right. In this case ***Justice Bhagwati*** said. The concept of open government is the direct emanation from the right to know which seems to implicit in the right of free speech and expression guaranteed under Article 19(1)(a)."[71]

12. HISTORICAL EVOLUTION OF RIGHT TO INFORMATION AROUND THE WORLD

The Right to Information has become a rampant phenomenon these days. This concept as a right is not confined to any single countries but it has spread to almost every democrat countries. Many country of the world are incorporating this right in their governance in one form or the other. At universal level, almost more than 85 countries[72] have accepted this right to information in their state laws by making legislation.

Historically, the right to access information held by the state has evolved from administrative law, which attempts to redress the imbalance of power between the individual and the state; James Michel explains these developments in the following terms[73].

Mostly statutes regarding freedom of information have evolved from administrative law. They reveal that first established basic rule that government is subject to law and that citizens have right to take legal actions against the state for beaches of the law and duties. A consequence of such a right that citizens have legally enforceable right to access to receive the information from the government that are relevant to their claims.

(i) Some Countries with Existing Legislation

1. *Albania*

Right to Information is a part of Albania Constitution. Article 23 of the 1998 constitution states:

1. The Right to Information is guaranteed.
2. Every one has the right, in compliance with law, to get information about the activity of state organs, as well as of person who exercise state functions.
3. Every body is given the possibility to follow the meeting of collectively elected organs.[74]

The Right to Information for official documents law was enacted in June 1999[75]. The law allows all persons to request information contained in official documents.

2. *Australia*

The Federal Freedom of Information Act provides for access to documents help by the Commonwealth agencies. The Act requires that agencies respond in thirty days. In Australia, the Freedom of Information Act was enacted in December 1982. It gave citizens more access to the Federal Government's documents. With this, manuals used for making decisions were also made available. But in Australia, the right is curtailed where an agency can establish that non-disclosure is necessary for protection of essential public interest and private and business affairs of a person about whom information is sought.[76]

3. *Bangladesh*

On October 21, 2008, the Caretaker Government of Bangladesh issued in the Bangladesh Gazette the Right to

Information Ordinance (No. 50 of 2008), based loosely on the Indian Right to Information Act, 2005[77]. The Ordinance is in effect until approved or withdrawn by the next elected Parliament.

4. *Canada*

The Access to Information Act, 1983 provides Canadian citizens and other permanent residents and corporations in Canada the right to apply for and obtain copies of record held by the government institutions. The institutions must reply is fifteen days.[78]

5. *China*

In April 2007, the State Council of the People's Republic of China promulgated the "Regulations of the People's Republic of China of Open Government Information", which came into effect on May 1, 2009[79]. However, the law has done very little to provide information on many of the Chinese government's practices.

6. *France*

The French law on access to administrative document was approved in July 1978 and has been enforce since December 1978. The 1978 law provides for a right to access administrative documents held by public bodies.[80]

The French Data Processing and Literties Act, 1978 apples to private organization changed by the state with operating public services. The 1978 Data Protection Act acts is in conjunction with the access law and allows individuals to obtain files that contain personal information about themselves and private bodies.

7. *Georgia*

The Constitution of Georgia includes two provisions specifying a right to access to information[81] Article 37(5). Individuals have a Right to get objective and timely information on their working and living conditions.

8. *Hong Kong*

In Hong Kong there are no laws specifically enacted to guarantee the freedom of information.

Since March 1995, the Government of Hong Kong has promulgated a "Code on Access to Information" to serve a similar purpose. This code, like other internal regulations of the Government, was not legislated by the Legislative Council and has minimal legal status. It requires government agencies listed in its appendix to appoint Access to Information Officers to answer citizens' requests for government records. A fee may be charged prior to the release of information.[82]

9. *Japan*

In Japan after twenty years of efforts, the law Concerning Access to Information held by Administrative Organs[83] was approved by the Diet in 1999 and came into effect from April 2001. The law allows any individual or company, Japanese or foreign to request administrative documents held by administrative agencies in printed or electronic form. The NGO Information Clearing house Japan founded in 1999 played an important role in pushing through this legislation. The Citizen's Movement for a Freedom of Information law, founded in 1980, is the parent organization of ICJ. The movement brought the Right to Information issue on the political agenda.

10. *Netherlands*

The Netherland Government Information (Public Access) Act[84] was adopted in 1991. Under the Act, any person can demand information related to an administrative matter if these are contained in documents held by public authorities and companies carrying out work for a public authority. The authority has two weeks to respond. Recommendations of advisory committees must be made public within four weeks.

11. *New Zealand*

Section 14 of the Bill of Rights Act states, "Everyone has the right to information of expression, including the freedom to seek, receive, and impart information and opinions of any kind in any form,[85] The Official Information Act, 1982 starts form the principle that all official information should be available.[86] Any resident or citizen or company in New Zealand can demand official information held by public bodies, state-owned enterprises and bodies which carry out public functions. Agencies have been required in some cases to take down notes of discussions that contributed to government decision-making if no documents are available. The body has no more than twenty days to respond.

12. Pakistan

Pakistan was first country in South Asia to pass Freedom of Information legislation in the 2002 Freedom of Information ordinance. Recently on 29th March 2008 Prime Minister ***Yusuf Raza Gilani*** announced that the new government, as part of its first 100 days programme; would present new Freedom of Information legislation and repeal the 2002 ordinance.

13. Poland

Article 61 of the Constitution of Poland provides for the right to information and mandates that Parliament enact a law setting out this right.

(1) A citizen shall have the right to obtain information on the activities of organs of public authority as well as persons discharging public functions. Such right shall also include receipt of information on the activities of self-governing economic or professional organs and other persons or organizational units relating to the field in which they perform the duties of public authorities and manage communal assets or property of the State Treasury.

(2) The right to obtain information shall ensure access to documents and entry to sittings of collective organs of public authority formed by universal elections, with the opportunity to make sound and visual recordings.

(3) Limitations upon the rights referred to in Paragraphs (1) and (2), may be imposed by statute solely to protect freedoms and right of other persons and economic subjects, public order, security or important economic interests of the State.

The Poland Parliament approved the Act on Access to Public Information in September 2001. It went into effect in January 2002.[87]

14. Slovakia

Constitution of the Slovak Republic[88] 1992 provides for a general right of access to information and a specific right of access to environmental information.

15. South Africa

South Africa Constitution contains an express guarantee of access to information, and is, one of the very few countries in the world, which, at the constitutional level. Article 32 of the South African constitution 1966 states that,

(1) Every one has a right to access to—
  (a) any information held by state; and
  (b) any information that is held by another person that is required for the exercise or protection or right.

(2) National legislation must be enacted to give effect to this right and may provide for reasonable measures to alleviate the financial and administrative burden of the state.[89]

The promotion of access to information Act was approved in parliament in 2000 and come in to enforce in 2001.[90] The South African Freedom of Information legislation is unique in that it allows access to information held by all private as well as public bodies. The inclusion of private bodies had much to do with active civil society participation in drafting legislation.

South Africa's Freedom of Information legislation emerged in the aftermath of the apartheid era and was designed in part to allow citizens access to information about that era—and also to mark a clear break from the highly secretive government of that time. While the Interim Constitution of 1994 provided for access to information from government/all public bodies, civil society activism led to this being expanded in the final 1996 Constitution to include: 'any information that is held by another person and is required for the exercise or protection of any right'.

Legislation to this effect, the Promotion of Access to Information Act, was finally passed in January 2000 after a six-year process during which many changes were made in the original bill, the Open Democracy Act. Civil society involvement in this legislative process stemmed from the fact that may had been involved in the fight against apartheid, and saw Freedom of Information legislation as crucial for the consolidation of participatory democracy and accountable government in South Africa.

16. Spain

The Constitution of Spain[91] provide the information law according to Article 105 of the Constitution states:

The law shall regulate: (b) access by the citizens to the administrative archives and registers except where it affects the security and defense of the State, the investigation of crimes, and the privacy of persons.[92]

The law signed in 1992 provides for access to government records and documents by Spanish citizens[93]. The documents must be part of a file which has been completed. Agencies must respond in three months.

Access can also be denied if the documents refer to government actions to constitutional responsibilities, national defense or national security, investigations, business or industrial secrecy or monetary policy. Access to documents that contain personal information are limited to the persons named in the documents.

17. Sweden

Sweden has a long history of freedom of information. The history of freedom of information law can be traced back to Sweden where, in 1766, the legislature passed the freedom of Press Act, which required the disclosure of official documents upon request.

The Freedom of the Press Act, is now part of the constitution. There freedom of the press Act recognizes that there are certain types of documents that ought to be kept secret and lists them as exemptions from the requirement of disclosure. The access to documents is to be restricted only if restrictions are necessary.

(a) for the security of the realm or its relations to a foreign State, or to an international organization, or (b) for the financial policy, the monetary policy or the foreign exchange policy of the realm; or (c) the activities of the public authority for the purpose of inspection, control or other supervision; or (d) the interest of prevention or prosecution of crime; or (e) the economic interest of the State or the communities; or (f) the protection of the personal integrity or the economic conditions of individuals; or (g) the interest of preserving animal or plant species.[94]

The Sweden government recently ran an "Open Sweden

Campaign" to encourage openness coordinated by representatives from the national government, Country Councils, municipalities and trade Unions.[95] The campion was aimed at increasing public-sector transparency, raising the level of public knowledge and awareness of information disclosure policies, and encouraging active citizen involvement and debate. Individuals have a right to access and correct personal information held by public and private bodies under the personal data Act.[96]

18. Thailand

Section 48 of the Constitution states:

> "Persons shall have the right to receive information or news from the government agency or state agency or public enterprise in order to check the performance of the government official or state official when such matter have or may have effects on the life of such persons as the law provided."[97]

The Official Information Act was approved in July 1997 and went into effect in December 1997.[98] The Act requires State agencies to publish or make available various types of information and allows citizens to demand official information that is not published. The agency must respond within a "reasonable time." They are also required to keep indices of documents.

19. United Kingdom

The Freedom of Information Act was approved in November 2000 after 20 years of campaigning.[99]

The Freedom of Information Act provides that any person have a general right of access to information held by a broad array of public authorities. State authorities are required to respond within twenty working days. Public authorities are also required to publish a number of categories of information about their structures and activities.

20. United States

The American country is with a long history of Right of Information legislation. American law regarding Right to

Information was not certain. But the United States of America enacted the Freedom of Information Act in 1966.[100]

Freedom of Information emerged during the water Gate revelation. Judge Swica and the Nixontape Case.[101] The water Gate battle for Information proved to be the water for the closeness in the US legal system. American Jurisprudence of freedom of information has often been treated as a paradigm of the evolution of the Right to Information. The freedom of Information Act was enacted in 1966 followed by its statutory causing the Private Act 1947 and the Sunshine Act, 1976.

The Supreme Court of the Union States also contributed to the development of the Right to Information. In ***Lamont v. Post Master General***[102] the American Supreme Court invalidated a provision of a statute conferring power on the post master. General to detain mailing printed or prepared in a foreign country and described by the secretary of treasury as communist political propaganda. The learned Justice Brennan said that it was true that the first Amendment contain no specific guarantee of access to publications.

The freedom of information Act was enacted in 1966 and has been amended several times most recently in 1966 by the electronic freedom of Information Act, which provides access to records in electronic form.[103]

The freedom of information Act allows any person or organization, regardless of citizenship or country of origin to ask for records held by federal government agencies. The government agencies include executive and military departments, government corporations and the entities which perform. Government functions except for congress, the courts or the president's immediate staff at the white house, including the national security council. According to the freedom of Information Act, 1966 Government agencies must respond in twenty working days.[104]

The freedom of Information Act, 1966 indicate the nine categories of exemptions including national security. Internal agency rules, information protected by other statutes, business information, inter and intra agency memos, personal privacy law enforcement records, financial institutions and oil well and data.

21. Zimbabwe

Parliament of Zimbabwe approved the Access to

Information and Privacy Bill in January 2002 and it was signed by President Mugabe in February 2002. The law creates a right to access by any citizen or resident (but not an unregistered media agency or foreign Government) to records held by a public body. The body must respond in 30 days.

There are exemptions for Cabinet documents and deliberations of local government bodies, advice given to public bodies, client-attorney privilege, law enforcement proceedings, national security, inter-governmental relations, public safety, commercial information, and privacy. There is a public-interest disclosure provision that allows the government to release information even if there is no request for a variety of reasons, including matters that threaten public order, the prevention, detection or suppression of crime; and national security.[105]

(ii) Countries with Pending Legislation

1. **In Argentina**, national freedom of information legislation is pending, though some individual regions have legislation on a local level.
2. **In Bangladesh**, the Caretaker Government that assumed power in January 2007 announced in the summer of 2007 that they would implement an RTI Act modeled after the Indian RTI Act of 2005.[106]
3. **In Barbados**, the Government headed by David Thompson has proposed to put in place a Freedom of Information Bill.[107] The Government has launched various initiatives to get the proposed bill with the citizens of the country for comment.
4. **In Botswana**, as of 2003, the government was quoted as saying "The Freedom of Information Bill is not a priority for the new ministry, but some activities like information gathering and initial planning will start."[108]
5. **In the Cayman Islands**, the Freedom of Information Regulations Act, 2008 is expected to go into effect on January 1, 2009.[109]
6. **In Fiji**, the constitution gives a general right of access, but enabling legislation has not yet been passed. A draft Freedom of Information Bill was circulated in

2000 but derailed by political unrest; the government has not yet begun work on a second bill.

7. **In Ghana**, the Right to Information Bill 2003[110] was resubmitted to the Cabinet in 2005.
8. **In Indonesia**, the House of Representatives drafted and submitted a freedom of information bill in 2004, but as of 2005 it remained dormant, with the government taking no action.
9. **In Kenya**, the draft Freedom of Information Act, 2007 will soon be tabled into Parliament.
10. **In the Maldives**, there is currently no freedom of information legislation. In 2004, the government announced that a bill was expected to be passed in that year, but this has not yet transpired.
11. **In Mozambique**, the government produced a draft Freedom of Information Bill in August 2005. It is expected to become law within two years.
12. **In Nauru**, the Freedom of Information Act, 2004 was laid before the parliament in that year, but was not passed. Further work on the legislation is currently being held back, pending a review of the country's Constitution.
13. **In Nigeria**, the Freedom of Information Bill[111] was approved by the Senate in November 2006. It must now be reconciled with the version approved by the House and signed by the President.
14. **In Sri Lanka**, the 2004 draft Freedom of Information Act[112] has been endorsed by both major parties, but had not been passed as of January 2005.

13. CONCLUSION

The history Right to Information has been very interesting. It is supposed that not only today but in primitive human society too, there was Right to Information according to that age. Though at different stages of civilization its nature has changed. It has been there in one or the other form be it in the form of declaration or holy sermons. The above mentioned contents have elaborate discussion regarding this where it can be found that there are numerous instances of Right to Information in different texts.

Notes and References

1. Dr. Madabhu Shri Sridhar, Right to Information, Ed. 2006, p. 7.
2. Kapila Khemundu, Centre for the Study of Social Systems, Jawaharlal Nehru University, New Delhi, pp. 344-45.
3. *Ibid*.
4. *Jurisprudence,* Manchester University Press, 1967.
5. Irdell Jenkins, The Concept of Right and Competence of Court, 18 AJ (1973), p. 1.
6. *Jurisprudence,* Vol. IV, p. 56.
7. Austin J, Lectures on Jurisprudence (5th Ed.), p. 344.
8. Gary, J.C., "The Nature and Sources of the Law, (2nd Ed), p. 10.
9. Holland, *Jurisprudence,* 13th Ed., p. 83.
10. W. Keeton, George, The Elementary Principles of Jurisprudence (London, 1929), p. 96.
11. Olivercrona, K, "The Concept of Right According to Hrotious and Pufendorf (1969), p. 214.
12. AIR 1968 MAD 355.
13. AIR 1977 SC 1361.
14. The Concise Oxford Dictionary.
15. Random House Webster's College Dictionary at p. 670.
16. Corpus Juris Secondum Dictionary.
17. Law Lexicon, Justice T.P. Mukharjee (Come. and Ed.) C.L.A., Vol. I, p. 687.
18. AIR 1957 Punjab 226 at 229, and Same I.L.R. 1957 Punjab 1253.
19. Sec. 2(F), Right to Information Act, 2005.
20. Sec. 3 Right to Information Act, 2005.
21. CHRI 2003 Report.
22. Transparency International Report, p. 8.
23. Kejriwal, A. "More Stories of Parivartan", India Together, April 2003.
24. www.indiatogather.org/2003.
25. Using the Right to information as an Anti-Corruption Tool, p. 8, www.transparency.org
26. Dr. Minial M. Bapat, Right to Information: Its Scope and Need, pp. 1 to 4.
27. Union of India *v.* Association for Democratic Reforms, AIR 2002 SC, pp. 21-26.
28. http://www.ebc-india.com Practicallawyer/index.pnp?option=com content and task=view and id=7309
29. htpp://www.ebc-indio.com/practicallawyer/index-pnp?option=com
30. Nigam Shalu, Right to Information Law and Practice, p. 27.
31. Patrick Birkinshaw, "Freedom of Information and Openness", Fundamental Human Rights, *Administrative Law Review,* 58:1, 2006, p. 194.

32. Foreword to 'Many Voices, One World', MacBride Report, by Director General of UNESCO, as quoted by Krishna Iyer, Justice V.R., Freedom of Information, EBC, 1990, p. IX.
33. Hursh Mandar and Abha Joshi, "The Right to Information Movement in India (Power People to Control Corruption (CHRI), New Delhi 1998.
34. *Ibid.*
35. Arthashastra 1/15.
36. P.V. Kane, History of Dharmashastra, Vol. II, p. 625.
37. Manu Smritis 6/147-150.
38. Yagyawalkya Smritis 1/344.
39. Kamandak Neetisar 11/53, 66-66.
40. 225/19.
41. Shanti 83|49 and Shanti 140|24A.
42. Yagyawalkya Smritis 11/343.
43. Arthashastra 10/6.
44. Ramcharit Manas, Ayodhya Kand 100/16.
45. Chandogupnishad 4/11/5.
46. Krishna Iyer, Justice V.R., Freedom of Information prolegomenom, EBC, 1990, p. XII.
47. Mahabhart, Vol I, Hindi Ed., Gita Press, Gorakhpur, pp. 675-85.
48. P.K. Das, Hand Book on the Right to Information Act, 2005, p. 50.
49. Mr. Abhimanya Ghosh, Open Government and Right to Information.
50. A division is an administrative unit comprising several districts.
51. A Network of Government Controlled 'ration shops' to supply foods at subsidized rates.
52. Kobu Region, now in the Chhattisgrah State.
53. Right to Information, A long way to go National Center for Advanced Study, Puna.
54. All draft law mentioned in this Section can be accessed from Right to Information Section of Chri's website.
55. Madabhushi Sridhar, Right to Information, 2006, p. 55.
56. Article 12 of Indian Constitution.
57. S.N. Shukla, 'Good Governance: Need for openness and Transparency, *IJPA*, Vol XLIV, 1998, p. 398.
58. *Ibid.*
59. Prithvis Chakravarti, Freedom of Information, *PCIR*, Vol 19, 1889, p. 63.
60. Vikram Khub Chand, Legislating Freedom of Information in India, CHRI, 1998.
61. New Delhi, December 1999 and August 2000.
62. Harare, January 1999, Dhaka, July 1999.
63. *Yojana*, Junuary 2006, Republic Day Special, pp. 4-5.
64. *Ibid.*
65. *Ibid.*

66. Nigam Shalu, Right to Information: Law and Practice, p. 95-96.
67. *Ibid.*
68. AIR 1975 SC 865.
69. Charulata Singh, New Life for Democracy, *Yojana,* January 2006, Republic Day Special, pp. 37.
70. AIR 1982 SC 149.
71. *Ibid.*
72. Till 20/9/2009.
73. J. Michel, "Freedom of Official Information", Vol. VI (www.article 19.org/docimages/116 html)
74. Constitution of Albania, 1998 http/www.tpls.org/serviçes/kusht/contents:html
75. The Law on the Right to Information over the offical documents, No. 8503, June 30, 1999.
76. Freedom of Information Act 1982 http://www.Australiaedu.au/au/legis/cth/consal act/Foia 1982222/
77. "Bangladesh Right to Information Ordinance, No. 50 of 2008 (Bangla)" (in Bangla), Ministry of Information, Press Information Department. 2008-10-21. http://www.bdpressinform.org/rti.htm. Retrieved, 2008-10-29.
78. Access to Information Act, CA-I
79. Regulations of the People's Republic of China on Open Government Information.
80. Freedom of Information Act, 5 USC 552, 1966.
81. Constitution of Republic of Georgia.
82. Code on Access to Information.
83. Law concerning Access to Information held by Administrative Organs.
84. Act of 31 October 1991, containing regulations governing public access to Government information. This replaced the Act on Public Access to Information of 9 November 1978, http://www.minbzk.nl./contents/pages/00012478/public_access_government_info_10-91.pdf
85. http://www.UNI-wuerzvurg.de/Law/nzo1000-.html
86. Official Information Act, 1982, http://www.ombudsmen.govt-nz/offical.html
87. Constitution of Poland, http://www.uni-wuerzburg.de/law/p100000_html
88. Constitution of the Slovak Republic, 1992, http://www.uni-wuerzburg.de/law/p100000_html
89. The Constitution of the Republic of South Africa, Act 108 of 1996, http://www.dity.org.zo/govdocs/constitution/Saconst.html
90. Promotion of access to Information Act, 2 of 2000, http://www.gov.za/gazette/acts/2000/a2-00.PdF.
91. Constitution of Spain, 1992.
92. Constitution of Spain, 1992, http://www.wverzvurg.de/Law/SP00000_html.

93. Ley30/1992, de26deNoviembre, de RegimenJuridicodelas Adminstrationes Publicasydel Procedimiento Administrative Comun, http://www.um.es/siu/marca/30
94. Quoted from Donald, C Rawat, "Law on Access to OFFICIAL DOCUMENTS XXV.
95. Home page http://www.oppnas verige.gov.SC/page/1/42.html
96. Personal Data Act (1998:2004) http://www.datainspektionen.se/PBF Filer/
97. Constitution of the Kingdom of Thailand, B.E 2534(1991), http://www.parbament.th/Files/Library/bes-b.htm
98. Official Information Act, BE2540 (1997)-http://www.krisdika.go.th/Law/text/lawpub/eo2092 s40/text.htm
99. Freedom of Information Act, 2000 http://www.CFio.org.vic/Foiact2000html
100. Freedom of Information Act, 5 WSC 1966 http://www.ePic.org/opengov/Foia/us_Foia_act, html.
101. (1974) 418 115, 683, 41 Law Ed. 2d 1039.
102. (1965) 14.L Ed. 2d. 398.
103. Freedom of Information Act, 5 USC 552, 1966.
104. *Ibid.*
105. Draft available at http.//www.privacyinternational.org/countries/zimbabwe/accessinfo-amend-102.
106. "Bangladesh Right to Information Ordinance, No. 50 of 2008.
107. Ministry of Information, Press Information Department. 2008-10-21. http://wẏw.bdpressinform.org/rti.htm. Retrieved 2008-10-29.
108. Uproar over Draconian Media Bill.
109. http://www.foi.gov.ky/pls/portal/docs/PAGE/FOIHOME/DRAFTBILL/DRAFTIMPLEMENTATIONPLAN11JAN08.P
110. Right to Information Bill, 2003.
108. Freedom of Information Bill, 2006.
109. Draft Freedom of Information Act, 2004.

CHAPTER

3

RIGHT TO INFORMATION AND LEGISLATIVE RESPONSE

I. INTRODUCTION

To bring transparence in society it was felt that the right to information must be given legal structure, legal personalities and legal status made this demand more forceful with their writing and speeches. Our Supreme Court too advocated for the law of Right to Information. Finally, the legislature gave the legal status to the Right to Information. In Indian context the basic law regarding Right to Information is found in Right to Information Act, 2005. But numerous scattered provisions are there found in different acts and statutes pertaining to Right to Information. The compilation of those is a really difficult task for which an endeavour has been made. Firstly, we can have the Right to Information in our constitution whether explicitly or implicitly. The legal part relating to right to information can be studied under below given heads:

(1) At National level
(2) At International level

At international level the roots or Right to Information can be traced in different treaties and covenants.

Whereas the law of Right to Information in India was scattered in different statutes before passing the act named as Right to Information Act, 2005. Before this act there were certain state enactments for Right to Information. Here the discussion is confined to those statutes in which there is a glimpse of Right to Information at national level.

2. RIGHT TO INFORMATION UNDER INDIAN CONSTITUTION

(i) Preamble and Right to Information

In the word of preamble WE, THE PEOPLE OF INDIA, having solemnly resolved to constitute India into a SOVEREIGN SOCIALIST SECULAR DEMOCRATIC REPUBLIC and to secure to all its citizens:

- JUSTICE, social, economic and political;
- LIBERTY of thought, expression, belief, faith and worship;
- EQUALITY of status and of opportunity; and to promote among them all;
- FRATERNITY assuring the dignity of the individual and the [unity and integrity of the Nation]; and
- IN OUR CONSTITUENT ASSEMBLY this twenty-sixth day of November, 1949, do HEREBY ADOPT, ENACT AND GIVE TO OURSELVES THIS CONSTITUTION.

The preamble of our constitution indicates the objective of the Constitution. It has been the best medium of expression of thoughts of our Constitution-makers. The different words used in our preamble explicitly and implicitly show that our Constitution is very alert and vigilant regarding right to information. Though there are no specific provisions pertaining to right to information in our Constitution, but still the term freedom of speech and expression used in the preamble of our constitution expressly declare that our constitution gives great importance to Right to Information.

(ii) Right to Information and Fundamental Right

Chapter III of Indian constitution dealing with fundamental right (Articles 12 to 35) does not have any direct bearing on Right to Information and has not even referred to in these words at all. But the judicial pronouncements of our Supreme Court and State High Courts have significantly contributed to providing a newer and finer perspective to Right to Information in the form of fundamental rights.

The court while dealing with Right to Information cases, have referred and based their judgments on Right to Equality (Article 14), Right to Freedom of Speech and Expression (Article 19(1)a), Right to Life (Article 21), Protection against arrest and detention (Article 22), Constitutional remedies (Article 32). There is a study of various aspects of Right to Information *vis-a-vis* fundamental rights provided under Chapter III of the Indian Constitution in this chapter.

(a) Right to Equality Clause Promotes Right to Information (Article 14)

Article 14 of Constitution of India can be told as cornerstone of our constitution. The philosophical aspect of our constitution is inherent in Act 14. The literal term of Art. 14 is as under—

> *"The state shall not deny to any person equality before the law or the equal protection of the law within the territory of India."*
>
> At first glance this article talks about equality before law and equal protection of law. But a thorough interpretation of Art. 14 show that this Article is the basis of Natural justice. As it is clear that there are two cardinal principles of Natural Justice, one amongst these is ***audi alteram partem***, which means hearing the other side party. This includes Right to Information because without information there can not be any hearing and without hearing natural justice could not be followed.

Moreover, Art. 14 is a shield against arbitrariness also. The Right to Information is a suitable and mighty weapon against arbitrariness. Infact, information itself suppresses the root cause of arbitrariness. So, it can be inferred that Art. 14 is associated with Right to Information.

(b) Freedom of Speech and Expression Clause Promotes Right to Information (Article 19)

Article 19(1)(a) of the Indian Constitution, through it guarantees Freedom of Speech and Expression. In the word of Article 19(1)(a) as under follows:

> Protection of Certain Rights regarding freedom of speech, etc.—(1) All citizens shall have the Right to Freedom of speech and expression.

Our Indian Constitution Art. 19(1)(a) provided the fundamental rights to free speech and expression, which by implication, includes within the right or access to Information. Therefore, the Right to Information becomes a Constitutional right, being an aspect of the Right to free speech and expression, which includes the right to receive and collect information. The Supreme Court of India thus deals with the right to information as implicit in the fundamental right to freedom of speech and expression in the absence of any information Act.

(c) Protection of Life and Personal Liberty Clause Promotes Right to Information (Article 21)

Article 21 of the Indian Constitution provided the Right to Life and Personal liberty. According to Article 21—

> **Protection of life and personal liberty,** *"No person shall be deprived of his life or personal liberty except according to procedure established by law."*

Actually Article 21 of our Constitution inherently has the right to information. This has been held by our Supreme Court in different decisions also. The Right to Information also seems to flow from Art. 21 of the constitution on the right to life and liberty. The expression right to life and personal liberty is a broad term, which includes within itself variety of rights and attributes. Article 21 confers on all persons a right to know which includes a right to receive information. The ambit and scope of Article 21 is much wider as compared to Art. 19(1)(a).[1]

(d) Preventive Detention Clause and Right to Information (Article 22)

Art. 22 is related to preventive detention. It gives right to information to detained persons. According to Art. 22(1) and 22(5) Protection against arrest and detention in certain cases:

No person who is arrested shall be detained in custody without being informed, as soon as may be of grounds for such arrest nor shall he be denied the right to consult, and to be defended by a legal practitioner of his choice.

And Article 22(5) of Indian Constitution provides persons detained under the law of preventive detention the right to be informed of the grounds of detention as soon as possible, also right to make a representation against their detention. The Constitution uses the words 'reasonable opportunity of being heard'. Grounds of detention must be communicated, and any lapse in this regard results in quashing of the detention order.[2] The grounds must be clear and relevant, and communication of the grounds should be adequate enough to enable them to state why they should not be detained. The arrested person must know the grounds of his arrest. So, that he may prepare grounds for his defence. The nature of Art. 22 is to issue a directive to the arresting authorities to disclose the grounds of arrest of a person immediately.[3]

(e) Constitutional Remedies Clause and Right to Information (Article 32)

This article is a constitutional guarantee to get enforced the fundamental right through Supreme Court of India, because by its different decisions our Supreme Court has elevated the status of Right to Information equivalent to any other fundamental right under Art. 19. So, this right can be enforced by our Supreme Court under Art. 32. More over, our Supreme Court has the power to issue different writs under Act 32 by which the court is entitled to have any information regarding the concerned matter.

The same above power of the High Court in Art. 226 of the Indian constitution. **According to Art. 226 :**

(1) Notwithstanding anything in Article 32, every High Court shall have powers, throughout the territories in relation to which it exercises jurisdiction, to issue to any person or authority, including in appropriate cases, any Government, within those territories directions, orders or writs, including writs in the nature of *habeas corpus, mandamus, prohibition, quo warranto* and certiorari,

or any of them, for the enforcement of any of the rights conferred by Part III and for any other purpose.

(2) The power conferred by clause (1) to issue directions, orders or writs to any Government authority or person may also be exercised by any High Court exercising jurisdiction in relation to the territories within which the cause of action, wholly or in part, arises for the exercise of such power, notwithstanding that the seat of such Government or authority or the residence of such person is not within those territories.

(3) Where any party against whom an interim order, whether by way of injunction or stay or in any other manner, is made on, or in any proceedings relating to, a petition under clause (1), without—

(a) furnishing to such party copies of such petition and all documents in support of the plea for such interim order; and

(b) giving such party an opportunity of being heard, makes an application to the High Court for the vacation of such order and furnishes a copy of such application to the party in whose favour such order has been made or the counsel of such party, the High Court shall dispose of the application within a period of two weeks from the date on which it is received or from the date on which the copy of such application is so furnished, whichever is later, or where the High Court is closed on the last day of that period, before the expiry of the next day afterwards on which the High Court is open; and if the application is not so disposed of, the interim order shall, on the expiry of that period, or, as the case may be, the expiry of the said next day, stand vacated.

(4) The power conferred on a High Court by this article shall not be in derogation of the power conferred on the Supreme Court by clause (2) of Article 32.

(iii) Directive Principles of State Policy and Right to Information

Chapter IV of the Indian Constitution (Articles 36 to 51) deals with the Directive Principles of State Policy. Some of them specifically deal with the various facets of Right to Information. These Directive Principles sometimes become complimentary to the fundamental rights and are enforced by courts of law. The following are some of the Directive Principles Indirectly related to Right to Information.

Promotion of International Peace and Security Clause and Right to Information : [Article 51(c)]

Article 51(c) indirectly promote to Right to Information. According to Art. 51(c) read as follows:

The state shall endeavour to—

(a) Promote international peace and security
(b) maintain just and honorable relations between nations;
(c) Foster respect for international law and treaty obligations in the dealings of organised people with one another; and
(d) encourage settlement of international dispute by arbitration.

India is a signatory to the UDHR 1948 Art. 19 or UDHR devoted to Right to Information. As a party to these obligations it is under an international obligations to effectively guarantee the right to information. Further, under provisions of Art. 51(c) in the constitution the state is duty bound to foster respect for international laws and treaty obligations. This bounds the Government of India to create suitable conditions to implement international laws and obligations with respect to the right to information. Further, there are other provisions in the constitution which indirectly seek to promote right to information.

(iv) Other Constitutional Provisions Relating to Right to Information

Many other provisions relating to Right to Information discuss as under following heads:

(a) Duties of Prime Minister as respect the Furnishing of Information to the President (Article 78)

Article 78 of the Indian Constitution imposes the duty of

the Prime Minister to provide relevant information to the President. According to Article 78 read, as follows:

Duties of Prime Minister as respects the furnishing of information to the President, etc.—It shall be the duty of the Prime Minister—

(a) to communicate to the President all decisions of the Council of Ministers relating to the administration of the affairs of the Union and proposals for legislation;
(b) to furnish such information relating to the administration of the affairs of the Union and proposals for legislation as the President may call for; and
(c) if the President so requires, to submit for the consideration of the Council of Ministers any matter on which a decision has been taken by a Minister but which has not been considered by the Council.

(b) Duties of Chief Minister as respects the Furnishing of Information to Governor (Article 167)

By the virtue of Art. 167 of our constitution the Chief Minister is under legal duty to give information to the Governor regarding the affairs and administration of the state. According to clause (2) of Art. 167, the Chief Minister shall have to made available those information which the Governor asks for regarding the affairs of state and administration.

In the words or Art. 167. Duties of Chief Minister as respects the furnishing of information to Governor, etc. It shall be the duty of the Chief Minister of each State—

(a) to communicate to the Governor of the State all decisions of the Council of Ministers relating to the administration of the affairs of the State and proposals for legislation;
(b) to furnish such information relating to the administration of the affairs of the State and proposals for legislation as the Governor may call for; and
(c) if the Governor so requires, to submit for the consideration of the Council of Ministers any matter on which a decision has been taken by a Minister but which has not been considered by the Council.

(c) Parliament Privileges and Right to Information (Article 105)

Article 105 of our constitution which is related to Parliamentary Privileges, there can be seen a glimpse of right to information in that also. Infact the Members of Parliament have the right to ask question to concerned Ministers and departments. This also shows nothing but the Right to Information.

(d) Dismissal, Removal or Persons Employed in Civil Capacities under the Union or a State and Right to Information [Article 311(2)]

Article 311(2) of the Indian Constitution says that no person who is a member of civil services under the Union Government or a state government shall be dismissed or removed or reduced in rank except after an inquiry in which he or she is informed of the charges against him or her and is given a reasonable opportunity of being heard in respect of those charges. These do not constitute an exhaustive list of situations where the rules of natural justice come into play. They are attracted whenever it is necessary to take a decision that may adversely affect a person.

Where none of the above Constitutional provisions is involved, and if the statute is silent on the need for a hearing, the Court decides whether even in the absence of an explicit provision for hearing, a hearing is necessary. So, we can have a glimpse of Right to Information in this article also.

3. RIGHT TO INFORMATION AND CERTAIN OTHER LEGISLATIVE RESPONSES

The present heads seeks to examine the legal framework provided for Right to Information in India. We discuss here a few of the earlier and recent legislations directed and undirected at Right to Information. Some relevant Act and Rules relating to Right to Information read as follows:

(i) The All India Services (Conduct) Rules, 1968

Section 9 of the India Services Rules, 1968 provided some relevant provisions Right to Information. Section 9 of Act read as follows:

Unauthorised communication of information : No member of the Service shall except in accordance with any general or special order of the Government or in the performance in good faith of the duties assigned to him, communicate directly or indirectly any official document or part thereof or information to any Government servant or any other person to whom he is not authorised to communicate such document or information.

Explanation : Quotation by a member of the Service (in his representations to the Head of Office or Head of Department or President) of, or from, any letter, circular or office memorandum or from the notes on any file to which he is not authorised to have access, or which he is not authorised to keep in his personal custody or for personally purposes, shall amount to unauthorised communication of information within the meaning of this rule.

(ii) The Atomic Energy Act, 1962

The Atomic Energy Act, 1962 provided the some relevant relating Right to Information. Section 18 of the Atomic Energy Act, 1962 read as follows:

Restriction on disclosure of information : (1) The Central government may by order restrict the disclosure of information, whether contained in a document, drawing photograph, plan, model, or in any other form whatsoever, which relates to, represents or illustrates—

(a) an existing or proposed plant used or proposed to be used for the purpose of producing, developing or using atomic energy, or

(b) the purpose or method of operation of any such existing or proposed plant, or

(c) any process operated or proposed to be operated in any such existing or proposed plant.

(2) No person shall—

(a) disclose, or obtain or attempt to obtain any information restricted under sub-section (1), or

(b) disclose, without the authority of the Central Government, any information obtained in the discharge of any functions under this Act or in the performance of his official duties.

(3) Nothing in this section shall apply—

(i) to the disclosure of information with respect to any plant of a type in use for purposes other than the production, development or use of atomic energy, unless the information discloses that plant of that type is used or proposed to be used for the production, development or use of atomic energy or research into any matters connected therewith; or

(ii) where any information has been made available to the general public otherwise than in contravention of this section, to any subsequent disclosure or that information.

(iii) The Bureau of Indian Standards Act, 1986

Section 30 of the Bureau of Indian Standards Act, 1986 provided some relevant provisions relating Right to Information.

Certain matters to be kept confidential: Any information obtained by an inspecting officer or the Bureau from any statement made or information supplied or any evidence given or from inspection made under the provisions of this Act shall be treated as confidential:

Provided that nothing in this section shall apply to the disclosure of any information for the purpose of prosecution under this Act.

(iv) The Central Civil Services (Conduct) Rules, 1964

Section 11 of the Central Civil Services (Conduct) Rules, 1964 provided some relevant provisions relating Right to Information. According to Section 11:

Unauthorised communication of information: No Government servant shall, except in accordance with any general or special order or the Government or in the performance in good faith of the duties assigned to him, communicate, directly or indirectly, any official document or any part thereof or information to any Government servant or any other person to whom he is not authorised to communicate such document or information.

Explanation: Quotations by a Government servant (in his representation to the Head of Office, or Head of Department or President) of or from any letter, circular or office memorandum or from the notes on any file, to which he is not authorised to have access, or which he is not authorised to keep in his personal custody or for personal purposes, shall amount to unauthorised communication of information within the meaning of this rule.

(v) The Code of Criminal Procedure, 1973

The Code of Criminal Procedure, 1973 is one of the earlier statutes dealing with the Right to Information. Some relevant Section read as follows:

Person arrested to be informed of grounds of arrest and of right to bail:[4]—(1) Every police officer or other person arresting any person without warrant shall forthwith communicate to him full particulars of the offence for which he is arrested or other grounds for such arrest.

(2) Where a police officer arrests without warrant any person other than a person accused of a non-bailable offence, he shall inform the person arrested that he is entitled to be released on bail and that he may arrange for sureties on his behalf.

Obligation of person making arrest to inform about the arrest, etc., to a nominated person:[5]—(1) Every police officer or other person making any arrest under this Code shall forthwith give the information regarding such arrest and place where the arrested person is being held to any of his friends, relatives or such other persons as may be disclosed or nominated by the arrested person for the purpose of giving such information.

(2) The police officer shall inform the arrested person of his rights under sub-section (1) as soon as he is brought to the police station.

(3) An entry of the fact as to who has been informed of the arrest of such person shall be made in a book to be kept in the police station in such form as may be prescribed in this behalf by the State Government.

(4) It shall be the duty of the Magistrate before whom such arrested person is produced, to satisfy himself that the requirements of sub-section (2) and sub-section (3) have been complied with in respect of such arrested person.

Supply to the accused of copy of police report and other documents:[6]—In any case where the proceeding has been instituted on a police report, the Magistrate shall without delay furnish to the accused, free of cost, a copy of each of the following:

(i) the police report;

(ii) the first information report recorded under section 154;

(iii) the statements recorded under sub-section (3) of section 161 of all persons whom the prosecution proposes to examine as its witnesses, excluding therefrom any part in regard to which a request for such exclusion has been made by the police officer under sub-section (6) of section 173;

(iv) the confessions and statements, if any, recorded under section 164;

(v) any other document or relevant extract thereof forwarded to the Magistrate with the police report under sub-section (5) of section 173;

Provided that the Magistrate may, after perusing any such part of a statement as is referred to in clause (iii) and considering the reasons given by the police officer for the request, direct that a copy of that part of the statement or of such portion thereof as the Magistrate thinks proper, shall be furnished to the accused:

Provided further that if the Magistrate is satisfied that any document referred to in clause (v) is voluminous, he shall, instead or furnishing the accused with a copy thereof, direct that he will only be allowed to inspect it either personally or through pleader in Court.

Supply of copies of statements and documents to accused in other cases triable by Court of Session:[7]—Where, in a case instituted otherwise than on a police report, it appears to the Magistrate issuing process under section 204 that the offence is triable exclusively by the Court of Section, the Magistrate shall without delay furnish to the accused, free of cost, a copy of each of the following:

(i) the statements recorded under section 200 or section 202, or all persons examined by the Magistrate;

(ii) the statements and confessions, if any, recorded under section 161 or section 164;

(iii) any documents produced before the Magistrate on which the prosecution proposes to rely:

Provide that if the Magistrate is satisfied that any such document is voluminous, he shall, instead of furnishing the accused with a coy thereof, direct that he will only be allowed to inspect it either personally or through pleader in Court.

(vi) The Companies Act, 1956

There are numerous provisions in companies Act, 1956 which are directly or indirectly associated with Right to Information. A brief description of those is as under:

Copies of memorandum and articles, etc., to be given to members:[8]—(1) A company shall, on being so required by a member, send to him within seven days of the requirement and subject to the payment of a fee of one rupee, a copy each or the following documents as in force for the time being—

(a) the memorandum;
(b) the articles, if any;
(c) every other agreement and every resolution referred to in section 192, if and insofar as they have not been embodied in the memorandum or articles.

(2) If a company makes default in complying with the requirements of section, the company, and every officer of the company who is in default, shall be punishable, for each offence, with fine which may extend to five hundred rupees.

Alteration of memorandum or articles, etc., to be noted in every copy:[9]—(1) Where an alteration is made in the memorandum or articles of a company, or any resolution, referred to in section 192, every copy of the memorandum, articles, agreement or resolution issued after the date of the alteration shall be in accordance with the alteration.

(2) If, at any time, the company issues any copies of the memorandum, articles, resolution or agreement, which are not in accordance with the alteration or alterations made therein before that time, the company, and every officer of the company who is in default, shall be punishable with fine which may extend to one hundred rupees for each copy so issued.

Service of documents on members by company:[10]—(1) A document may be served by a company on any member thereof either personally, or by sending it by post to him to his registered address, or if he has no registered address in India, to the address, if any, within India supplied by him to the company for the giving of notice to him.

(2) Where a document is sent by post,—

(a) service thereof shall be deemed to be effected by properly addressing, prepaying and posting a letter containing the document, provide that where a member has intimated to the company in advance that documents should be sent to him under a certificate of posting or by registered post with or without acknowledgment due and has deposited with the company a sum sufficient to defray the expenses of doing so, service of the document shall not be deemed to be effected unless it is sent in the manner intimated by the member; and

(b) such service shall be deemed to have been effected—

(i) in the case of a notice of a meeting, at the expiration of forty-eight hours after the letter containing the same is posted, and

(ii) in any other case, at the time at which the letter would be delivered in the ordinary course of post.

(3) A document advertised in a newspaper circulation in the neighborhood of the registered office of the company shall be deemed to be duly served on the day on which the advertisement appears, on every member of the company who has no registered address in India and has not supplied to the company an address within India for the giving of notices to him.

(4) A document may be served by the company on the joint-holders of a share by serving it on the joint-holder named first in the register in respect of the share.

(5) A document may be served by the company on the persons entitled to a share in consequence of the death or insolvency of a member by sending it through the post in a prepaid letter addressed to them by name or by the title or representatives of the deceased, or assignees of the insolvent, or by any like description at the address, if any, in India supplied for the purpose by the persons claiming to be so entitled, or until such an address has been so supplied, by serving the document

in any manner in which it might have been served if the death or insolvency had not occurred.

Authentication of documents and proceedings:[11]—Save as otherwise expressly provided in this Act, a document or proceeding requiring authentication by a company may be signed by a director, the manager, the secretary or other authorised officer of the company, and need not be under its common seal.

Information memorandum:[12]—(1) A public company making an issue of securities may circulate information memorandum to the public prior to filing of a prospectus.

(2) A company inviting subscription by an information memorandum shall be bound to file a prospectus prior to the opening of the subscription lists and the offer as a red-herring prospectus, at least three days before the opening of the offer.

(3) The information memorandum and red-herring prospectus shall carry same obligations as are applicable in the case of a prospectus.

(4) Any variation between the information memorandum and the red-herring prospectus shall be highlighted as variations by the issuing company.

Explanation—For the purposes of sub-sections (2), (3) and (4), "red-herring prospectus" means a prospectus which does not have complete particulars on the price of the securities offered and the quantum of securities offered.

(5) Every variation as made and highlighted in accordance with sub-section (4) above shall be individually intimated to the persons invited to subscribe to the issue of securities.

(6) In the event of the issuing company or the underwriters to the issue have invited or received advance subscription by way of cash or post-dated cheques or stock-invest, the company or such underwriters or bankers to the issue shall not encash such subscription moneys or post-dated cheques or stock-invest before the date of opening of the issue, without having individually intimated the prospective subscribers of the variation and without having offered an opportunity to such prospective subscribers to withdraw their application and cancel their post-dated cheques or stock-investor return of subscription paid.

(7) The applicant or proposed subscriber shall exercise his right to withdraw from the application on any intimation of variation within seven days from the date of such intimation and

shall indicate such withdrawal in writing to the company and the underwriters.

(8) Any application for subscription which is acted upon by the company or underwriters or bankers to the issue without having given enough information of any variations, or the particulars of withdrawing the offer or opportunity for cancelling the post-dated cheques or stock invest or stop payments for such payments shall be void and the applicants shall be entitled to receive a refund or return of its post-dated cheques or stock-invest or subscription moneys or cancellation of its application, as if the said application has never been made and the applications are entitled to receive back their original application and interest at the rate of fifteen per cent from the date of encashment till payment or realisation.

(9) Upon the closing of the offer of securities, a final prospects stating therein the total capital raised, whether by way of debt or share capital and the closing price of the securities and any other detail as were not complete in the red-herring prospectus shall be filed in a case of a listed public company with the Securities and Exchange Board and Registrar, and in any other case with the Registrar only.

Terms of contract mentioned in prospectus or statement in lieu of prospectus, not to be varied:[13]—A company shall not, at any time, vary the terms of a contract referred to in the prospectus or statement in lieu of prospectus, except subject to the approval of, or except on authority given by, the company in general meeting.

Criminal liability for mis-statements in prospectus:[14]—(1) Where a prospectus issued after the commencement of this Act includes any untrue statement, every person who authorised the issue of the prospectus shall be punishable with imprisonment for a term which may extend to two years, or with fine which may extend to fifty thousand rupees, or with both, unless he proves either that the statement was immaterial or that he had reasonable ground to believe, and did up to the time of the issue of the prospectus believe, that the statement was true.

(2) A person shall not be deemed for the purposes of this section to have authorised the issue of a prospectus by reason only of his having given—

(a) the consent required by section 58 to the inclusion therein of a statement purporting to be made by him as an expert, or

(b) the consent required by sub-section (3) of section 60.

Document containing offer of shares or debentures for sale to be deemed prospectus:[15]—(1) Where a company allots or agrees to allot any shares in or debentures of the company with a view to all or any of those shares or debentures being offered for sale to the public, any document by which the offer for sale to the public is made shall, for all purposes, be deemed to be prospectus issued by the company; and all enactments and rules of law as to the contents of prospectus and as to liability in respect of statements in and omissions from prospectuses, or otherwise relating to prospectuses, shall apply with the modification specified in sub-sections (3), (4) and (5), and have effect accordingly, as if the shares or debentures had been offered to the public for subscription and as if persons accepting the offer in respect of any shares or debentures were subscribers for those shares or debentures, but without prejudice to the liability, if any, of the persons by whom the offer is made in respect of misstatements contained in the document or otherwise in respect thereof.

(2) For the purposes of this Act, it shall, unless the contrary is proved, be evidence that an allotment of, or an agreement to allot, shares or debentures was made with a view to the shares or debentures being offered for sale to the public if it is shown—

(a) that an offer of the shares or debentures or of any of them for sale to the public was made within six months after the allotment or agreement to allot; or

(b) that at the date when the offer was made, the whole consideration to be received by the company in respect of the shares or debentures had not been received by it.

(3) Section 56 as applied by this section shall have effect as if it required a prospectus to state in addition to the matters required by that section to be stated in a prospectus—

(a) the net amount of the consideration received or to be received by the company in respect of the shares or debentures to which the offer relates; and

(b) the place and time at which the contract under which the said shares or debentures have been or are to be allotted may be inspected.

(4) Section 60 as applied by this section shall have effect as if the persons making the offer were persons named in a prospectus as directors of a company.

(5) Where a person making an offer to which this section relates is a company or a firm, it shall be sufficient if the document referred to in sub-section (1) is signed on behalf of the company or firm by two directors of the company or by not less than one-half of the partners in the firm, as the case may be; and such director or partner may sign by his agent authorised in writing.

Right to obtain copies of and inspect trust deed:[16]—(1) A copy of any trust deed for securing any issue of debentures shall be forwarded to the holder or any such debentures or any member of the company, at his request and within seven days of the making thereof, on payment—

(a) in the case of a printed trust deed of such sum as may be prescribed; and

(b) in the case of a trust deed which has not been printed, of such sum as may be prescribed for every one hundred words or fractional part thereof required to be copied.

(2) If a copy is refused, or is not forwarded within the time specified in sub-section (1), the company, and every officer of the company who is in default, shall be punishable, for each offence, with fine which may extend to five hundred rupees and with a further fine which may extend to two hundred rupees for every day during which the offence continues.

(3) The Central Government may also, by order, direct that the copy required shall forthwith be sent to the person requiring it.

(4) The trust deed referred to in sub-section (1) shall also be open to inspection by any member or debenture-holder of the

company in the same manner, to the same extent, and on payment of the same fees, as if it were the register of members of the company.

Right to inspect copies of instruments creating charges and company's register of charges:[17]—(1) The copies of instruments creating charges kept in pursuance of section 136, and the register of charges kept in pursuance of section 143, shall be open during business hours (but subject to such reasonable restrictions as the company in general meeting may impose, so that not less than two hours in each day are allowed for inspection) to the inspection of any creditor or member of the company without fee, at the registered office of the company.

(2) The register of charges kept in pursuance of section 143 shall also be open, during business hours but, subject to the reasonable restrictions aforesaid, to the inspection of any other person on payment of a fee of such sum as may be prescribed of each impaction, at the registered office of the company.

(3) If inspection of the said copies or register is refused the company, and every officer of the company who is in default, shall be punishable with fine which may extend to five hundred rupees and with a further fine which may extend to two hundred rupees for every day during which the refusal continues.

(4) The Central Government may also by order compel an immediate inspection of the said copies or register.

Publication of reports of proceedings of general meetings:[18]—(1) No document purporting to be a report of the proceedings of any general meeting of a company shall be circulated or advertised at the expense of the company, unless it includes the matters required by section 193 to be contained in the minutes of the proceedings of such meeting.

(2) If any report is circulated or advertised in contravention of sub-section (1), the company, and every officer of the company who is in default, shall be punishable, in respect of each offence, with fine which may extend to five thousand rupees.

Construction of references to documents annexed to accounts:[19]— References in this Act to documents annexed or required to be annexed to a company's accounts or any of them shall not include the Board's report, the auditors' report or any document attached or required to be attached to those accounts.

Provided that any information which is required by this

Act to be given in the accounts, and is allowed by it to be given in a statement annexed to the accounts, may be given in the Board's report instead of in the accounts; and if any such information is so given, the report shall be annexed to the accounts and this Act shall apply in relation thereto accordingly, except that the auditors shall report thereon only insofar as it gives the said information.

Certain companies to publish statement in the Form in Table F in Schedule I:[20]—(1) Every company which is a limited banking company, an insurance company or a deposit, provident or benefit society, shall, before it commences business and also on the first Monday in February and the first Monday in August in every year during which it carries on business, make a statement in the Form in Table F in Schedule I, or in a Form as near thereto as circumstances admit.

(2) A copy of the statement, together with a copy of the last audited balance-sheet laid before the members of the company; shall be displayed and until the display of the next following statement, shall be kept displayed, in a conspicuous place in the registered office of the company, and in every branch office or place where the business of the company is carried on.

(3) Every member and every creditor, of the company shall be entitled, on payment of a sum of eight annas, to be furnished with a copy of the statement, within seven days of such payment.

(4) If default is made in complying with any of the requirements of this section, the company, and every officer of the company who is in default, shall be punishable with fine which may extend to five hundred rupees for every day during which the default continues.

(5) This section shall not apply to a life assurance company or provident insurance society to which the provisions of the Insurance Act, 1938 (4 of 1938), as to the annual statements to be made by such company or society, apply with or without modifications, if the company or society complies with those provisions.

Duty of directors, etc., to make disclosure:[21]—(1) Every director, managing director, manager or secretary of any company, who is appointed to or relinquishes, the office of director, managing director, manager or secretary of any other body corporate, shall, within twenty days of his appointment to, or as the case may be, relinquishment of, such office, disclose to the company aforesaid the particulars relating to the office in the other body corporate which are required to be specified under sub-section (1) of section 303; and if he fails to do so, he shall be punishable with fine which may extend to five thousand rupees.

(2) The provisions of sub-section (1) shall also apply to a person deemed to be a director of the company by virtue of the Explanation *to sub-section (1) of section 303 when such person in appointed to, or relinquishes, any of the offices in the other body corporate referred to in sub-section (1).*

Register to be kept by Registrar and inspection thereof:[22]—(1) The Registrar shall keep a separate register or registers in which there shall be entered the particulars received by him under sub-section (2) of section 303 in respect of companies, so however that all entries in respect of each such company shall be together.

(2) The register or registers aforesaid shall be open to inspection by any member of the public at any time during office hours, on payment of the prescribed fee.

Register of directors' shareholdings, etc.:[23]—(1) Every company shall keep a register showing, as respects each director of the company, the number, description and amount of any shares in, or debentures of, the company or any other body corporate, being the company's subsidiary or holding company, or a subsidiary of the company's holding company, which are held by him or in trust for him, or of which he has any right to become the holder whether on payment or not.

(2) Where any shares or debentures have to be recorded in the said register or to be omitted therefrom, in relation to any director, by reason of a transaction entered into after the commencement of this Act and while he is a director, the register shall also show the date of, and the price or other consideration for, the transaction:

Provided that where there is an interval between the agreement for any such transaction and the completion thereof, the date so shown shall be that of the agreement.

(3) The nature and extent of any interest or right in or over any shares or debentures recorded in relation to a director in the said register shall, if he so requires be indicated in the register.

(4) The company shall not, by virtue of anything done for

the purposes of this section, be affected with notice, of, or be put upon inquiry as to, the right of any person in relation to any shares or debentures.

(5) The said register shall, subject to the provisions of this section, be kept at the registered office of the company, and shall be open to inspection during business hours (subject to such reasonable restrictions as the company may, by its articles or in general meeting, impose, so that not less than two hours in each day are allowed for inspection) as follows:

(a) during the period beginning fourteen days before the date of the company's annual general meeting and ending three days after the date of its conclusion, it shall be open to the inspection of any member or holder or debentures of the company; and

(b) during that or any other period, it shall be open to the inspection of any person acting on behalf of the Central Government or of the Registrar.

In computing the fourteen days and the three days mentioned in this sub-section any day which is a Saturday, a Sunday or a public holiday shall be disregarded.

(6) Without prejudice to the rights conferred by sub-section (5), the Central Government or the Registrar may, at any time require a copy of the said register, or any part thereof.

(7) The said register shall also be produced at the commencement of every annual general meeting of the company and shall remain open and accessible during the continuance of the meeting to any person having the right to attend the meeting.

If default is made in complying with this sub-section the company, and every officer of the company who is in default, shall be punishable with fine which may extend to five thousand rupees.

(8) If default is made in complying with sub-section (1) or (2), or if any inspection required under this section is refused, or if any copy required thereunder is not sent within a reasonable time, the company, and every officer of the company who is in default, shall be punishable with fine which may extend to fifty thousand rupees and also with a further fine which may extend to two hundred rupees for every day during which the default continues.

(9) In the case of any such refusal, the Central Government or Tribunal, as the case may be, may also, by order, compel an immediate inspection of the register.

(10) For the purpose of this section—

(a) any person in accordance with whose directions or instructions the Board of directors of a company is accustomed to act, shall be deemed to be a director of the company; and

(b) a director of a company shall be deemed to hold, or to have and interest or a right in or over, any shares or debentures, if a body corporate other than the company holds them or has that interest or right in or over them, and either—

(i) that body corporate or its Board of directors is accustomed to act in accordance with his directions or instructions; or

(ii) he is entitled to exercise or control the exercise of one-third or more of the total voting power exercisable at any general meeting of that body corporate.

Duty of directors and persons deemed to be directors to make disclosure of shareholdings:[24]—(1) Every director of a company, and every person deemed to be a director of the company by virtue of sub-section (10) of section 307, shall give notice to the company of such matters relating to himself as may be necessary for the purpose of enabling the company to comply with the provisions of that section.

(2) Any such notice shall be given in writing, and if it is not given at a meeting of the Board, the person giving the notice shall take all reasonable steps to secure that it is brought up and read at the meeting of the Board next after it is given.

(3) Any person who fails to comply with sub-section (1) or (2) shall be punishable with imprisonment for a term which may extend to two years, or with fine which may extend to fifty thousand rupees, or with both.

Information as to compromises or arrangements with creditors and members:[25]—(1) Where a meeting of creditors or any class of creditors, or of members or any class of members, is called under section 391—

(a) with every notice calling the meeting which is sent to a creditor or member, there shall be sent also a statement setting forth the terms of the compromise or arrangement and explaining its effect; and in particular, stating any material interest of the directors, managing director or manager of the company, whether in their capacity as such or as members or creditors of the company or otherwise, and the effect on those interests of the compromise or arrangement if, and in so far as, it is different from the effect on the like interests of other persons; and

(b) in every notice calling the meeting which is given by advertisement, there shall be included either such a statement as aforesaid or a notification of the place at which and the manner in which creditors or members entitled to attend the meeting may obtain copies of such a statement as aforesaid.

(2) Where the compromise or arrangement affects the rights of debenture-holders of the company, the said statement shall give the like information and explanation as respects the trustees of any deed for securing the issue of the debentures as it is required to give as respects the company's directors.

(3) Where a notice given by advertisement includes a notification that copies of a statement setting forth the terms of the compromise or arrangement proposed and explaining its effect can be obtained by creditors or members entitled to attend the meeting , every creditor or member so entitled shall, on making an application in the manner indicated by the notice, be furnished by the company, free of charge, with a copy of the statement.

(4) Where default is made in complying with any of the requirements of this section, the company, and every officer of the company who is in default, shall be punishable with fine which may extend to fifty thousand rupees; and for the purpose of this sub-section any liquidator of the company and any trustee of a deed for securing the issue of debentures of the company shall be deemed to be an officer of the company:

Provided that a person shall not be punishable under this sub-section if he shows that the default was due to the refusal of any other person, being a director, managing director, manager or trustee for debenture-holders, to supply the necessary particulars as to his material interests.

(5) Every director, managing director, or manager of the company, and every trustee for debenture-holders of the company, shall give notice to the company of such matters relating to himself as may be necessary for the purposes of this section; and if he fails to do so, he shall be punishable with fine which may extend to five thousand rupees.

Power of Tribunal to call for periodic information:[26]—On receipt of reference under section 424A, the Tribunal may call for any periodic information from the company as to the steps taken by the company to make its net worth exceed the accumulated losses or to make repayment of its debts referred to in that section, as the case may be, and the company shall furnish such information.

Books to be kept by liquidator:[27]—(1) The liquidator shall keep, in the manner prescribed, proper books in which he shall cause entries or minutes to be made of proceedings at meetings and of such other matters as may be prescribed.

(2) Any creditor or contributory may, subject to the control of the Tribunal, inspect any such books, personally or by his agent.

Publication of resolution to wind up voluntarily:[28]—(1) When a company has passed a resolution for voluntary winding up, it shall, within fourteen days of the passing of the resolution, give notice of the resolution by advertisement in the Official Gazette, and also in some newspaper circulating in the district where the registered office of the company is situated.

(2) If default is made in complying with sub-section (1), the company, and every officer of the company who is in default, shall be punishable with fine which may extend to five hundred rupees for every day during which the default continues.

For the purposes of this sub-section, a liquidator of the company shall be deemed to be an officer of the company.

Declaration of solvency in case of proposal to wind up voluntarily:[29]—(1) Where it is proposed to wind up a company voluntarily, its directors, or in case the company has more than two directors, the majority of the directors, may, at a meeting of the Board, make a declaration verified by an affidavit, to the effect that they have made a full inquiry into the affairs of the company, and that, having done so, they have formed the opinion that the company has not debts, or that it will be able to pay its debts in full within such period not exceeding three years from the commencement of the winding up as may be specified in the declaration.

(2) A declaration made as aforesaid shall have no effect for the purpose of this Act, unless—

(a) it is made within the five weeks immediately, preceding the data of the passing of the resolution for winding company and it delivered to the Registrar for registration before that date; and

(b) it is accompanied by a copy of the report of the auditors of the company (prepared, as far as circumstances admit, in accordance with the provisions of this Act) on the profit and loss account of the company for the period commencing from the date up to which the last such account was prepared and ending with the latest practicable date immediately before the making of the declaration and the balance sheet of the company made out as on the last-mentioned date and also embodies a statement of the company's assets and liabilities as at that date.

(3) Any director of a company making a declaration under this section without having reasonable grounds for the opinion that the company will be able to pay its debts in full within the period specified in the declaration, shall be punishable with imprisonment for a term which may extend to six months, or with fine which may extend to fifty thousand rupees, or with both.

(4) If the company is wound up in pursuance of a resolution passed within the period of five weeks after the making of the declaration, but its debts are not paid or provided for in full within the period specified in the declaration, it shall be presumed, until the contrary is shown, that the director did not have reasonable grounds for his opinion.

(5) A winding up in the case of which a declaration has been made and delivered in accordance with this section is in this Act referred to as "a members' voluntary winding up", and a winding up in the case of which a declaration has not been so

made and delivered is in this Act referred to as a "a creditors' voluntary winding up."

Provisions applicable to a members' voluntary winding up:[30]—The provisions contained in section 490 to 198, both inclusive shall subject to the provisions of section 498, apply in relation to a members' voluntary winding up.

Books and papers of company to be evidence:[31]— Where a company is being wound up, all books and papers of the company and of the liquidators shall, as between the contributories of the company be *prima facie* evidence of the truth of all matters purporting to be therein recorded.

Inspection of books and papers by creditors and contributories:[32]—(1) At any time after the making of an order for the winding up of a company by the Tribunal, any creditor or contributory of the company may, if the Supreme Court, by rules prescribed so permit and in accordance with and subject to such rules but not further or otherwise, inspect the books and papers of the company.

(2) Nothing in sub-section (1) shall be taken as excluding or restricting any rights conferred by any law for the time being in force—

(a) on the Central or a State Government; or

(b) on any authority or officer thereof; or

(c) on any person acting under the authority of any such Government or of any such authority or officer.

Information as to pending liquidations.[33]—(1) If the winding up of a company is not concluded within one year after its commencement, the liquidator shall, unless he is exempted from so doing either wholly or in part by the Central Government, within two months of the expiry of such year and thereafter until the winding up is concluded, at intervals of not more than one year or at such shorter intervals if any, as may be prescribed, file a statement in the prescribed form and containing the prescribed particulars duly audited, by a person qualified to act as auditor of the company, with respect to the proceedings in, and position of, the liquidation,—

(a) in the case of a voluntary winding up by the Tribunal, in Tribunal; and

(b) in the case of a voluntary winding up, with the Registrar:

Provided that no such audit as is referred to in this sub-section shall be necessary where the provisions of section 462 apply.

(2) When the statement is filed in Tribunal under clause (a) of sub-section (1), a copy shall simultaneously be filed with the Registrar and shall be kept by him along with the other records of the company.

(2A) Where a statement referred to in sub-section (2) relates to a Government company in liquidation, the liquidator shall forward a copy thereof,—

(a) to the Central Government, if that Government is a member of the Government company; or

(b) to any State Government, if that Government is a member of the Government company; or

(c) to the Central Government and any State Government, if both the Governments are members of the Government company.

(3) Any person stating himself in writing to be a creditor or contributory of the company shall be entitled, by himself or by his agent, at all reasonable times, on payment of the prescribed fee, to inspect the statement, and to receive a copy thereof or an extract therefrom.

(4) Any person untruthfully stating himself to be a creditor or contributory for the above purpose shall be deemed to be guilty of an offence under section 182 of the Indian Penal Code, and shall, on the application of the liquidator, be punishable accordingly.

(5) If a liquidator fails to comply with any of requirements of this section, he shall be punishable with fine which may extend to five thousand rupees for every day during which the failure continues:

Provided that if the liquidator makes wilful default in causing the statement referred to in sub-section (1) to be audited by a person qualified to act as auditor of the company, the liquidator shall be punishable with imprisonment for a term which may extend to six months, or with fine which may extend to ten thousand rupees, or with both.

Inspection, production and evidence of documents kept by Registrar:[34]—(1) Save as otherwise provided elsewhere in this Act, any person may—

(a) inspect any document kept by the Registrar in accordance with the rules made under the Destruction of Records Act, 1917 being documents filed or registered by him in pursuance of this Act, or making a record of any fact required or authorised to be recorded or registered in pursuance of this Act, on payment for each inspection, of such fee as may be prescribed; and

(b) require a certificate of the incorporation of any company, or a copy or extract of any other document or any part of any other document to be certified by the Registrar, on payment in advance of such fees as may be prescribed.

Provided that the rights conferred by this sub-section shall be exercisable—

(i) in relation to documents delivered to the Registrar with a prospectus in pursuance of sub-clause (i) of clause (b) of sub-section (1) of section 60, only during the fourteen days beginning with the date of publication of the prospectus; and at other times, only with the permission of the Central Government; and

(ii) in relation to documents so delivered in pursuance of clause (b) of sub-section (1) of section 605, only during the fourteen days beginning with the date of the prospectus; and at other times, only with the permission of the Central Government.

(2) No process for compelling the production of any document kept by the Registrar shall issue from any Court or the Tribunal except with the leave of the Court or the Tribunal; and

such process, if issued, shall bear thereon a statement that it is issued with the leave of the Court or the Tribunal.

(3) A copy of, or extract from, any document kept and registered at any of the offices for the registration of companies under this Act, certified to be a true copy under the hand of the Registrar (whose official position it shall not be necessary to prove), shall, in all legal proceedings, be admissible in evidence as of equal validity with the original document.

Admissibility of micro-films, facsimile copies of documents, computer printouts and documents on computer media as documents and as evidence:[35]—(1) Notwithstanding anything contained in any other law for the time being in force,—

(a) a micro-film of a document or the reproduction of the image or images embodied in such micro-film (whether enlarged or not); or

(b) a facsimile copy of a document; or

(c) a statement contained in a document and included in a printed material produced by a computer (hereinafter referred to as a "computer printout"), if the conditions mentioned in sub-section (2) are satisfied,

shall be deemed to be also a document for the purpose of this Act and the rules made thereunder and shall be admissible in any proceedings thereunder, without further proof or production of the original, as evidence of any contents of the original or of any fact stated therein of which direct evidence should be admissible.

(2) The conditions referred to in sub-section (1) in respect of a computer printout shall be the following, namely—

(a) the information contained in the statement reproduces or is derived from returns and document filed by the company on paper or on computer network, floppy, diskette, magnetic cartridge tape, CD-rom or any other computer readable media;

(b) while receiving returns or documents on computer media, necessary checks by scanning the documents filed on computer media will be carried out and media will be duly authenticated by the Registrar; and

(c) the Registrar shall also take due care to preserve the computer media by duplicating, transferring, mastering or storage without loss of data.

Power of Central Government to direct companies to furnish information or statistics:[36]—(1) The Central Government may, by order, require companies generally, or any class of companies, or any company, to furnish such information or statistics with regard to their or its constitution or working, and within such time, as may be specified in the order.

(2) (a) Every order under sub-section (1) addressed to companies generally or to any class of companies, shall be published in the Official Gazette, and in such other manner, if any, as the Central Government may think fit.

(b) The date of publication of the order in the Official Gazette shall be deemed to be the date on which the demand for information or statistics is made on such companies or class companies, as the case may be.

(3) Every order under sub-section (1) addressed to an individual company shall be served on it in the manner laid down in section 51.

(4) For the purpose of satisfying itself that any information or statistics furnished by a company in pursuance of any order under sub-section (1) is correct and complete, the Central Government may require such company—

(a) to produce such records or documents in its possession or under its control for inspection, before such officer and at such time as may be specified by the Central Government; or

(b) to furnish such further information as may be specified by the Central Government and within such time as may be fixed by it.

(5) The Central Government may also, by order, direct an inquiry to be made by any person or persons named in the order—

(a) for the purpose of obtaining any information or statistics which a company has failed to furnish as required of it by an order under sub-section (1); or

(b) for the purpose of satisfying itself that any information or statistics furnished by a company in pursuance of an order made under sub-section (1) is correct and complete; and insofar as such information or statistics may be found to be incorrect or incomplete, for the purpose of obtaining such information or statistics as may necessary to make the information or statistics furnished correct and complete,

and a person or persons so appointed shall, for the purposes of such inquiry, have such powers as may be prescribed.

(6) If any company fails to comply with an order made under sub-sections (1) or (4), or knowingly furnishes any information or statistics which is incorrect or incomplete in any material respect, the company, and every officer hereof who is in default, shall be punishable with imprisonment which may extend to three months, or with fine which may extend to ten thousand rupees, or with both.

(7) An order requiring any information or statistics to be furnished by a company may also be addressed to any person who is, or has at any time been, an officer or employee of the company, and all the provisions of this section, so far as may be, shall apply in relation to such person as they apply in relation to the company:

Provided that no such person shall be punishable under sub-section (6), unless the court is satisfied that he was in a position to comply with the order and made wilful default in doing so.

(8) Where a body corporate incorporated outside India and having established an office within India, carries on business in India, all references to a company in this section shall be deemed to include references to the body corporate in relation, and only in relation, to such business.

Production and inspection of books where offence suspected:[37]— (1) If, on an application made to a Judge of a High Court in chambers or Tribunal, as the case may be, by the Public

Prosecutor of the State or by the Central Government, or by a company prosecutor appointed under section 624A, it is shown that there is reasonable cause to believe that any person has, while, he was an officer of a company, committed an offence in connection with the management of the company's affairs, and that evidence of the commission of the offence is to be found in any books or papers of or under the control of the company, an order may be made—

(i) authorising any person named therein to inspect the said books or paper or any of them for the purpose of investigating, and obtaining evidence of the commission of, the offence; or
(ii) requiring the manager of the company or such other officer thereof as may be named in the order, to produce the said books or papers or any of them to a person, and at a place and time, named in the order.

(2) Sub-section (1) shall apply also in relation to any books or papers of a person carrying on the business of banking so far as they relate to the company's affairs, as it applies to any books or papers of or under the control of the company, except that no such order as is referred to in clause (ii) thereof shall be made by virtue of this sub-section.

(3) No appeal shall lie from the decision of a Judge of the High Court or Tribunal, as the case may be, under this section.

Penalty for false statements:[38]—If in any return, report, certificate, balance sheet, prospectus, statement or other document required by or for the purposes of any of the provisions of this Act, any person makes a statement—

(a) which is false in any material particular, knowing it to be false; or
(b) which omits any material fact knowing it to be material, he shall, save as otherwise expressly provided in this Act, be punishable with imprisonment for a term which may extend to two years, and shall also be liable to fine.

(vii) The Delimitation Act, 2002

Sections 10 and 11 of the Delimitation Act, 2002 provided relevant provisions relating Right to Information. According to Sections 10 and 11—

Publication of orders and their date of operation:[39]— (1) The Commission shall cause each of its orders made under section 8 or section 9 to be published in the Gazette of India and in the Official Gazette of the States concerned and simultaneously cause such orders to be published at last in two vernacular newspapers and publicize on radio, television and other possible media available to the public and after such publication in the Official Gazettes of the States concerned, every District Election Officer shall cause to be affixed, the Gazette version of such orders relating to the area under his jurisdiction, on a conspicuous part of his office for public notice.

(2) Upon publication in the Gazette of India, every such order shall have the force of law and shall not be called in question in any court.

(3) As soon as may be after such publication, every such order shall be laid before the House of the People and the Legislative Assemblies of the States concerned.

(4) Subject to the provisions of sub-section (5), the readjustment of representation of the several territorial constituencies in the House of the People or in the Legislative Assembly of a State and the delimitation of those constituencies provide for in any such order shall apply in relation to every election to the House or to the Assembly, as the case may be, held after the publication in the Gazette of India of that order and shall so apply in supersession of the provisions relating to such representation and delimitation contained in any other law for the time being in force or any order or notification issued under such law in so far as such representation and delimitation are inconsistent with the provision of this Act.

(5) Nothing in this section shall affect the representation in the House of the People or in the Legislative Assembly of a State until the dissolution of the House or of the Assembly, as the case may be, existing on the date of publication in the Gazette of India of the final order or orders of the Commission relating to the delimitation of parliamentary constituencies or, as the case may be, of the assembly constituencies of the State and any bye-election

to fill any vacancy in such House or in any such Assembly shall be held on the basis of the provisions of the laws and orders superseded by sub-section (4) as if the said provisions had not been superseded.

(6) The Commission shall endeavour to complete and publish each of its orders referred to in sub-section (1) in the manner provide in that sub-section, within two years of the constitution of the Commission under section 3.

Power to maintain delimitation orders up-to-date:[40]—(1) The Election Commission may, from time to time, by notification in the Gazette of India and in the Official Gazette of the State concerned—

(a) correct any printing mistake in any of the orders made by the Commission under section 9 or any error arising therein from an inadvertent slip or omission; and

(b) where the boundaries or name of any district or any territorial division mentioned in any of the said orders are or is altered, make such amendments as appear to it to be necessary or expedient for bringing the orders up-to-date, so however, that the boundaries or areas or extent of any constituency shall not be changed by any such notification.

(2) Every notification under this section shall be laid, as soon as may be after it is issued, before the House of the People and the Legislative Assembly of the State concerned.

(viii) The Designs Act, 2000

This is comparatively new enactment which contains provisions related to Right to Information which are as under—

Effect of disclosure on copyright:[41]—The disclosure of a design by the proprietor to any other person, in such circumstances as would make it contrary to good faith for that other person to use or publish the design, and the disclosure of a design in breach of good faith by any person, other than the proprietor of the design, and the acceptance of a first and confidential order for articles bearing a new or original textile design intended for registration, shall not be deemed to be a publication of the design sufficient to invalidate the copyright thereof if registration thereof is obtained subsequently to the disclosure or acceptance.

Inspection of registered designs:[42]—(1) During the existence of copyright in a design, any person on furnishing such information as may enable the Controller to identify the design and on payment of the prescribed fee may inspect the design in the prescribed manner.

(2) Any person may, on an application to the Controller and on payment of such fee as may be prescribed, obtain a certified copy of any registered design.

Information as to existence of copyright:[43]—On the request of any person furnishing such information as may enable the Controller to identity the design, and on payment of the prescribed fee, the Controller shall inform such person whether the registration still exists in prospect of the design, and if so, in respect of what classes of articles, and shall state the date of registration, and the name and address of the registered proprietor.

(ix) The Environment (Protection) Act, 1986

The Environment (Protection) Act, 1986 and the Environmental Impact Assessment Regulations provide for instances of public consultation and allow access to information about the pollution caused by industries covered by the regulations. The Environmental Impact Assessment Regulations allow for a procedure for public hearings and publication of the executive summary of any proposal for any project affecting the environment by the person seeking to execute that project. The relevant provision regarding this is as under:

Power of Central Government to take measures to protect and improve environment:[44]—(1) Subject to the provisions of this Act, the Central Government shall have the power to take all such measures as it deems necessary or expedient for the purpose of protecting and improving the quality of the environment and preventing, controlling and abating environmental pollution.

(2) In particular, and without prejudice to the generality of the provisions of sub-section (1), such measures may include measures with respect to all or any of the following matters, namely—

(i) co-ordination of actions by the State Governments, officers and other authorities—
   (a) under this Act, or the rules made thereunder, or
   (b) under any other law for the time being in force which is relatable to the objects of this Act,

(ii) planning and execution of a nation-wide programme for the prevention, control and abatement of environmental pollution;

(iii) laying down standards for the quality of environment in its various aspects;

(iv) laying down standards for emission or discharge of environmental pollutants from various sources whatsoever:

   Provided that different standards for emission or discharge may be laid down under this clause from different sources having regard to the quality or composition of the emission or discharge of environmental pollutants from such sources;

(v) restriction of areas in which any industries, operations or processes or class of industries, operations or processes shall not be carried out or shall be carried out subject to certain safeguards;

(vi) laying down procedures and safeguards for the prevention of accidents which may cause environmental pollution and remedial measures for such accidents;

(vii) laying down procedures and safeguards for the handling of hazardous substances;

(viii) examination of such manufacturing processes, materials and substances as are likely to cause environmental pollution;

(ix) carrying out and sponsoring investigations and research relating to problems of environmental pollution;

(x) inspection of any premises, plant, equipment, machinery, manufacturing or other processes, materials or substances and giving, by order, of such directions to such authorities, officers or persons as it may consider necessary to take steps for the prevention, control and abatement of environmental pollution;

(xi) establishment or recognition of environmental laboratories and institutes to carry out the functions entrusted to such environmental laboratories and institutes under this Act;

(xii) collection and dissemination of information in respect of matters relating to environmental pollution;

(xiii) preparation of manuals, codes or guides relating to the prevention, control and abatement of environmental pollution; and

(xiv) such other matters as the Central Government deems necessary or expedient for the purpose of securing the effective implementation of the provisions of this Act.

(3) The Central Government may, if it considers it necessary or expedient so to do for the purpose of this Act, by order, published in the Official Gazette, constitute an authority or authorities by such name or names as may be specified in the order for the purpose of exercising and performing such of the powers and functions (including the power to issue directions under section 5) of the Central Government under this Act and for taking measures with respect to such of the matters referred to in sub-section (2) as may mentioned in the order and subject to the supervision and control of the Central Government and the provision of such order, such authority or authorities may exercise the power or perform the functions or take the measures so mentioned in order as if such authorities had been empowered by this Act to exercise those powers or perform those functions or take such measures.

Appointment of officers and their powers and functions:[45]—(1) Without prejudice to the provisions of sub-section (3) of section 3, the Central Government may appoint officers with such designations as it thinks fit for the purpose of this Act and may entrust to them such of the powers and functions under this Act as it may deem fit.

(2) The officers appointed under sub-section (1) shall be subject to the general control and direction of the Central Government or, if so directed by that Government, also of the authority or authorities, if any, constituted under sub-section (3) of section 3 or of any other authority or officer.

(x) The Factories Act, 1948

The Factories Act, 1948 provides for compulsory disclosure of information to factory workers regarding dangers, including health hazards, and the measures to overcome such hazards arising from their exposure to dangerous materials. While this is a excellent provision, in practice it is violated with impunity. The relevant provision regarding this is as under:

Compulsory disclosure of information by the occupier:[46]—(1) The occupier of every factory involving a hazardous process shall disclose in the manner prescribed all information regarding dangers, including health hazards and the measures to overcome such hazards arising from the exposure to or handling of the materials or substances in the manufacture, transportation, storage and other processes, to the workers employed in the factory, the Chief Inspector, the local authority within whose jurisdiction the factory is situated and the general public in the vicinity.

(2) The occupier shall, at the time of registering the factory involving a hazardous process, lay down a detailed policy with respect to the health and safety of the workers employed therein and intimate such policy to the Chief Inspector and the local authority and, thereafter, at such intervals as may be prescribed, inform the Chief Inspector and the local authority of any change made in the said policy.

(3) The information furnished under sub-section (1) shall include accurate information as to the quantity, specifications and other characteristics of wastes and the manner of their disposal.

(4) Every occupier shall, with the approval of the Chief Inspector, draw up and on-site emergency plan and detailed disaster control measures for his factory and make known to the workers employed therein and to the general public living in the vicinity of the factory the safety measures required to be taken in the event of an accident taking place.

(5) Every occupier of a factory shall,—

(a) if such factory engaged in a hazardous process on the commencement of the Factories (Amendment) Act, 1987, within a period of thirty days or such commencement; and

(b) if such factory proposes to engage in a hazardous process at any time after such commencement, within a period of thirty days before the commencement of such process,

inform the Chief Inspector of the nature and details of the process in such form and in such manner as may be prescribed.

(6) Where any occupier of a factory contravenes the provisions of sub-section (5), the licence issued under section 6 to such factory shall, notwithstanding any penalty to which the occupier of factory shall be subjected to under the provisions of this Act, be liable for cancellation.

(7) The occupier of a factory involving a hazardous process shall, with the previous approval of the Chief Inspector, lay down measures for the handling, usage, transportation and storage of hazardous substances inside the factory premises and the disposal of such substances outside the factory premises and publicise them in the manner prescribed among the workers and the general public living in the vicinity.

(xi) Civil Procedure Code, 1908

Civil Procedure Code is an important legislation dealing with the procedural administration of civil justice. It is also contains certain provisions pertaining to Right to Information. *Relevant provisions of Civil Procedure Code, 1908, Order XI, R. 14 to 19 reads: A brief discussion of those is as under.*

Production of documents[47]:—It shall be lawful for the Court, at any time during the pendency of any suit, to order the production by any party thereto, upon oath of such of the documents in his possession or power, relating to any matter in question is such suit, as the Court shall think right; and the Court may deal with such documents, when produced, in such manner as shall appear just.

Inspection of documents referred to in pleadings or affidavits:[48]—Every party to a suit shall be entitled [at or before the settlement of issues] to give notice to any other party, in whose pleadings or affidavits reference is made to any document [or who has entered any document in any list annexed to his pleadings] or produce such document for the inspection of the party giving such notice, or of his pleader, and to permit him or them to take copies thereof; and any party not complying with such notice shall not afterwards be at liberty to put any such document in evidence on his behalf in such suit unless he shall satisfy the Court that such document relates only to his own title, he being a defendant to the suit, or that he had some other cause or excuse which the Court shall deem sufficient for not complying with such notice, in which case the Court may allow the same to be put in evidence on such terms as to costs and otherwise as the Court shall think fit.

Notice to produce:[49]—Notice to any party to produce any documents referred to in his pleading or affidavits shall be in Form No. 7 in Appendix C, with such variations as circumstances may require.

Time for inspection when notice given:[50]—The party to whom such notice is given shall, within ten days from the receipt of such notice, deliver to the party giving the same a notice stating a time within three days from the delivery thereof at which the documents, or such of them as he does not object to produce, may be inspected at the office of his pleader, or in the case of banker's books or other books of account or books in constant use for the purpose of any trade or business, at their usual place of custody, and stating which (if any) of the documents he objects to produce, and on what ground. Such notice shall be in Form No. 8 in Appendix C, with such variations as circumstances may require.

Order for inspection:[51]—(1) Where the party served with notice under Rule 15 omits to give such notice of a time for inspection or objects to give inspection, or offers inspection elsewhere than at the office of his pleader, the Court may, on the application of the party desiring it, make an order for inspection in such place and in such manner as it may think fit:

Provided that the order shall not be made when and so far as the Court shall be of opinion that it is not necessary either for disposing fairly of the suit or for saving costs.

(2) Any application to inspect documents, except such as are referred to in the pleadings, particulars or affidavits of the party against whom the application is made or disclosed in his affidavit of documents, shall be founded upon an affidavit showing of what documents inspection is sought, that the party applying is entitled to inspect them, and that they are in the possession or power of the other party. The Court shall not make

such order for inspection of such documents when and so far as the Court shall be of opinion that it is not necessary either for disposing fairly of the suit or for saving costs.

Verified copies:[52]—(1) Where inspection of any business books is applied for, the Court may, if it thinks fit, instead of ordering inspection of the original books, order a copy of any entries therein to be furnished and verified by the affidavit of some person who has examined the copy with the original entries and such affidavit shall whether or not there are in the original book any and what erasures, interlineations or alterations:

Provided that, notwithstanding that such copy has been supplied, the Court may order inspection of the book from which the copy was made.

(2) Where on an application for an order for inspection privilege is claimed for any document, it shall be lawful for the Court to inspect the document for the purpose of deciding as to the validity of the claim of privilege [unless the document relates to matters of State.]

(3) The Court may, on the application of any party to a suit at any time, and whether an affidavit of documents shall or shall not have already been ordered or made, make an order requiring any other party to state by affidavit whether any one or more specific documents, to be specified in the application, is or are, or has or have at any time been, in his possession or power, and, if not then in his possession, when he parted with the same and what has become thereof. Such application shall be made on an affidavit stating that in the belief of the deponent the party against whom the application is made has, or has at some time had, in his possession or power the document or documents specified in the application, and that they relate to the matters in question in the suit, or to some of them.

(xii) The Indian Evidence Act, 1872

The Indian Evidence Act, 1872 has provided to relevant provision of right to information, Section 76 of the Evidence Act, 1872 has been termed as freedom of information, in boronic form, this provision requires public official to provide copies of public documents to any one who has a right inspect them. Further, other than this some relevant Sections read as follows:

Evidence as to affairs of State:[53]—No one shall be

permitted to give any evidence derived from unpublished official records relating to any affairs of State, except with the permission of the officer at the head of the department concerned, who shall give or without such permission as he thinks fit.

Official communications:[54]—No public officer shall be compelled to disclose communications made to him in official confidence, when he considers that the public interests would suffer by the disclosure.

Informations as to commission of offences:[55]—No Magistrate or Police Officer shall be compelled to say whence he got any information as to the commission of any offence, and no Revenue Officer shall be compelled to say whence he got any information as to the commission of any offence against the public revenue.

Explanation: 'Revenue Officer' in this section means an officer employed in or about the business of any branch of public revenue.

Professional communictions:[56]—***No barrister, attorney, pleader or* vakil *shall at any time be permitted, unless with his client's express consent, to disclose any communication made to him in the course and for the purpose of his employment as such barrister, pleader, attorney or* vakil, *by or on behalf of his client, or to state the contents or condition of any document with which he has become acquainted in the course and for the purpose of his professional employment, or to disclose any advice given by him to his client in the course and for the purpose of such employment.***

Provided that nothing in this section shall protect from disclosure—

(1) Any such communication made in furtherance of any illegal purpose; and

(2) Any fact observed by any barrister, pleader, attorney or vakil, in the course of his employment as such, showing that any crime or fraud has been committed since the commencement of his employment.

It is immaterial whether the attention of such barrister, pleader, attorney or vakil was or was not directed to such fact by or on behalf of his client.

(xiii) The Geographical Indications of Goods (Registration and Protection) Act, 1999

Section 78 of the Geographical Indications of Goods Act. 1999 deals provision relating Right to Information. Some important provisions read as follows:

Documents open to public inspection:—(1) The following documents, subject to such conditions as may be prescribed, be open to public inspection at the Geographical Indications Registry, namely—

(a) the register and any document upon which any entry in the register is based;

(b) every notice of opposition to the registration of a geographical indication, application for rectification before the Registrar, counter-statement thereto, and any affidavit or document filed by the parties in any proceedings before the Registrar;

(c) the indexes mentioned in section 77; and

(d) such other documents as the Central Government may, by notification in the Official Gazette, specify;

Provided that where such register is maintained wholly or partly on computer, the inspection of such register under this section shall be made by inspecting the computer print out the relevant entry in the register so maintained on computer.

(2) Any person may, on an application to the Registrar and on payment of such fee as may be prescribed, obtain a certified copy of any entry in the register or any document referred to in sub-section (1).

(xiv) The Information Technology Act, 2000

With the advent of new technologies it was felt that these must be certain apt law to regulate it. By this way the Information Technology Act, 2000 come into existence which categorically recognises certain electronic instruments which have come in existence during recent time of information. This Act deals with number of provisions relating Right to Information.

Authentication of electronic records:[57]—(1) Subject to the provisions of this section, any subscriber may authenticate an electronic record by affixing his digital signature.

(2) The authentication of the electronic record shall be effected by the use of asymmetric crypts system and hash function which envelop and transform the initial electronic record into another electronic record.

Explanation: For the purpose of this sub-section. "hash function" means an algorithm mapping or translation of one sequence of bits into another, generally smaller, set known as "hash result" such that an electronic record yields the same hash result every time the algorithm is executed with the same electronic record as its input making it computationally infeasible—

(a) to derive or reconstruct the original electronic record from the hash result produced by the algorithm; and
(b) that two electronic records can produce the same hash result using the algorithm.

(3) Any person by the use of a public key of the subscriber can verify the electronic record.

(4) The private key and the public key are unique to the subscriber and constitute a functioning key pair.

Legal recognition of electronic records:[58]—(1) Where any law provides that information or any other matter shall be in writing or in the typewritten or printed form, then, notwithstanding anything contained in such law, such requirement shall be deemed to have been satisfied if such information or matter is—

(a) rendered or made available in an electronic form; and
(b) accessible so as to be usable for a subsequent reference.

Legal recognition of digital signatures:[59]—Where any law provides that information or any other matter shall be authenticated by affixing the signature or any document shall be signed or bear the signature of any person, then, notwithstanding anything contained in such law, such requirement shall be deemed to have been satisfied, if such information or matter is authenticated by means of digital signature affixed in such manner as may be prescribed by the Central Government.

Explanation—For the purpose of this section, "signed", with its grammatical variations and cognate expressions, shall, with reference to a person, mean affixing of his hand written signature or any mark on any document and the expression "signature" shall be construed accordingly.

Use of electronic records and digital signatures in Government and its agencies:[60]—(1) Where any law provides for-

(a) the filing of any form, application or any other document with any office, authority, body or agency owned or controlled by the appropriate Government in a particular manner;
(b) the issue or grant of any licence, permit, sanction or approval by whatever name called in a particular manner; and
(c) the receipt or payment of money in a particular manner,

then, notwithstanding anything contained in any other law for the time being in force, such requirement shall be deemed to have been satisfied if such filing, issue, grant, receipt or payment, as the case may be, is effected by means of such electronic form as may be prescribed by the appropriate Government.

(2) The appropriate Government may, for the purpose of sub-section (1), by rules, prescribe—

(a) the manner and format in which such electronic records shall be filed, created or issued; and
(b) the manner or method of payment of any fee or charges for filing, creation or issue any electronic record under clause (a).

Retention of electronic records:[61]—(1) Where any law provides that documents, records or information shall be retained for any specific period, then, that requirement shall be deemed to have been satisfied if such documents, records or information are retained in the electronic form, if—

(a) the information contained therein remains accessible so as to be usable for a subsequent reference;

(b) the electronic record is retained in the format in which it was originally generated, sent or received or in a formal which can be demonstrated to represent accurately the information originally generated, sent or received; and

(c) the details which will facilitate the identification of the origin, destination, date and time of despatch or receipt of such electronic record are available in the electronic record:

Provided that this clause does not apply to any information which is automatically generated solely for the purpose of enabling an electronic record to be despatched or received.

(2) Nothing in this section shall apply to any law that expressly provides for the retention of documents, records or information in the form of electronic records.

Publication of rule, regulation, etc., in Electronic Gazette:[62]—Where any law provides that any rule, regulation, order, bye-law, notification or any other matter shall be published in the Official Gazette, then, such requirement shall be deemed to have been satisfied if such rule, regulation, order, bye-law, notification or any other matter is published in the Official Gazette or Electronic Gazette:

Provided that where any rule, regulation, order, bye-law, notification or any other matter is published in the Official Gazette or Electronic Gazette, the date of publication shall be deemed to be the date of the Gazette which was first published in any form.

Section 6, 7 and 8 not to confer right to insist document should be accepted in electronic form:[63]—Nothing contained in section 6, 7 and 8 shall confer a right upon any person to insist that any Ministry or Department of the Central Government or the State Government or any authority or body established by or under any law or controlled or funded by the Central or State Government should accept, issue, create, retain and preserve any document in the form of electronic records or effect any monetary transaction in the electronic form.

Attribution of electronic records:[64]—An electronic record shall be attributed to the originator,—

(a) if it was sent by the originator himself;

(b) by a person who had the authority to act on behalf of the originator in respect of that electronic record; or
(c) by an information system programmed by or on behalf of the originated to operate automatically.

Acknowledgments of receipt:[65]—(1) Where the originator has not agreed with the addressee that the acknowledgment of receipt of electronic record be given in a particular form or by a particular method, an acknowledgment may be given by—

(a) any communication by the addressee, automated or otherwise; or
(b) any conduct of the addressee, sufficient to indicate to the originator that the electronic record has been received.

(2) Where the originator has stipulated that the electronic record shall be binding only on receipt of an acknowledgment of such electronic record by him, then, unless acknowledgment has been so received, the electronic record shall be deemed to have been never sent by the originator.

(3) Where the originator has not stipulated that the electronic record shall be binding only on receipt of such acknowledgment, and the acknowledgment has not been received by the originator within the time specified or agreed or, if no time has been specified or agreed to within a reasonable time, then, the originator may give notice to the addressee stating that no acknowledgment has been received by him and specifying a reasonable time by which the acknowledgment must be received by him and if no acknowledgment is received within the aforesaid time limit he may after giving notice to the addressee, treat the electronic record as though it has never been sent.

Time and place of despatch and receipt of electronic record:[66]—(1) Save as otherwise agreed to between the originator and the addressee, the despatch of an electronic record occurs when it enters a computer resource outside the control of the originator.

(2) Save as otherwise agreed between the originator and the addressee, the time of receipt of an electronic record shall be determined as follows, namely:—

(a) If the addressee has designated a computer resource for the purpose of receiving electronic records,—

(i) receipt occurs at the time when the electronic record enters the designated computer resource; or

(ii) if the electronic record is sent to a computer resource of the addressee that is not the designated computer resource, receipt occurs at the time when the electronic record is retrieved by the addressee;

(b) if the addressee has not designated a computer resource along with specified timings, if any, receipt occurs when the electronic record enters the computer resource of the addressee.

(3) Save as otherwise agreed to between the originator and the addressee, an electronic record is deemed to be despatched at the place where the originator has his place of business, and is deemed to be received at the place where the addressee has his place of business.

(4) The provisions of sub-section (2) shall apply notwithstanding that the place where the computer resource is located may be different from the place where the electronic record is deemed to have been received under sub-section (3).

(5) For the purposes of this section—

(a) if the originator of the addressee has more than one place of business, the principal place of business, shall be the place of business;

(b) if the originator or the addressee does not have a place of business, his usual place of residence shall be deemed to be the place of business; and

(c) "usual place of residence", in relation to a body corporate, means the place where it is registered.

Secure electronic record:[67]—Where any security procedure has been applied to an electronic record at a specific point of time, then such record shall be deemed to be a secure electronic record from such point of time to the time of verification.

Secure digital signature:[68]—If, by application of a security procedure agreed to by the parties concerned, it can be verified that a digital signature, at the time it was affixed, was—

(a) unique to the subscriber affixing it;
(b) capable of identifying such subscriber; and
(c) created in a manner using a means under the exclusive control of the subscriber and is linked to the electronic record to which it relates in such a manner that if the electronic record was altered the digital signature would be invalidated,

then such digital signature shall be deemed to be a secure digital signature.

Access to computers and date:[69]—(1) Without prejudice to the provisions of sub-section (1) of section 68, the Controller or any person authorised by him shall, if he has reasonable cause to suspect the any contravention of the provisions of this Act, rules or regulations made thereunder has been committed, have access to any computer system, any apparatus, data or any other material connected with such system, for the purpose of searching or causing a search to be made for obtaining any information or data contained in or available to such computer system.

(2) For the purposes of sub-section (1), the Controller or any person authorised by him may, by order, direct any person incharge of, or otherwise concerned with the operation of, the computer system, data apparatus or material, to provide him with such reasonable technical and other assistance as he may consider necessary.

Certifying Authority to follow certain procedures:[70]—Every Certifying Authority shall,—

(a) make use of hardware, software, and procedures that are secure from intrusion and misuse;
(b) provide a reasonable level of reliability in its services which are reasonably suited to the performance of intended functions;
(c) adhere to security procedures to ensure that the secrecy and privacy of the digital signatures are assured; and
(d) observe such other standards as may be specified by regulations.

Disclosure:[71]—(1) Every Certifying Authority shall disclose in the manner specified by regulations—

(a) its Digital Signature Certificate which contains the public key corresponding to the private key used by that Certifying Authority to digitally sign another Digital Signature Certificate;
(b) any certification practice statement relevant thereto;
(c) notice of the revocation or suspension of its Certifying Authority certificate, if any; and
(d) any other fact that materially and adversely affects either the reliability of a Digital Signature Certificate, which that Authority has issued, or the Authority's ability to perform its services.

(2) Where in the opinion of the Certifying Authority any event has occurred or any situation has arisen which may materially and adversely affect the integrity of its computer system or the conditions subject to which a Digital Signature Certificate was granted, then, the Certifying Authority shall—

(a) use reasonable efforts to notify any person who is likely to be affected by that occurrence; or
(b) act in accordance with the procedure specified in its certification practice statement to deal with such event or situation.

Publishing of information which is obscene in electronic form:[73]—Whoever publishes or transmits or causes to be published in the electronic form, any material which is lascivious or appeals to the prurient interest or if its effect is such as to tend to deprave and corrupt persons who are likely, having regard to all relevant circumstances, to read, see or hear the matter contained or embodied in it, shall be punished on first conviction with imprisonment of either description for a term which may extend to five years and with fine which may extend to one lakh rupees and in the event of a second or subsequent conviction with imprisonment of either description for a term which may extend to ten years and also with fine which may extend to two lakh rupees.

Protected system:[73]—(1) The appropriate Government may, by notification in the Official Gazette, declare that any computer, computer system or computer network to be a protected system.

(2) The appropriate Government may, by order in writing, authorise the person who are authorised to access protected systems notified under sub-section (1).

(3) Any person who secures access or attempts to secure access to a protected system in contravention of the provisions of this section shall be punished with imprisonment of either description for a term which may extend to ten years and shall also be liable to fine.

Penalty for Breach of confidentiality and privacy:[74]—Save as otherwise provided in this Act or any other law for the time being in force, if any person who, in pursuance of any of the powers conferred under this Act, rules or regulations made thereunder, has secured access to any electronic record, book, register, correspondence, information, document or other material without the consent of the person concerned discloses such electronic record, book, register, correspondence, information, document or other material to any other person shall be punished with imprisonment for a term which may extend to two years, or with fine which may extend to one lakh rupees, or with both.

(xv) The Protection of Plant Varieties and Farmers' Rights Act, 2001

This Act is intended to protect farmers in the era of global competition. It too has provision for Right to Information which is as under:

Document open to public inspection:[75]—Any person may, on an application to the Authority or the Registrar, as the case may be, and on payment of such fees as may be prescribed, obtain a certified copy of any entry in the Register or any other document in any proceeding under this Act pending before such Authority or Registrar or may inspect such entry or document.

Government to be bound:[76]—The provisions of this Act shall be binding on the Government.

(xvi) The Protection of Plant Varieties and Farmers' Rights Rules, 2003

Further certain rules have been made in compliance of this Act read as follows:

Size, etc., of documents[77]:—All documents and copies of documents, except affidavits and drawings, sent to or left at the office of the Authority or otherwise furnished to the Registrar shall be written, typewritten, lithographed, or printed (either in the Hindi or in the English language unless otherwise directed or allowed by the Authority or the Registrar-General) in large and legible characters with deep indelible ink with lines widely spaced upon one side only of strong white paper of a size of approximately 33.00 centimeters by 20.50 centimeters (13 inches by 8 inches) or 29.7 centimeters by 21 centimeters (11¾ inches by 8¼ inches) with a margin of at least four centimeters (one and a half inches) on the left-hand part thereof.

(xvii) The Representation of the People Act, 1951

Our's is the world's largest democracy. The Democratic Setup is mainly based on free and fair election. There is a constitutional body in our country named as 'Election Commission" to conduct free and fair election. To further this cause there is a legislation the representation of the People Act, 1951. This incorporations numerous provisions for Right to Information which has been dealt as under:

Right to information:[78]—(1) A candidate shall, apart from any information which he is required to furnish, under this Act or the rules made thereunder, in his nomination paper delivered under sub-section (1) of section 33, also furnish the information as to whether—

(i) he is accused of any offence punishable with imprisonment for two years or more in a pending case in which a charge has been framed by the court of competent jurisdiction; and

(ii) he has been convicted of an offence other than any offence referred to in sub-section (1) or sub-section (2), or covered in sub-section (3), of section 8 and sentenced to imprisonment for one year or more.

(2) The candidate or his proposer, as the case may be, shall, at the time of delivering to the returning officer the nomination paper under sub-section (1) of section 33, also deliver to him an affidavit sworn by the candidate in a prescribed form verifying the information specified in sub-section (1).

(3) The returning officer shall, as soon as may be after the furnishing of information to him under sub-section (1), display the aforesaid information by affixing a copy of the affidavit, delivered under sub-section (2), at a conspicuous place at his office for the information of the electors relating to a constituency for which the nomination paper is delivered.

Candidate to furnish information only under the Act and the rules:[79]—Notwithstanding anything contained in any judgment, decree or order of any court or any direction, order or any other instruction issued by the Election Commission, no candidate shall be liable to disclose or furnish any such information, in respect of his election, which is not required to be disclosed or furnished under this Act or the rules made thereunder.

Publication of list of contesting candidates:[80]—(1) Immediately after the expiry of the period within which candidature may be withdrawn under sub-section (1) of section 37, the returning officer shall prepare and publish in such form and manner as may be prescribed a list of contesting candidates, that is to say, candidates who were included in the list of validly nominated candidates and who have not withdrawn their candidature within the said period.

(2) For the purpose of listing the names under sub-section (1), the candidates shall be classified as follows, namely:—

(i) candidates or recognised political parties;
(ii) candidates of registered political parties other than those mentioned in clause (i); and
(iii) other candidates.

(3) The categories mentioned in sub-section (2) shall be arranged in the order specified therein and the names of candidates in each category shall be arranged in alphabetical order and the addresses of the contesting candidates as given in the nomination papers together with such other particulars as may be prescribed.

Publication of results of elections to the Council of States and of names of persons nominated by the President:[81]—After the elections held in any year in pursuance of the notifications issued under section 12, there shall be notified by the appropriate authority in the Official Gazette the names of members elected by the elected members of the Legislative Assemblies of the State and by the members of the electoral colleges for the various Union territories at the said elections together with the names of any persons nominated by the President of the Council of State under sub-clause (a) of clause (1) of article 80 or under any other provisions.

Publication of results of general elections to the House of the People and the State Legislative Assemblies and of names of persons nominated thereto:[82]—Where a general election is held for the purpose of constituting a new House of the People or a new State Legislative Assembly, there shall be notified by the Election Commission in the Official Gazette, as soon as may be after the results of the elections in all the constituencies other than these in which the poll could not be taken for any reason on the date originally fixed under clause (d) of section 30 or for which the time for completion of the election has been extended under the provisions of section 153 have been declared by the returning officer under the provisions of section 53 or, as the case may be, section 66, the names of the members elected for those constituencies and upon the issue of such notification that House or Assembly shall be deemed to be duly constituted:

Provided that the issue of such notification shall not be deemed—

(a) to preclude—
   (i) the taking of the poll and the completion of the election in any Parliamentary or Assembly constituency or constituencies in which the poll could not be taken for any reason on the date originally fixed under clause (d) of section 30; or
   (ii) the completion of the election in any Parliamentary or Assembly constituency or constituencies for which time has been extended under the provisions of section 153; or

(b) to affect the duration of the House of the People or the State Legislative Assembly, if any, functioning immediately before the issue of the said notification.

Publication of results of elections the State Legislative

Councils and of names of persons nominated to such Councils:[83]—After the elections held in pursuance of the notifications issued under section 15A or in any year in pursuance of the notifications issued under section 16, there shall be notified by the appropriate authority in the Official Gazette the names of the members elected for the various Council constituencies and by the members of the Legislative Assembly of the State at the said elections together with the names of any persons nominated by the Governor under sub-clause (e) of clause (3) of Article 171.

Declaration of assets and liabilities:[84]—(1) Every elected candidate for a House of Parliament shall, within ninety days from the date on which he makes and subscribes an oath or affirmation, according to the form set out for the purpose in the Third Schedule to the Constitution, for taking his seat in either House of Parliament, furnish the information, relating to—

(i) the movable and immovable property of which he, his spouse and his dependant children are jointly or severally owners or beneficiary;
(ii) his liabilities to any public financial institution; and
(iii) his liabilities to the Central Government or the State Government,

to the Chairman of the Council of State or the Speaker of the House of the People, as the case may be.

(2) The information under sub-section (1) shall be furnished in such form and in such manner as may be prescribed in the rules made under sub-section (3).

(3) The Chairman of the Council of States or the Speaker of the House of the People, as the case may be, may make rules for the purposes of sub-section (2).

(4) The rules made by the Chairman of the Council of States or the Speaker of the House of the People, under sub-section (3) shall be laid, as soon as may be after they are made, before the Council of States or the House of the People, as the case may be, for a total period of thirty days which may be comprised in one session or in two or more successive sessions and shall take effect upon the expiry of the said period of thirty days unless they are sooner approved with or without modifications or disapproved

by the Council of States or the House or the People and where they are so approved, they shall take effect on such approval in the form in which they were laid or in such modified form, as the case may be, and where they are so disapproved, they shall be of no effect.

(5) The Chairman of the Council of States or the Speaker of the House of the People, as the case may be, may direct that any wilful contravention of the rules made under sub-section (3) by an elected candidate for a House of Parliament referred to in sub-section (1) may be dealt with in the same manner as a breach of privilege of the Council of States or the House of the People, as the case may be.

Explanation—For the purposes of this sections,—

(i) "immovable property" means the land and includes any building or other structure attached to the land or permanently fastened to anything which is attached to the land;

(ii) "movable property" means any other property which is not the immovable property and includes corporeal and incorporeal property of every description;

(iii) "public financial institution" means a public financial institution within the meaning of section 4A of the Companies Act, 1956 (1 of 1956) and includes bank;

(iv) "bank" referred to in clause (iii) means—

(a) State Bank of India constituted under section 3 of the State Bank of India Act, 1955 (23 of 1955);

(b) subsidiary bank having the meaning assigned to it in clause (k) of section 2 of the State Bank of India (Subsidiary Banks) Act, 1959 (38 of 1959);

(c) Regional Rural Bank established under section 3 of the Regional Rural Banks Act, 1976 (21 of 1976);

(d) corresponding new bank having the meaning assigned to it in clause (da) of section 5 of the Banking Regulation Act, 1949 (10 of 1949);

(e) co-operative bank having the meaning assigned to it in clause (cci) of section 5 of the Banking Regulation Act, 1949 (10 of 1949) as modified by sub-section (i) of clause (c) of section 56 of that Act; and

(v) "dependant children" means sons and daughters who have no separate means of earning and are wholly dependant on the elected candidate referred to in sub-section (1) for their livelihood.

Free supply of copies of electoral rolls:[85]—(1) The Government shall, at any election to be held for the purposes of constituting the House of the People or the Legislative Assembly of a State, supply, free of cost, to the candidate of recognised political parties such number of copies of the electoral roll, as finally published under the Representation of the People Act, 1950 (43 of 1950) and such other material as may be prescribed.

(2) The material referred to in sub-section (1) shall be supplied-

(i) subject to such conditions as may be imposed by the Central Government in constituting with the Election Commission with respect to the reduction of the maximum expenditure which may be incurred by the candidate under section 77; and

(ii) through such officers as may be specified by the Election Commission shall, act in accordance with such general or special directions as may be given by the Election Commission.

Supply of certain items to candidates, etc.:[86]—(1) The Election Commission shall, at any time between the date of publication of the notification calling the election for the purpose of constituting the House or the People or the Legislative Assembly of a State and the date on which the poll is to be taken, supply or cause to be supplied, such items as the Central Government may, by order, determine in consultation with the Election Commission, to the electors in the constituencies concerned or to the candidates set-up by the recognised political parties.

(2) Where the Election Commission supplies the items to the candidates under sub-section (1), the Central Government may, in consultation with the Election Commission, impose conditions with respect to the reduction of the maximum expenditure which may be incurred by the candidate under section 77.

Explanation—For the purposes of section 39A, this Chapter and clause (hh) of sub-section (2) of section 169, the expression "recognised political party", has the meaning assigned to it in the Election Symbols (Reservation and Allotment) Order, 1968.

(xviii) The Semiconductor Integrated Circuits Layout-design Act, 2000

The Semiconductor Integrated Circuits Act, 2000 provides some information relating Right to Information. The important provisions read as follows:

Documents open to public inspection:[87]—(1) Save as otherwise provided in sub-section (4) of section 25,—

(a) the register and any document upon which any entry in the register is based;

(b) every notice of opposition to the registration of a layout-design application for rectification before the Registrar, counter-statement thereto, and any affidavit or document filed by the parties in any proceedings before the Registrar; and

(c) the indexes mentioned in section 86 and such other documents as the Central Government may, by notification in the Official Gazette, specify;

shall, subject to such conditions as may be prescribed, be open to public inspection at the Semiconductor Integrated Circuits Layout-Design Registry.

(2) Any person may, on an application to the Registrar and on payment of such fees as may be prescribed, obtain a certified copy of any entry in the register or any document referred to in sub-section (1).

(xix) The Trademarks Act, 1999

This Act is chiefly for stopping unscrupulous use of trade marks and this is done by making the information public, which is an aspect of Right to Information. Certain provisions are as under:

Documents open to public inspection:[88]—(1) Save as otherwise provided in sub-section (4) of section 49,—

(a) the register and any document upon which any entry in the register is based;
(b) every notice of opposition to the registration of a trade mark application for rectification before the Registrar, counter-statement thereto, and any affidavit or document filed by the parties in any proceedings before the Registrar;
(c) all regulations deposited under section 63 or section 74, and all applications under section 66 or section 77 for varying such regulations;
(d) the indexes mentioned in section 147; and
(e) such other documents as the Central Government may, by notification in the Official Gazette, specify,

shall, subject to such conditions as may be prescribed, be open to public inspection at the Trade Marks Registry:

Provided that when such register is maintained wholly or partly on computer, the inspection of such register under this section shall be made by inspecting the computer print-out of the relevant entry in the register so maintained on computer.

(2) Any person may, on an application to the Registrar and on payment of such fees as may be prescribed, obtain a certified copy of any entry in the register or any document referred to in sub-section (1).

4. SPECIFIC LAW ON RIGHT TO INFORMATION

(i) Background

Disclosure of Government Information in India is governed by a law enacted during the British rule over large parts of what is now India, the Official Secrets Act of 1889 which was amended in 1923.[89] This law secures information related to security of the State, sovereignty of the country and friendly relations with foreign states, and contains provisions which prohibit disclosure of non-classified information. The Right to Information Act, 2005 (Act No. 22/2005) is a law enacted by the Parliament of India giving citizens of India access to records of the Central Government and State Governments. This law was passed by Parliament on 15 June 2005 and came fully into force on 13 October 2005. Information disclosure in India was hitherto restricted by the Official Secrets Act, 1923 and various other special laws, which the new Right to Information Act now relaxes.

(ii) State-level Laws on Right to Information

While the debate on the national level legislation goes on, a few states have, since 1997, enforced their own Right to Information laws, with varying degree of impeccability. Tamil Nadu was the first State to set an example by introducing the Right to Information Act on 17th April, 1996.

The Right to Information Laws were first successfully enacted by the state governments:—Tamil Nadu (1997)[90], Goa (1997), Rajasthan (2000), Karnataka (2000), Delhi (2001), Maharashtra (2002), Madhya Pradesh (2003), Assam (2002) and Jammu and Kashmir (2004). The Acts were diverse and disparate in critical provisions, particularly with respect to appeals and penalties for non-compliance. The Maharashtra and Delhi State level enactments are considered to have been the most widely used. The Delhi Right to Information Act is still in force. Jammu & Kashmir, has its own Right to Information Act of 2009, the successor to the repealed Jammu and Kashmir Right to Information Act, 2004 and its 2008 amendment.

(iii) Freedom of Information Act, 2002

Passage of a national level law, however, proved to be a difficult task. Given the experience of state governments in passing practicable legislation, the Central Government appointed a working group under H. D. Shourie and assigned it the task of drafting legislation. The Shourie draft, in an extremely diluted form, was the basis for the Freedom of Information Bill, 2000 which eventually became law under the Freedom of Information Act, 2002. An Act to provide for freedom to every citizen to secure access to information under the control of public authorites, consistent with public interest, in order to promote openness, transparency and accountability in administration and in relation to matters connected therewith or incidental thereto.

This Act was severely criticised for permitting too many exemptions, not only under the standard grounds of national security and sovereignty, but also for requests that would involve "disproportionate diversion of the resources of a public authority." There was no upper limit on the charges that could be levied. There were no penalties for not complying with a request for information. The Freedom of Information Act, 2002 consequently, never came into effective force.

(iv) The Right to Information Act, 2005

(a) General

The Right to Information promotes transparency; empowers the citizen; reduces corruption; increases efficiency; makes their accountable, and puts an end to their indifference, arrogance and corruption. Unless the citizens are informed of their rights in the form of information, probably they cannot assert their rights and make the government accountable for its actions.

The Government of India passed the Right to Information Act, 2005. The basic premise is that the informed citizenry and transparency of information is necessary to contain corruption and make the government accountable. The Act not only recognizes this right but also provides for mechanisms to realize this right. The Act makes this right a statutory positive right, which lays the corresponding positive duty on the public authority to supply information. The Act also provides for procedure for procuring information and penalty for giving insufficient and wrong information or not providing information or providing not in the manner in which it is sought. This Act is kept at high pedestal as all other enactments are to be read subject to this Act.

(b) Important Provisions

The Act in its **Preamble** says to provide for the setting up of the practical regime of right to information for all citizens to secure access to information under the control of public authorities in order to promote transparency and accountabilities in the working of every public authority. The whole Act is in light of democratic approach of participating government. This Act is an attempt in the direction of achieving the goal of promoting transparency and accountability in the working of every public authority. This Act turns into reality the right of citizens to secure access to information under the control of public authorities.

HIGHLIGHTS OF RIGHT TO INFORMATION ACT, 2005

1.	FEE	Cost of copying plus a fee of Rs. 10/ generally. Poor citizens are exempted from fee.
2.	EXEMPTIONS	No. of exemptions increased to 11 clauses only 20 years old information also has 3 restrictions. Class exemtions are provided.
3.	TIME LIMIT	30 days for grating or refusing.
4.	URGENT REQUEST	Information regarding rise and liberty has to be given within 48 hours.
5.	*SUO MOTO* DESCLOSURE	Public Authority has an obligation to disclose. See. 4.
6.	APPEALS	Appeal is provided to Appellate Authority and thereafter to Information Commission.
7.	PRIVATE BODIES	Private bodies are left out of pruview.
8.	MEANS OF COMMUNICATION	Disclosure in websites, printing of modules, workbooks, manuals, etc. to made mandatory.
9.	PUBLICATION & ACT	It is mandatory.
10.	TRAINING	It is mandatory.
11.	PENALTIES	Rs. 250 per day not exceding Rs. 25,000 can be imposed for delay, unjustified denial, etc., and departmental action in recommended. (Imprisonment provisions removed)
12.	REGULATORY BODY	Information Commission is created as a Regulatory at centre and state levels, with independent powers.

According to Section 2(i) of Right to Information Act, 2005, **record includes** any mode of information in any form of record, document, e-mail, circular, press releases, contact, sample electronic data, etc.

The Act defines **Information**[91] as any material in any form including records, documents, memos, e-mails, opinions, advises, press releases, circular, orders, logbooks, contracts, reports, papers, samples, models, data material held in any electronic form and information relating to any private body which can be accessed by a public authority under any other law for the time being in force.

Further the Act define word ***"Right to Information"***[92] means the Right to Information accessible under this Act which is held by or under the control of any public authority and includes the right to—inspection of work, documents, records; taking notes, extracts, or certified copies of documents or records; taking certified samples of material; obtaining information in the form of diskettes, floppies, tapes, video cassettes or in any other electronic mode or through printouts where such information is stored in a computer or in any other device;

As a preparatory step the Act makes it mandatory for all the public authorities to collect, document and computerize all the information they have and publish the same in all media possible including the web within 120 days from the enactment of this Act.[93] The Act also mandates all the public authorities to constantly endeavor to take steps to provide as much information suo motu as possible to the public at regular intervals so that citizens have minimum resort to this Act.

Section 5 mandates the public authorities to designate some of its officers as Central/State Public Information Officers and Assistant Information Officer as the case may be at each sub-divisional or sub-district level within 100 days of the enactment of this Act.

Section 6 of this Act provide **Request for Obtaining Information.** According to this Section a person, who desires to obtain any information under this Act, shall make a request in writing or through electronic means in English or Hindi in the official language of the area in which the application is be being made, accompanying such fee as may be prescribed to, where such request cannot be made in writing, the Central Public Information Officer or State Public Information Officer, as the case may be, shall render all reasonable assistance to the person making the request orally to reduce the same in writing.

An applicant making request for information shall not be required to give any reason for requesting the information or any other personal details except those that may be necessary for contacting him.

Section 7 of this Act is related to the Disposal of Request. The Central Public Information Officer or State Public Information Officer, as the case may be on receipt of a request under Section 6 shall, as expeditiously as possible, and in any case within thirty days of the receipt of the request, either provide the information on payment of such fee as may be prescribed or reject the request for any of the reasons specified in Section 8 and 9.

Provided that where the information sought for concerns the life or liberty of a person, the same be provided within forty-eight hours of the receipt of the request. No such fee shall be charged from the person who are of below poverty line as may be determined by the appropriate Government.

The Act provides for around ten exemptions against the disclosure of information out of which six are absolute where there is not option for the public information officer but to refuse to make information available.[94] According to Section 8, Information which can not be given, we can see the following flow chart:

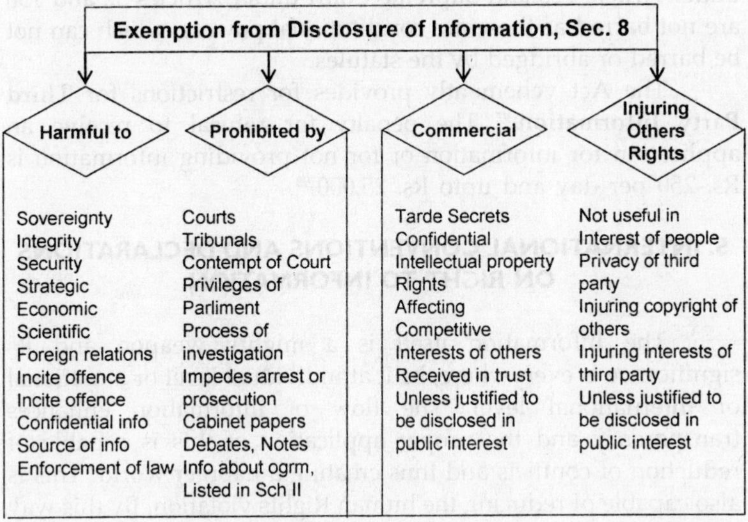

The Act provides for the constitution of Central Information Commission[95] and State Information Commission[96] at the Centre and State levels respectively. It consists of Chief Information Commissioner and not more than ten information commissioners. The Act also provides for appointment, terms of office, conditions of and removal from service, the chief and other information commissioners. Section 18 deals with power and function of Commission.

Under Section 19, the Act provides for Appeals Against the Decisions of the information officer to the officer senior in rank on the grounds that the decision of the information officer is not received within time under section 7(1) or (3) (a) or is aggrieved by a decision of the information officer. Against the decision of the appellate authority, a second appeal may be filed to the Central or State commissions as the case may be.

The decision of the Central Information Commission or State Information Commission, as the case may be, shall be binding. Section 23 of the Act bars the jurisdiction of the courts to entertain any suit, application or other proceeding in respect of any other made under Act. This bars the jurisdiction of not only the lower courts but also the High Court in its original and appellate jurisdiction. But, the writ jurisdiction of the High Courts under Article 226 and Supreme Court under Articles 32 and 136 are not barred as these are constitutional powers, which can not be barred or abridged by the statutes.

The Act vehemently provides for restrictions for **Third Party Information.**[97] The penalty for refusal to receive an application for information or for not providing information is Rs. 250 per day and upto Rs. 25,000.[98]

5. INTERNATIONAL CONVENTIONS AND DECLARATIONS ON RIGHT TO INFORMATION

The Information itself is a mighty weapon and its significance is everywhere, be it at individual level or at national or international level. The flow of information enhances transparency and the proper application of this is capable of reduction of conflicts and thus creating a happier world. This is also capable of reducing the human Rights violation. By this way this right to information at international level is a great service to mankind.

At the International level, the Right to Information finds articulation as inalienable fundamental human right in basic human rights documents, namely, the Universal Declaration of Human Rights, the International Covenant on Civil and Political Rights and the International Covenant on Economic, Social and Cultural Rights.

(i) United Nations Charter on Right to Information

Right to Information was recognised by the United Nations at its very inception in 1946, when the General Assembly resolved: "Freedom of Information is a fundamental human right and the touchstone for all freedoms to which the United Nations consecrated[99]."

(ii) Universal Declaration of Human Rights, 1948 on Right to Information

The Universal Declaration of Human Right of 1948 adopted on 10 December 1948.[100] The annual Assembly accepted and recognized importance of Freedom of Information when it was included under universal declaration of human right. Article 19 of the universal declaration of human rights, 1948 directly related to right to information, Article 19 read as under follows:

> "Everyone has the right to freedom of opinion and expression; this right includes freedom to hold opinions without interference and to seek, receive and impart information and ideas through any media and regardless of frontiers."

(iii) International Covenant on Civil and Political Rights, 1966[101] and Right to Information

It is legally binding treaty was adopted by the UN General Assembly in 1966. It declared right of people to be fully and reliable informed and so as to improve their understanding through free flow of information and opinion. This covenant is done under the agencies of the United Nations for the protection of civil and political rights at international level. This also include some relevant provisions of Right to Information which are as under:

The International covenant of civil and political right, 1966 broadly referred to the Article 19.[102] According to:

1. Everyone shall have the right to hold opinions without interference.
2. Everyone shall have the right to freedom of expression; this right shall include freedom to seek, receive and impart information and ideas of all kinks,

regardless of frontiers, either orally, in writing or in print, in the form of Art., or through any other media of his choice.

3. The exercise of the rights provided for in paragraph 2 of the Article carries with it special duties and responsibilities. It may therefore be subject to certain restrictions, but these shall only be such as are provided by law and are necessary:
   (a) for respect of the rights or reputations of others;
   (b) for the protection of national security or of public order (order public), or of public health or morals.

(iv) International Convention on the Elimination of all Forms of Racial Discrimination, 1966 and Right to Information

Another convention for elimination of all types of social discrimination was made at international level under the auspices of United Nations, which has certain inherent provision for Right to Information. The International Convention of the Elimination of all Forms of Racial Discrimination[103] was adopted in 1966.

Article 7 of International Convention on of the Elimination of all Forms of Racial Discrimination, 1966 broadly referred to Right to Information in different fields of society. Article 7 read as follows:

States Parties undertake to adopt immediate and effective measures, particularly in the fields of teaching, education, culture and information, with a view to combating prejudices which lead to racial discrimination and to promoting understanding, tolerance and friendship among nations and racial or ethnical groups, as well as to propagating the purpose and principles of the Charter of the United Nations, the Universal Declaration of Human Rights, the United Nations Declaration on the Elimination of All Forms of Racial Discrimination, and this Convention.

(v) American Declaration of the Rights of Man, 1948

American declaration of the rights of man, 1948 Adopted by the 9th International Conference of American States. Some Relevant Provisions of the Declaration relating Right to Information read as follows:

Right to Life, Liberty and Personal Security[104]

Every human being has the right to life, liberty and the security of his person.

Right to Freedom of Investigation, Opinion, Expression and Dissemination[105]

Every person has the right to freedom of investigation, of opinion, and of the expression and dissemination of ideas, by any medium whatsoever.

(vi) American Convention on Human Rights ('Pact of San Jose, *Costa Rica*') 1969

American convention on human rights ('pact of San Jose, costa rica') came into force on 18th July, 1978. Some Relevant Provisions of the Convention relating Right to Information reads as follows:

Obligation to Respect Rights[106]

1. The States Parties to this Convention undertake to respect the rights and freedoms recognized herein and to ensure to all person subject to their jurisdiction the free and full exercise of those rights and freedoms, without any discrimination for reasons of race, color, sex, language, religion, political or other opinion, national or social origin, economic status, birth, or any other social condition.

2. For the purposes of this Convention, "person" means every human being.

Freedom of Thought and Expression[107]

1. Everyone has the right to freedom of thought and expression. This right includes freedom to seek, receive, and impart information and ideas of all kinds, regardless of frontiers, either orally, in writing, in print, in the form of Art., or through any other medium of one's choice.

2. The exercise of the right provided for in the foregoing paragraph shall not be subject to prior censorship but shall be subject to subsequent imposition of liability, which shall be expressly established by law to the extent necessary to ensure:

(a) respect for the rights or reputations of others; or
(b) the protection of national security, public order, or public health or morals.

3. The right of expression may not be restricted by indirect methods or means, such as the abuse of government or private controls over newsprint, radio broadcasting frequencies, or equipment used in the dissemination of information, or by any other means tending to impede the communication and circulation of ideas and opinions.

4. Notwithstanding the provisions of paragraph 2 above, public entertainments may be subject by law to prior censorship for the sole purpose of regulating access to them for the moral protection of childhood and adolescence.

5. Any propaganda for war and any advocacy of national, racial, or religious hatred that constitute incitements to lawless violence or to any other similar action against any person or group of persons on any grounds including those of race, color, religion, language, or national origin shall be considered as offenses punishable by law.

(vii) African Charter on Human and Peoples' Rights, 1981 and Right to Information

African charter on human and peoples' rights, 1981 come into force for each member state which has accepted it in accordance with its constitutional procedure, three months after the Secretary-General has received the notice of acceptance. Article 9 of the African Charter on Human and Peoples' Rights, 1981 promote the Right to Information. These Articles read as under follows:

1. Every individual shall have the right to receive information.
2. Every individual shall have the right to express and disseminate his opinions within the law.

(viii) Rome Convention for the Protection of Human Rights and Fundamental Freedoms, 1950

Rome convention for the protection of human rights and fundamental freedoms, 1950 held at Rome, 4th November, 1950; came into force on 3rd September, 1953. Some Relevant Provisions of the Rome Convention relating Right to Information reads as follows:

Freedom of Expression[108]

1. Everyone has the right to freedom of expression. This right shall include freedom to hold opinions and to receive and impart information and ideas without interference by public authority and regardless of frontiers. This Article shall not prevent States from requiring the licensing of broadcasting, television or cinema enterprises.

2. The exercise of these freedoms, since it carries with its duties and responsibilities, may be subject to such formalities, conditions, restrictions or penalties as are prescribed by law and are necessary in a democratic society, in the interests of national security, territorial integrity or public safety, for the protection of the reputation or rights of others, for preventing the disclosure of information received in confidence, or for maintaining the authority and impartiality of the judiciary.

6. CONCLUSION

The development of law and society are interdependent on each other. Both of these go almost hand in hand and change their form according to other. In fact, we can not imagine a lawless society. There is the existence of certain sets of rules to govern the conduct of different instruments of society. So that the people can live peacefully in society with the change in time we found certain laws for the strengthening of individual. This fact applies to Right to Information. It has become a law of almost universal application. This law is also being supplemented by other legislation which contain in themselves provisions for Right to Information.

In the present time, most of the countries have their own Right to Information. In our country we have a specific law, namely, Right to Information. Other than this law other enactment also protect the Right to Information. There is a great deal of contribution of our constitution in protecting information Right. Now-a-days we can find that it has been tried to take this Right to Information law at grass-root level for help and protection of general public.

The present scenario is witness to the fact that Right to Information has become a global phenomenon. It has covered a long distance since its inception at international level. It was in its recent stage at the time of Universal Declaration of Human Right. Since then it has become a prominent figure these days, as has been discussed in above details. The Information sharing at international level is so important that to dispense with this would give rise to conflicts. Though we still do not have a good enough transparent mechanism for Right to Information at international level. If we would succeed in doing so, there would be less corrupt world and more transparent fearless universe.

Notes and References

1. Shalu Nigam, Let us Know: Right to Information: Law and Practice, 2006, p. 65.
2. Sunil Dutt *v.* Union of India, AIR 1982 SC 53.
3. Hanshmukh *v.* State, AIR 1981 SC 28.
4. Section 50.
5. Section 50(A).
6. Section 207.
7. Section 208.
8. Section 39.
9. Section 40.
10. Section 53.
11. Section 54.
12. Section 60B.
13. Section 61.
14. Section 63.
15. Section 64.
16. Section 118.
17. Section 144.
18. Section 197.
19. Section 222.
20. Section 223.
21. Section 305.
22. Section 306.
23. Section 307.
24. Section 308.
25. Section 393.
26. Section 424.
27. Section 461.
28. Section 485.
29. Section 488.
30. Section 489.

31. Section 548.
32. Section 549.
33. Section 551.
34. Section 610.
35. Section 610A.
36. Section 615.
37. Section 627.
38. Section 628.
39. Section 10.
40. Section 11.
41. Section 16.
42. Section 17.
43. Section 18.
44. Section 3.
45. Section 4.
46. Section 41B.
47. Order XI, Rule 14.
48. Order XI, Rule 15.
49. Order XI, Rule 16.
50. Order XI, Rule 17.
51. Order XI, Rule 18.
52. Order XI, Rule 19.
53. Section 123.
54. Section 124.
55. Section 125.
56. Section 126.
57. Section 3.
58. Section 4.
59. Section 5.
60. Section 6.
61. Section 7.
62. Section 8.
63. Section 9.
64. Section 11.
65. Section 12.
66. Section 13.
67. Section 14.
68. Section 15.
69. Section 29.
70. Section 34.
71. Section 34.
72. Section 67.
73. Section 70.
74. Section 72.

75. Section 84.
76. Section 86.
77. Section 9.
78. Section 33A.
79. Section 33B.
80. Section 38.
81. Section 71.
82. Section 73.
83. Section 74.
84. Section 75A.
85. Section 78A
86. Section 78B.
87. Section 87.
88. Section 148
89. The Official Secrets Act, 1923. IndiaLawInfo.com. http://www.indialawinfo.com/bareacts/OSA.html
90. "Comparative Table of RTI Laws in India." Commonwealth Human Rights Initiative. http://www.humanrightsinitiative.org/programs/ai/rti/india/Comparative%20Table%20-%20Indian%20RTI%20laws.htm.
91. Section 2F.
92. Section 2J.
93. Section 4.
94. Section 8.
95. Section 12.
96. Section 15.
97. Section 11.
98. Section 20.
99. UN General Assembly (1946), Resolution 59(1), 65th Plenary Meeting, December 14.
100. Vide United Nations General Assembly Resolution 217A (III), dated 10 December, 1948.
101. Vide United Nations General Assembly Resolution 2200A (XXI), dated 16 December, 1966.
102. International Covenant on Civil and Political Rights, 1966.
103. Opened for signature and New York, dated 7 March 1966.
104. Article 1.
105. Article 4.
106. Article 1.
107. Article 13.
108. Article 10.

CHAPTER 4

RIGHT TO INFORMATION IN DEMOCRACY

I. INTRODUCTION

"If liberty and equality, as is thought by some are chiefly to be found in democracy, they will be best attained when all persons alike share in the government to the utmost."

—(*Aristotle—Greek philosopher*)

After a long period of slavery we got independence. At that time there was a great deal of advocacy for the right to freedom and equality in the whole world. It was possible only when we incorporated a democratic form of government in our national ruling system. In British period the oppression of Indians was at its peak, and equality and freedom was highly ignored. So, after independence our great leaders emphasized a democratic government governed by the principle of liberty and equality. Finally, when we adopted, enacted and gave to ourselves our Constitution on 26th of Nov. 1949. We incorporated liberty and equality in its preamble.

It is an undisputed fact that we have adopted a democratic form of government and we are the largest democracy in the world. Because the democratic government is an open government with no room for secrecy, and the citizens have the right to know about the different activities of government and administration. Infact, for a healthy and accountable democracy the Right to Information is a must. Without this the democracy can not survive flourish in full. The basis of good democracy is right to information. If there is a lack of right to information in democracy that is not a democracy in true sense. In this chapter different aspects of Right to Information regarding democracy have been discussed and this chapter therefore utmost importance also.

The democracy rests on good governance founded on transparency, openness and accountability. Democracy is the best form of government for a country, more especially with a large population like us, which is based on the principle of 'government of the people, for the people and by the people'. A democratic form of government is administered through the peoples' participation and such government is presumed to work for excellence and betterment of the common man. As such, transparency, is a fundamental component of democracy. Democracy prohibits any form of secrecy in governance. Happening in the Government cannot be withheld by a section of people to another section of the people. No democratic Government can survive without transparency and accountability and the basic need for result-oriented functioning of the democracy is that people should have information about each and every act of the Government. To make democracy meaningful, access of information to the citizen is a must. It is the only source to promote openness, transparency in a democracy.[1]

We live in a democratic age. Over the last century the world has been shaped by one trend above all others—the rise of democracy. In 1900 not a single country had what we would today consider a democracy: a government created by elections in which every adult citizen could vote. Today 119 countries do, comprising 62 percent of all countries in the world. What was once a peculiar practice of a handful of states around the North Atlantic has become the standard form of government for humankind. Monarchies are antique, fascism and communism utterly discredited. Even Islamic theocracy appeals only to a fanatical few. For the vast majority of the world, democracy is the sole surviving source of political legitimacy.

We live in a democratic age in an even broader sense. From its Greek root, "democracy" means "the rule of the people." And every where we are witnessing the shift of power downward. I call this "democratization," even though it goes far beyond politics, because the process is similar: hierarchies are breaking down, closed systems are opening up, and pressures from the masses are now the primary engine of social change. Democracy has gone from being a form of government to a way of life.

Consider the economic realm. What is truly distinctive and new about today's capitalism is not that it is global or information rich or technologically driven—all that has been true at earlier points in history—but rather that it is *democratic*. Over the last half-century economic growth has enriched hundreds of millions in the industrial world, turning consumption, saving, and investing into a mass phenomenon. This has forced the social structures of societies to adapt. Economic power, which was for centuries held by small groups of businessmen, bankers, and bureaucrats, has as a result, been shifting downward. Today most companies—indeed most countries—woo not the handful that are rich but the many that are middle class. And rightly so, for the assets of the most exclusive investment group are dwarfed by those of a fund of workers' pensions.

Culture has also been democratized. What was once called "high culture" continues to flourish, of course, but as a niche product for the elderly set, no longer at the center of society's cultural life, which is now defined and dominated by popular music, blockbuster movies, and prime-time television. Those three make up the canon of the modern age, the set of cultural references with which everyone in society is familiar. The democratic revolution coursing through society has changed our very definition of culture. The key to the reputation of, say, a singer in an old order would have been *who* liked her. The key to fame today is *how many* like her. And by that yardstlck Madonna will always trump Jessye Norman. Quantity has become quality. What has produced this dramatic shift? As with only large-scale social phenomenon, many forces have helped produce the democratic wave—a technological revolution, growing middle-class wealth, and the collapse of alternative systems and ideologies that organized society. To these grand systemic causes add another: America. The rise and dominance of America—a country whose politics and culture are deeply democratic—has made democratization seem inevitable. Whatever its causes, the democratic wave is having predictable effects in every area. It is breaking down hierarchies, empowering individuals, and transforming societies well beyond their politics. Indeed much of what is distinctive about the world we live in is a consequence of the democratic idea. We often read during the roaring 1990s that technology and information had been democratized. This is a relatively new phenomenon.[2]

2. MEANING OF DEMOCRACY

A superficial definition of democracy would be 'rule by the people' as the word, first used in the fifth century BC, combines the Greek words of *demos* (the people) and *kratein* (to rule).[3] However, this rule by the people is no longer literal. Democracy has now evolved to require rule by the people's representatives.

Democracy is defined by Abraham Lincon as the government, of the people, for the people and by the people.[4] It is a system that is the most acceptable. Every single individual in the country is a part of the process of governing the legislature is elected by the people. It makes laws for the people. The executive, selected from the legislature, runs the country for the people. If it is corrupt or failing in this duty it will not be re-elected the next time. This does not mean that democracy is an ideal system for which makes the functioning of the government flawless. Democracy has also its failure. It does not guarantee social justice. Sometimes those in powers are corrupt. At the time the governing bodies keep their actions a secret and do not take the people into the confidence. It is slow in functioning and is incapable of coping up with emergency but in spite of all this defects democracy is the most effective form of government.

If the democracy is to be effective the people have to be alert. They must continuously keep tack of the activities of those to whom they have entrusted the reins of government. They must to raise a voice against injustice and atrocities. Democracy gives them this height and opportunity. But most important they must perform their functions as citizens faithfully and to the best of their abilities. If an individual is corrupt he cannot accept those in power to be free from corruption. Democracy is better than other forms of government. Other forms of government are monarchy and dictatorship of an individual, of a foreign imperialist government, of a military or of a political party. In both monarchy and dictatorship, the ruler-individual or group-wields absolute power and people have no remedy against its misuse. Absolute power corrupts absolutely. There is no individual freedom, freedom of speech or expression. But the most important attribute of democracy is that everyone is treated equally before the law, irrespective of caste, creed or sex. Everyone is entitled to freedom of speech, worship, occupation and to move throughout the country.

3. HISTORY OF DEMOCRACY

(i) Origin of Democracy

The beginnings of democracy can be credited to the Greeks of the sixth century BC. The word comes from two Greek words: demos, meaning "the people," and kratein, meaning "to rule." These two words are joined together to form democracy, literally meaning "rule by the people" (Pious). The Greek system of government was perhaps closer to a true democracy or rule by the people than any other in history. The Greeks viewed dictatorship as the worst possible form of government, so their government evolved as the exact opposite. Their civilization was broken down into small city-states, and all the men voted on all issues of government. There were no representatives in the Greek system of government. Instead, they ruled themselves directly; each man was a life long member of the decision-making body. This was almost a total democracy except for the fact that women and slaves were not considered citizens and were not allowed to vote. Despite this, no other civilization has come as close to democracy as its creators, the Greeks, and many later civilizations have incorporated this Greek idea as part of the foundation for their government.[5]

The term ***democracy*** first appeared in ancient Greek political and philosophical thought. The philosopher Plato contrasted democracy, as the system of "rule by the governed", with the alternative systems of monarchy, oligarchy and timocracy. Ideas of democracy similar to that of the Greeks were used by the Romans, though not to the same extent. The Roman Empire took some of their governmental ideals from the Greeks. Their government was a representative democracy, which had representatives from the nobility in the Senate and representatives from the commoners in the Assembly. Governmental power was divided between these two branches and they voted on various issues. Many Roman political thinkers were fond of democracy. The Roman Statesman, Cicero was one. Cicero suggested that all people have certain rights that should be preserved. He and other political philosophers of the time taught that governmental and political power should come from the people. After the trend of democracy was started by the Greeks and carried on by the Romans, it has been seen in many later governmental systems throughout history.[6]

Although Athenian democracy is today considered by many to have been a form of direct democracy, originally it had two distinguishing features:

Firstly, the allotment (selection by lot) of ordinary citizens to government offices and courts, and

Secondly, the assembly of all the citizens. All the male Athenian citizens were eligible to speak and vote in the Assembly, which set the laws of the city-state; citizenship was not granted to women, or slaves. Of the 250,000 inhabitants only some 30,000 on average were citizens. Of those 30,000 perhaps 5,000 might regularly attend one or more meetings of the popular Assembly. Most of the officers and magistrates of Athenian government were allotted; only the generals and a few other officers were elected.[7]

The island of Arwad, settled in the early 2nd millennium BC by the Phoenicians, has been cited as one of the first known examples of a democracy in the world. In Arwad, the people, rather than a monarch, are described as sovereign. In Greek, Arwad was known as Arado or Arados. Another possible example of primitive democracy may have been the early Sumerian city-states. Vaishali in what is now Bihar, India is also one of the first governments in the world to have elements of what we would today consider democracy, similar to those found in ancient Greece (although it was not a monarchy, ancient Vaishali is perhaps better described as an oligarchy). A similar proto-democracy or oligarchy existed temporarily among the Medes in the 6th century BC, but which came to an end after the Achaemenid Emperor Darius the Great declared that the best monarchy was better than the best oligarchy or best democracy.[8]

A serious claim for early democratic institutions comes

from the independent "republics" of India, *sanghas* and *gram*, which existed as early as the sixth century BCE and persisted in some areas until the fourth century CE. The evidence is scattered and no pure historical source exists for that period. In addition, Diodorus (a Greek historian at the time of Alexander the Great's excursion of India), without offering any detail, mentions that independent and democratic states existed in India. However, modern scholars note that the word *democracy* at the third century BC had been degraded and could mean any autonomous state no matter how oligarchic it was.[9]

(ii) Democracy in the Meddle Age

Democracy was not directly instituted in the Middle Ages, many democratic ideas were prevalent throughout the period. Because Christianity, which taught that men were created equal in the eyes of God, was deeply ingrained into the society of the Middle Ages, the democratic idea of equality was understood by many of the people. The Middle Ages, however, utilized another form of government, which was developed during this period called feudalism. Feudalism stressed that all people have certain rights and developed a system of courts to defend these rights. From these courts came the modern day judicial branch of the American government along with many of the ideas such as king's councils, assemblies and eventually parliamentary systems.[10]

During the Middle Ages, there were various systems involving elections or assemblies, although often only involving a minority of the population, such as the election of Uthman in the Rashidun Caliphate, the election of Gopala in Bengal, the Polish-Lithuanian Commonwealth, the Althing in Iceland, certain medieval Italian city-states such as Venice, the tuatha system in early medieval Ireland, the Veche in Novgorod and Pskov Republics of medieval Russia, Scandinavian Things, The States in Tyrol and Switzerland and the autonomous merchant city of Sakai in the 16th century in Japan. However, participation was often restricted to a minority, and so may be better classified as oligarchy. Most regions in medieval Europe were ruled by clergy or feudal lords.

A little closer to modern democracy were the Cossack republics of Ukraine in the 16th-17th centuries: Cossack

Hetmanate and Zaporizhian Sich. The highest post - the Hetman was elected by the representatives from country's districts. Because these states were very militarised, the right to participate in Hetman's elections was largely restricted to those who serve in the Cossack Army and overtime was curtailed effectively limiting these rights to higher army ranks.

The Parliament of England had its roots in the restrictions on the power of kings written into Magna Carta. The first elected parliament was De Montfort's Parliament in England in 1265. However, only a small minority actually had a voice; Parliament was elected by only a few percent of the population, and the system had problematic features such as rotten boroughs. The power to call parliament was at the pleasure of the monarch (usually when he or she needed funds). After the Glorious Revolution of 1688, the English Bill of Rights was enacted in 1689, which codified certain rights and increased the influence of the Parliament. The franchise was slowly increased and the Parliament gradually gained more power until the monarch became largely a figurehead.

Democracy was also seen to a certain extent in bands and tribes such as the Iroquois Confederacy. However, in the Iroquois Confederacy only the males of certain clans could be leaders and some clans were excluded. Only the oldest females from the same clans could choose and remove the leaders. This excluded most of the population. An interesting detail is that there should be consensus among the leaders, not majority support decided by voting, when making decisions. Band societies, such as the Bushmen, which usually number 20-50 people in the band often do not have leaders and make decisions based on consensus among the majority. In Melanesia, farming village communities have traditionally been egalitarian and lacking in a rigid, authoritarian hierarchy. Although a "Big man" or "Big woman" could gain influence, that influence was conditional on a continued demonstration of leadership skills, and on the willingness of the community. Every person was expected to share in communal duties, and entitled to participate in communal decisions. However, strong social pressure encouraged conformity and discouraged individualism.[11]

(iii) Contribution of John Locke and Jacques Rousseau Theories

The concept of democracy continued to be prevalent in Europe with the philosophies of an English philosopher by the name of John Locke and a French philosopher named Jean Jacques Rousseau. Locke's book, *Two Treatises,*[12] stated that under the "social contract," the government's job was to protect "natural rights", which included "the right to life, liberty, and the ownership of property." Rousseau expanded on this idea with his book, *The Social Contract*, in 1762. In essence, these two philosophers said that the people should have input on how their government is run. This school of thought paved the way for modern day American Democracy.

(iv) Democracy in 18th and 19th Century

Although not described as a democracy by the founding fathers, the United States founders shared a commitment to the principle of natural freedom and equality. The United States Constitution, adopted in 1788, provided for an elected government and protected civil rights and liberties. However, in the colonial period before 1776, only adult white male property owners could vote; enslaved Africans, free black people and women were not extended the franchise. On the American frontier, democracy became a way of life, with widespread social, economic and political equality. However, the frontier did not produce much democracy in Canada, Australia or Russia. By the 1840s almost all property restrictions were ended and nearly all white adult male citizens could vote; and turnout averaged 60-80% in frequent elections for local, state and national officials. The system gradually evolved, from Jeffersonian Democracy to Jacksonian Democracy and beyond. In Reconstruction after the Civil War (late 1860s) the newly freed slaves became citizens with (in the case of men) a nominal right to vote.

In 1789, Revolutionary France adopted the Declaration of the Rights of Man and of the Citizen and, although short-lived, the National Convention was elected by all males. Liberal democracies were few and often short-lived before the late nineteenth century, and various nations and territories have also claimed to be the first with universal suffrage.

(v) Modern Democracy

The American Revolution is another important event in the history of democracy. The first step, of course, in America's pursuit of democracy was the Declaration of Independence in 1776. In this great document, written by Thomas Jefferson, many ideas are taken from the aforementioned philosophers, Locke and Rousseau. From Locke, Jefferson borrowed the idea that all men are created equal, and he altered the right to life, liberty and property to "the right to life, liberty and the pursuit of happiness." Jefferson borrowed a little from Rousseau as well when he said that all men should have the right to take up arms against the government if it did not respect these rights. In the French Revolution, a similar cause was espoused. Political thinkers and philosophers such as Montesquieu, Voltaire, and Rousseau inspired the people by building off of American ideas and insisting that freedom comes only after the legislative, judicial and executive branches of the government are separated. The people of France overthrew the king, then set forth the "Declaration of the Rights of Man," which changed Locke's right to life, liberty and property to the right to "liberty, property, security, and resistance to oppression." (The resistance of oppression probably came from Rousseau.) These ideas, like the ones in the American Declaration of Independence, ended themselves to a partially democratic system where the powers of the king are limited and the people have some say in their government.

All over the world, revolutions began to spring up against monarchies, and democratic governments began to develop. Before the end of the 19th century, almost all of the Western European monarchies had adopted a constitution limiting the power of the Royal Family and giving some power to the people. Parliamentary type representative legislatures were also developed in many of these countries, giving the people more power to rule.[13]

20th century transitions to liberal democracy have come in successive "waves of democracy," variously resulting from wars, revolutions, decolonization, religious and economic circumstances. World War I and the dissolution of the Ottoman and Austro-Hungarian empires resulted in the creation of new nation-states in Europe, most of them at least nominally democratic. In the 1920s democracy flourished, but the Great

Depression brought disenchantment, and most of the countries of Europe, Latin America, and Asia turned to strong-man rule or dictatorships. Fascism and dictatorships flourished in Nazi Germany, Italy, Spain and Portugal, as well as non-democratic regimes in the Baltics, the Balkans, Brazil, Cuba, China, and Japan, among others.[14]

World War II brought a definitive reversal of this trend in Western Europe. The successful democratization of the American, British, and French sectors of occupied Germany, Austria, Italy, and the occupied Japan served as a model for the later theory of regime change. However, most of Eastern Europe, including the Soviet sector of Germany was forced into the non-democratic Soviet bloc. The war was followed by decolonization, and again most of the new independent states had nominally democratic constitutions. India, however emerged as the world's largest democracy and continues to be so. Currently, there are 123 countries that are democratic, and the trend is increasing . As such, it has been speculated that this trend may continue in the future to the point where liberal democratic nation-states become the universal standard form of human society. The United Nations has declared September 15 as the International Day of Democracy.[15]

4. THE RIGHT TO INFORMATION : TOUCH STONE FOR DEMOCRACY

> **"The great democratizing power of information has given us all the chance to effect change and alleviate poverty in ways we cannot even imagine today. Our task.... is to make that change real for those in need, wherever they may be. With information on our side, with knowledge a potential for all, the path to poverty can be reversed."**
>
> —(***Kofi Annan***, *Former Secretary-General, United Nations*)

This is the age of information affluence. Technology, with its capacity for storing simplifying and communicating information with astonishing speed has, more then ever, put information at the entire of development. Information is a global resource of unlimited potential for all government is a vost shore house of this resource. The information kept by government held the memory of the nation and provides a full portrait of its activities, performance and future plans.[16]

The "Right to Information" is fundamental to the realization of economic, social, civil, political right and an effective democracy, which requires informed participation by all. The right to information has now been recognized as a fundamental human right, which in turn is linked to respect for the inherent dignity of all human beings and as an essential component of participatory democracy and is described as the *"oxygen of democracy."*[17]

The core issues of the Right to Information lie in:

(1) People's participation in governance and the democratic process as a means of ensuring effective democracy.
(2) Accountability of the Government to the public.
(3) Acting as a check on rampant corruption and abuse of power including those powers, which are discretionary in nature.
(4) Ensuring transparency in the functioning of the Government.
(5) Protecting and upholding human rights, which are fundamental to realizing the inherent dignity of man.

In a country like ours the focal point of the movement for the right to information has been developmental issues. Health, safety, environment, food security and human rights are all directly linked to the "Right to Information."

Public participation in the democratic and governmental process becomes meaningful when citizens have adequate access to official information.

> *"No democratic government can survive without accountability and the basic postulate of accountability is that the people should have information about the functioning of the government. That an open society is the new democratic culture towards which every liberal democracy is moving and our society should be no exception. The concept of the open government is the direct emanation from the right to know which seems to be implicit in*

> *the right of free speech and expression guaranteed under Article 19(1)(a). Therefore, disclosure of information in regards to functioning of the government must be the rule and secrecy in exception, justified only when the strictest requirement of public interest so demands.*[18]

The essence of an effective representative democracy is the participation of a well-informed citizenry in the democratic process. In the matter of ***PUCL* v. *Union of India***[19] court said that:

> "Right to participate by casting vote at the time of election would be meaningless unless the voters are well informed about all sides of the issues, in respect of which they are called upon to express their views by casting their votes. Disinformation, misinformation and non-information all equally create an uninformed citizenry which would finally make democracy a mobacracy and a farce....the voter has to cast intelligent and rational vote according to his own criteria. A well-informed voter is the foundation of a democratic structure. That information to a voter, who is a citizen of this country, is one facet of the fundamental right under Article 19(1)(a).

A liberal information-sharing regime guaranteed by law is the practical answer to the present search for deeper democracy and people-centred development. Right to Information is both a practical short cut to achieving the goals of poverty eradication and good governance and a long recognized human right. Human beings need information in order to realize their full social, political and economic potential. Information is a public resource, collected and stored by government in trust for people. The challenge is to share it equitably and manage it to the best advantage of all of society.

Information is the currency that every citizen requires to participate in the life and governance of society and the various legislations, which provide the Right to Information, represent the substratum on which the superstructure of effective representative democracy can grow and flourish.

5. RIGHT TO INFORMATION IS A NEW LIFE FOR DEMOCRACY

> **The Right to Information or access to information is basic to the democratic way of life. In Act, real democracy cannot function with out a free and unfettered exercise of this right.[20]**
>
> —*Justice Baghwati*

In the modern world democracy signifies that the ultimate authority in political affairs rightfully belongs to the people. Whereas in centuries past indeed up to world war-I there were principle opponents of democratic political rule, today it is only the rare intellectual who expresses opposition to it. *We are all democrats now,* fairly summarizes the semantic allegiance of politicians and statesmen, throughout the world. Dictators, absolute ruler's even hereditary monarchs use the democratic idioms to characterize their regimes and their aspirations. A result has been a proliferation in the meanings of democracy. *There are organic democracies, guided democracies, and new high and socialist democracies.*[21]

In democratic countries at the present movement, the accent is on open government. Of course, there are quite a few things which must be kept confidential in the interest of public security or national interest sometime the law may impose secrecy in the interest of the individual. But then the secrecy ought not to be more than what is absolutely necessary. In this area, with an accent on the latter. There are many reasons suggesting an open government. Participation in government by the people is regarded as an important aspect of democracy and people cannot participate unless they have information as to what is going on in the country. A modern democratic state being answerable to the people, the people are entitled to know what policies and programs, how, and why, are being followed by the government. People have to pass verdict every three or five years on the performance of the government, and decide whether it should stay in office or not, people cannot exercise their choice intelligently unless they are given adequate information about the functioning of the government. Another factor justifying openness by the government is that being on activist entity, government gathers a vast arsenal of powers in a welfare state.[22]

Freedom of expression and right to information are considered as integral concepts in modern democracies. Since the last decades of the last century, there has been an unstoppable global trend towards the recognition of right to information or knowledge and freedom of speech or expression among the people of all countries and inter-governmental organizations. In a democracy, the greater the access to information, the greater the responsiveness of government to the needs of the community. The right to information and freedom of expression have been recognized as fundamental human rights, which upholds the dignity of all human beings. Free speech is protected by international human rights law, under Article 19 of the Universal Declaration of Human Rights. In our country, the largest democracy in the world in every sense of the term, the enactment of the Right to Information Act, marks a significant step towards our goal of greater democracy. In a democracy those who manage the affair of the society are supposed to be the trustees of the people and have to be accountable for their acts and omissions. That is why in democratic countries at the present movement, the accent is on *"open government."* That is why the access to the relevant materials having a bearing on the commission and omissions of the government are emerging as prerequisites of democratic governance. A Government, which reveals in secrecy not only, acts against democratic decency, basic human rights but equally busies itself with its own burial. The people consent is the justification for continuance of the Government in power. Thus in every democratic set-up everyone shall have the right to freedom of expression and this right shall include freedom to seek, receive and impart information and ideas of all kinds. The means of acquiring information without which there can be no well information citizenry is through freedom of access to the materials in the possession of the Government and also to proceeding of the Government.

The plea for freedom of speech and expression was raised for the first time in the history of democracy by the Athenian orator Secretes (B.C. 436-386), who committed suicide after his country was defeated and conquered by Philip of Macedon at the Battle of Chaeronea. His immortal speech "Logos Areopagicos" was a strong plea for restoring democracy and freedom of expression in Athens. In modern times imposing restrictions on freedom of expression and suppression of information was initiated by the British, claimed to be the creators of modern parliamentary democracy. The much famed "Long Parliament" of the United Kingdom (1640-60), which carried out the executions of a number of aides of the emperor of the empire of never setting sun, issued ordinances prohibited free speech for the first time in the history of human civilization. The Parliament ordered, "it is therefore ordered by the lords and commons in Parliament, that no order or declaration or both, of either house of Parliament shall be printed by any but by order by both the houses." This order of the British democracy led John Milton, the most famous epic poet of modern time, to issue the classic pamphlet "Areopagitica" in 1644, pleading for the restoration of basic fundamental rights. Now people remember the ordnance of the British Parliament only because of the plea against it.

Of course, it took 77 years for us to transform from a system legitimized by the colonial official secrets Act to one where citizens can demand the right to information. The absence of communication tools, and law levels of literacy compounded the poor flow of information. With offices full of dusty files all over, the standard of keeping records is abysmally poor. But the growth of information technology has now made things easier and many states are competing with each other to attract more investment with open window systems, now we entered another era of democracy where everything is transparent.

In India, the movement for the right to information has been vibrant for a long time. The common man, academician and the media have been raising the voice since independence, as many of the basic and survival needs like food security, shelter and employment are closely linked to the right to information.

Throughout twentieth century, *'Democracy'* being the common creed amongst the nations, no contemporary analysis of the 'Rule of law' can afford to ignore the vast expansion of the government functions which has occurred as a result both of the growing complexity of modern life and the minimum postulates of political philosophy and social justice. That is why almost in all democratic countries at the present moment the accent is on an open government and transparency. It is the basic postulate of democracy that government shall be based on consent of the government. The consent of the governed implies not only that consent shall be free but also that it shall be grounded on an adequate information and discussion aided by the widest possible dissemination of from diverse and antagonistic sources,[23] consequently, citizens must have access to information, ***'Right to Know'*** about the functioning of the government and public functionaries. As no democratic government can survive without accountability and transparency. The basic postulate of accountability is that the people should have information about the functions of Government. If cannot be over emphasized that even from a conceptual standpoint, the public right to information is an indispensable prerequisite of democracy. To ensure such accountability, the people must have right to know about the policies, programmes, doings, or misdoings or their representatives in the legislative and executive branches of the administration.[24]

Right to Information is as crucial as freedom of expression in any democracy. It is only through information and resultant expressions that people can influence the government of the people, for the people and by the people. It is essential for the discovery of truth and transparency. Furthers the search for truth and helps in achieving the age old Bharatiya concept of "Vasudhaiva Kudumbakam." Suppressing or hiding information can ruin a family, relationships or individuals with each other and the same is applicable to a nation also. Moreover, it is integral to tolerance, which is considered by many as a basic value in society. Gandhiji taught us to be tolerant towards all types of violence. To be tolerant is to develop a sense of imaginative sympathy in every person. When a person is informed, he or she can imagine himself or herself in the place of the other. That itself may lead to solutions for many a problems and issues. Such tolerance serves as a model that encourages more tolerance.

According to statistics more than 85 countries have comprehensive laws to facilitate access to state records. The collapse of authoritarian states since the 1960s and emergence of new democracies and technologies and information revolution provided a new sense on the right to informed among the people. Modern consumerism also played a vital role. International bodies like Worked Bank and International Monetary Fund and other market players are also pressing nations to be more transparent in their dealings. In a global economy things should be transparent. And people naturally have a right to information about what is happening to their lives and in the society in which they live. India, as a vibrant economy and democracy is entering a new era, where she is going to be a global power. There is not stop now or no looking back. The world is going to accept her as a key player in every sense.

One of the fundamentals of democratic government is that government must be sensitive to public opinion. Public opinion can be formed only when the public have the knowledge about the functioning of the Government. It is, therefore, necessary that the people should have access to the full knowledge about the functioning of the Government. Right to Information the facts about the functioning of Administration is therefore is, one of the important and valuable Rights of a Citizen in Democratic State. In parliamentary democracy, people are ruled in the form of the executive by the political parties elected by them once in four or five years. The functioning of various democracies and the representative governments are gradually establishing the fact that at best, they form *Rule for the people* and not *Role by the people.* The system of accountability of the government does not seem to be as sound and effective as it ought to have been. Democracies of this type become essentially weak and superficial, thereby, generating a lot of hardships to the common man. In a democracy, those who manage the affairs of the society are supposed to be the trustees of the people and have to be accountable for their acts and omissions, that stands the essence of participative democracy and a representative government. The access to the relevant materials have a bearing on the commission and the Commissions of the government. It is a pre-requisite of the democratic governance.

In Democracy Right to Information is the power to the people. Instead of being dependent on vague suppositions and assumptions, people armed with sound factual information have the confidence to take on those in power. Even the most marginalities can act in their own interests. For example, a daily wage earner can ask to see work registers to check if they are being paid what a contractor is claiming on their behalf from the government. A parent can challenge the basis on which school admission is given. A pensioner can check if personal records held by government are accurate or misinterpret their entitlements. A small business can sue for compensation if it discovers that a tender it lost was corruptly awarded to another bidder. A resident can question the quality of a road being laid in their locality against specifications stated in the government contract. A citizens group can examine the viability of a development project because it can access documents that indicate if a project would have a detrimental impact on the environment.[25]

6. RIGHT TO INFORMATION AND PANCHAYATS

(i) Meaning and Concept of Panchayat

When the Panchayati Raj movement was launched about 48 years ago, it was hope and faith of the nation that it will make bulworks of democracy, nurseries of public leadership and the powerhouse of people's action. But thanks to the lack of confidence in the system resulting in the weakening of political will and support of country's ruling elites, role of bureaucracy in dissociating the Panchayati Raj Institutions from the development process, structural inadequacies and lack of conceptual clarity.[26] Panchayati Raj Institutions have yet to fulfil their promise and yet to translate that faith into a living and pulsating reality so that people's power is harnessed from the *Gram Sabha* to the *Lok Sabha* in a steady progression.[27]

As a matter of fact, the use of the title *Panchayat* is misleading because the ancient Panchayats were self-reliant and controlled by the concept of *Panch-Parmeshwar*, i.e., detached divine justice. In the process, by important use of term Panchayat in the Constitution, we sponsored a myth, irrelevant to our reality. The founding fathers created another myth, i.e., Parliamentary Democracy which sidetracked the true nature of Policy enshrined in the Directive Principles of State Policy, i.e., Elected oligarchies to conserve and maintain 'dual society' plus some democratic freedom. The Panchayat system did not form an integral part of the Indian polity.

In the view of **Balwant Rai Mehta Committee** was aware of the objective to initiate "a process of transformation of social and economic life of the villages and to cultivate self-reliant initiative of the people", and the *Method* as "democratic decentralisation", they got involved in the consideration of the role of local-bodies, who were never an instrument of social change. They merely attempted to distinguish the "delegation of power from decentralisation." But they forgot that "the concept of decentralisation can mainly be based on the concept of self-reliance." According to the Committee, "the Government will have to devolve all its functions in defined fields (of development) on these bodies, reserving to itself the functions of *guidance supervision,* and *higher planning* and where necessary, providing extra-finances." This is nothing more than *administrative decentralisation* or centralisation in disguise. This means a system of bodies (*Zila Parishad, Panchayat Samitis* and *Panchayats*) under the control of the Government.

Gandhi's Concept of Panchayat

To Gandhi, Panchayat symbolises the power of the people. This is his concept of Swaraj: "Every village will be a republic or Panchayat having all powers... every village has to be self-sustained capable of managing its affairs... This does not exclude dependence on and willing help from neighbours or from the world." In this structure composed of innumerable villages, there will be ever-widening, never ascending circles, "Life will not be a pyramid with the apex sustained by the bottom. But it will be an oceanic circle whose centre will be the individual." In short, by 'Swaraj', he meant "Government by the consent of largest number of such voters."[28] Father of Nation Mahatma Gandhi was utopian and more practical. So he visualised the phases by which the weaker sections of the society could be organised and made effective through organised non-cooperation and *satyagraha*. In this way, he advocated non-violent class-struggle. For example, he said, "what can the poor zamindar do when they say that they will simply not work on the land unless they are paid enough to feed, cloth and educate themselves and their children in a decent manner."[29]

(ii) Panchayat under Indian Constitution

(a) Directive Principles of State Policy

Certain Directive Principles of State Policy based on social, political and economic justice are laid down for the guidance of the legislatures as well as the government authorities. They are intended to be kept in mind both by the legislatures in enacting laws and by the executive authorities in executing the laws. They give an indication of the policy which the Union and the State ought to follow. It is not clear how far these principles or injunctions are to be kept in mind by the judiciary in the interpretation of legislation. As they are fundamental in the governance of the country, they may be used in case of doubt in the interpretation of legislation.[30]

These principles are mostly those which the framers of the Constitution conceived as the basic principles of a new social and economic order.

(i) Organisation of Village Panchayats

Panchayats is a part of democracy at the gross-root level. **Article 40** of our Constitution provides that ***"the state shall take steps to organize village panchayats and endow them with such powers and authority as may be necessary to enable then to function as units of self-government."*** The object of the provision is to introduce democracy at the grass-roots level. These panchayats are expected to be the training grounds for the developments of democratic traditions. Village panchayats has been introduced throughout the country. The Constitutions-makers have unwillingly misled the country for four decades and in the process sidetracked the concept of self-reliance enshrined in the ancient concepts of Panchayats.

(b) 73rd and 74th Amendments of the Constitution

The 73rd and 74th amendments to the Constitution provide Constitutional sanction to democracy at the grass-root level by the incorporating in the Constitution newparts. IX and IXA relating to panchayats and urban local bodies. The 73rd Constitutional amendment provides for a three tier of Panchayat Raj system at the village intermediate and district levels. The 74th Constitutional amendment act provides constitutional sanction to urban self-governing institutions. It provides for three types of municipal corporations for urban areas according to population.

(iii) Right to Information Promote Panchayats

In India public funds are directly routed to Panchayats and Municipal bodies for the implementation of development programmes and welfare schemes and the distribution of subsidies. The Right to Information movements across the country have on their own steam unearthed mismanagement of public funds and even in the absence of Right to Information laws. The Right to Information provides new strength to redouble these efforts and empowers the tax payer to question the manner in which public authorities spend the money he/she pays in the form of taxes. Yet the Right to Information needs to be seen as an opportunity not just to unearth corruption but also prevent its occurrence.

The Right to Information can help the *gram sabha* and the elected bodies of Panchayats at the intermediary and district levels to plan and priorities development.

True participation of the people in governance will be realized the day when using the Right to Information citizens in remote villages, towns and cities will be able to identity the most needy and underprivileged, provide for their needs in the developmental plans, monitor the implementation of developmental programmes and evaluate outcomes on the basis of actual improvement at the ground level and not merely in annual statistical reports. This is our chance to make use of a law that was crafted in a participatory manner for the benefit of those people who have suffered generations of deprivation. If we fail to do so, the Right to Information will become another addition to the ever expanding stature book of the State and a golden opportunity to truly entrench participatory democracy and developmental planning will be lost. "Eternal vigilance is the price of liberty" said Lord Action. Indeed, eternal vigilance on the part of every citizen tax payer is the only means to ensure that governance is carried out in a manner that promotes the democratic ideal and secures the fulfilments of human rights to all citizens. The Right to Information is now the foremost democratic tool, may weapon, in the hands of citizens to make this happen.

7. CONCLUSION

In the democratic form of government there is the participation of public in government. Because of this, this form of government is supposed to be a good form of government. The democracy gets its strength from people, and flow of information in democracy makes this participation more strange. Through

Right to Information public participation has increased in day to day functioning of government and administration. On the one hand where by this right the foundation of democracy is strengthened and on the other hand people's faith in democracy has increased.

In today's changing scenario this Right to Information has proved to be a mile stone. At the lowest level of democracy, i.e., Gram Panchayat, too, this Right to Information is very useful and effective. A very common application of this Act is seen in the form that the public is asking the authorities for the accounts and other things of development projects initiated by government.

Notes and References

1. Justice A.H. Saikia, The Right to Information Act, 2005 an instrument to strengthen democracy, *Gauhati Law Times*, Vol. I, 2006.
2. *Ibid.*
3. B. Holden Understanding Liberal Democracy, Oxford, Philip Allan 1988, p. 5.
4. At the Gettysburg Address, 1863.
5. A More Perfect Union—History of Democracy, p. 1.
6. *Ibid.*
7. Democracy—Wikipedia, the free encyclopedia.
8. *Ibid.*
9. *Ibid.*
10. A More Perfect Union—History of Democracy, p. 3.
11. Melanesia Historical and Geographical: the Solomon Islands and the New Hebrides", Southern Cross n°1, London: 1950.
12. Published in 1690.
13. A More Perfect Union History of Democracy, p. 3.
14. Democracy From Wikipedia, the free encyclopedia.
15. *Ibid.*
16. CHRI 2003 Report.
17. Saxsena Ambrish, Right to Information and freedom of press, Ist ed., p. 7.
18. S.P. Gupta *v.* Union of India, AIR 1981 SC 2148.
19. 2003 4 SCC 399.
20. AIR 1997 SC, pp. 73-74.
21. Encyclopedia American, p. 684.
22. Jain and Jain, "Principles of Administrative Law", 4th Ed. 1993, pp. 810-91.
23. Soli Sorabjee, Enforcing the Right to Know *exct Juris*, 1986, p. 10.

24. Justice R.S. Sarkaria, Right to Information, p. 4, *Press Council of India Review*, 1993, Vol. 14.
25. CHRI 2003 Report.
26. Report of the Committee on Panchayati Raj Institutions, New Delhi, p. 6.
27. *Ibid.*, Annexure 2, Para III, 6, p. 207.
28. Gandhi, M.K., *Harijan*, 29.1.1946.
29. Gandhi, M.K., *Harijan*, 20.7.1941.
30. G.N. Joshi, The Constitution of India, 7th Ed, 1983, p. 108.

CHAPTER

5

PUBLIC ADMINISTRATION AND RIGHT TO INFORMATION

I. INTRODUCTION

"Every thing secret degenerates, even the administration of Justice; nothing is safe that does not show it can bear discussion and publicly."

—*J.R. Wiggens*

After centuries long development process administrative law is before us in its present form. Basically, as a concept in practice administrative law endeavors to incorporate transparency and accountability. This is necessary and required for a healthy administration. When we talk about transparency and accountability in administrative law, we find this somewhat near to the concept of Right to Information. Right to Information is the most basic requirement for transparency and accountability in public administration. If a Right to Information is denied in public administration, we shall be left with anarchy and corruption in administration. So the present scenario the changing dimension of Right to Information has become an integral part of public administration.

During the last hundred years, the concept of State and its functions has undergone a change. The emphasis on paternal form of government has shifted to maternal form of government. Besides confining itself to defense, public order and enforcement of criminal law and few other general matters, the modern states have assumed the role of social welfare State. It has undertaken the elaborate task of social services and public utilities. The 18th century individualism has gone. The doctrine of *'laissez faire'* emphasised by *Locke* no longer remains the governing principle of modern State. The doctrine has given place to the concept of a welfare State and this has led to the proliferation of administrative powers and functions. The growth in the range of activities of the State has thus ushered in an era of administrative law. It is a harsh fact of life that the phenomenal growth of administrative power as a by-product of an intensive form of government, though necessary for development and growth, at times spells negation of people's rights and values. Profligate and pachydermic administration emboldened by the anesthetised public conscience does not hesitate to trample upon the civil liberties of the people. Thus, administrative adventurists impatient of democratic process may slip into authoritationism, making all material growth a pretence for tyranny. Here comes the need, importance and purpose of administrative law. Administrative law, thus, becomes dharma which conduces to the stability and growth of the society and the maintenance of a just social order and welfare of mankind by reconciling power with liberty. Thus administrative law goes beyond legalism and represents a principled regulation of administrative space, whether domestic or global, which can be practically regulated for the expansion of human freedoms. Therefore, today, administrative law represents the way of conceptualising and articulating a new domestic and global socioeconomic order. Against this backdrop, administrative law has a tremendous social function to perform. Without a good system of administrative law any society would die because of its own administrative weight like a Black Hole—which is a dying neutron star collapses due to its own gravity. Administrative law, therefore, becomes that body of reasonable limitations and affirmative action parameters which are developed and operationalised by the legislature and the courts to maintain and sustain rule of law society.[1]

At an earlier stage 18th century had witnessed a phenomenal growth in the powers and function of the State. The

State no longer confined itself to its traditional functions such as defence, administration of justice or maintenance of law and order. It undertook to provide social security and social welfare for the common man, regulate industrial relations with a view to maintaining industrial peace, regulate industry, trade and business with a view to protecting as well as promoting public interest (which included the interest of the citizens) and embarked upon economic planning for development. Elimination of poverty and exploitation were the main ends of development. The State had to promote literacy, reduce poverty and remove social and gender injustice. It had to provide cheap housing to the poor. It had to provide employment and social insurance against death, sickness or accident. Even the colonial state was not entirely *laissez faires* and took responsibility for certain welfare functions.[2]

Now-a-day's administrative law has become more participatory because such regulatory authorities are involving the people in their decision-making processes. The State has to intervene mainly for fufiling the following objectives:[3]

(i) protection of the poor and the disadvantaged from exploitation and social injustice by providing for education, health services, social security and opportunities of employment and by abolishing poverty and exploitation;

(ii) preservation and strengthening of the democratic process and the democratic institutions;

(iii) protection of environment and conservation and economic utilisation of the natural resources;

(iv) promoting development which will bring about economic and social progress of all geographical regions and all sections of society.

(v) protection of the consumer and the investor;

(vi) ensuring free competition and preventing restrictive trade practices and unfair trade practices and promoting corporate democracy; and

(vii) protection of environment and conservation and economic utilisation of the natural resources.

The traditional governmental functions such as defending the territory of the State against invasion, maintenance of law and order, and collection of revenue, continue to be performed by the State. The growth of terrorism in which violence is unleashed by anonymous elements against anonymous people as a weapon for political ends has added to the responsibility of the State. The need to combat terrorism without sacrificing individual liberty is the most formidable challenge before a democratic government.[4]

The modern welfare State cannot invoke the doctrine of sovereign immunity when it performs its functions. Even a traditional State did not throw immunity on its officers if they wrongfully acted against any citizen. In the modern context, the liability of the State and its employees for acts done on behalf of the State has acquired greater importance. Administrative law of accountability of the public authorities for their arbitrary and *ultra vires* actions has now reached a critical stage.[5] Where powers and functions of the executive increase, there is always a danger that the authority may exceed its power or may act arbitrarily. The purpose of administrative law is to see that the authorities act within their powers, according to fair procedure and do not abuse their power. A democratic State must have a transparent and accountable government. The growth of administrative law was, therefore, rightly described as an 'outstanding legal development of the Twentieth Century'. Administrative law ensures the rule of law by insisting that the powers given to various legal functionaries be used for the purpose for which they are given. There is a tendency on the part of those in whom discretionary power is vested, to exercise it either illegally or ostensibly for a legal purpose, but in reality for serving personal or class interests. It gives us a mechanism for preventing abuse or non-use of power as well as empowers the people by providing them access to remedies against the misuse or abuse of power by the authorities. The growth of public interest litigation and judicial activism which has led to the articulation of various people's rights such as the right to an honest and efficient governance, right to natural resources such as water and fresh air and the right to development have doubtlessly strengthened administrative law.[6]

2. MEANING OF ADMINISTRATIVE LAW

The term "Administrative Law" has three possible meanings. According to the renowned writer U.P.D. Keshrai[7], the term administrative law have been classified in three following possible meaning as under—

(1) The rules of law promulgated by Executive Department, with the consent and by the authority of the Central legislation. In this sense Administrative law is nothing more than a form of delegated legislation, framed by a subordinate law-making body. Recently, in consequence of vast increase of legislative activity in all States, due to changing social conditions, this type of subordinate or delegated legislation has increased greatly in bulk and scope. Moreover, legislations and specially Parliament of India, have shown—a disposition to confer very wide powers of law-making upon different departments of State.

(2) Administrative law may also mean that part or public law which describes the nature of the activity of the Executive Department of the government in action. In this sense, it may also be termed the law relating to public administration. It deals with the organs of Government in their relations with the subject, whereas, constitutional law deals with the same organs from the standpoint or structure, and of their relations with one another. Thus, administrative law in this sense would deal with the relations of Central to local Government and with the promotion of the welfare of the citizen of a State.

(3) Administrative law may denote that portion of nation's legal system which determines the legal status and liabilities of all State officials which defines the rights and liabilities of private individuals in their dealings with public officials and which specifies the procedure by which those rights and liabilities are enforced. When the term is used in this sense, it is customary to retain the French designation

> of *droit administratif.* Partly because the system and partly because the French term expresses a good deal more than "Administrative Law." It implies the French acceptance of the doctrine of the separation of powers and the difference in nature between disputes of officials and private citizens.

For the present purpose Administrative Law may be taken to the law governing organization, procedures, powers and duties of the organs or public authorities other than the legislature and courts. It studies the law made by, as well as the law which controls administration.

Broadly, administrative law deals with composition and powers or different organs of administration, the limits of their powers; the procedure which the administrative authorities adopt in the exercise of their powers and the various modes of control including particularly judicial control over the different kinds of powers exercised by them. Precisely it deals with the *quasi*-legislative and *quasi*-judicial powers of the administrative authorities as also their executive powers and their control. It is true that there is greater emphasis upon the study of various modes of judicial control of administrative action in the present administrative law.[8]

3. MEANING OF PUBLIC ADMINISTRATION

Public Administration is a branch of the wider field of administration. It may be said that Public Administration is a species while Administration is the genus. Public Administration is any kind of Administration in the public interest, and the word *public* should be emphasised over the word *administration* or, Public Administration may simply be called governmental administration.

Public administration can be broadly described as the development, implementation and study of branches of government policy. The pursuit of the public good by enhancing civil society, ensuring a well-run, fair, and effective public service are some of the goals of the field.

Even in this field the term 'Public Administration' is used in two senses:

(i) In its broader sense, it is concerned with the conduct affairs of the government generally; and

(ii) In its narrower sense, it defines the operations of the administrative branch only. However, Public Administration as government in action has been integrally tied to the nature of government in a specific context.

Public administration is also an academic field. In comparison with related fields such as political science, public administration is relatively new, having emerged in the 19th century. Multidisciplinary in character, it draws on theories and concepts from political science, economics, sociology, administrative law, management, and a range of related fields.

Public administration theory is the domain in which discussions of the meaning and purpose of government, bureaucracy, budgets, governance, and public affairs takes place. In recent years, public administration theory has periodically connoted a heavy orientation toward critical theory and postmodern philosophical notions of government, governance, and power. However, many public administration scholars support a classic definition of the term emphasizing constitutionality, service, bureaucratic forms of organization, and hierarchical government.

The goals of the field of public administration are related to the democratic values of improving equality, justice, security, efficiency, effectiveness of public services; business administration is primarily concerned with profit.

4. CONCEPT CONTRIBUTING OF THE DEVELOPMENT THE RIGHT TO INFORMATION

(a) Doctrine of the Rule of Law

'Rule of Law' is the supreme manifestation of human civilization and culture and is a new 'lingua franca' of global moral thought. It is an eternal value of constitutionalism and an inherent attribute of democracy and good governance.

(i) Origin of Rule of Law

The concept of the Rule of Law is of old origin. Edward

Coke is said to be the originator of this concept, when he said that the King must be under God and Law and thus vindicated the supremacy of law over the pretensions of the executives. The term 'Rule of Law' is derived from the French phrase *la prinipe de legalite* (the principle of legality) which refers to a government based on principles of law and not of men. In this sense the concept of *la principle de legalite* was opposed to arbitrary powers.

(ii) Development of Rule of Law

In India, concept of Rule of Law can be traced to Upanished. It provides—Law is the King of Kings. It is more powerful and rigid than they (Kings). There in nothing higher than law. By its powers the weak shall prevail over the strong and justice shall triumph. Thus in monarchy, the concept of law developed to control the exercise of arbitrary powers of the monarchs who claimed divine powers to rule. In a democracy, the concept has assumed different dimension and means that the holders of public power must be able to justify publicly that the exercise of power is legally valid and socially just. **A.V. Dicey** later developed on this concept in the course of his lectures at the Oxford University. Dicey was an individualist; he wrote about the concept of the Rule of Law at the end of the golden Victorian era of *laissez-faire* in England. That was the reason why Dicey's concept of the Rule of Law contemplated the absence of wide powers in the hands of government officials. According to him, wherever there is discretion there is room for arbitrariness.

The Rule of Law is a viable and dynamic concept and, like many other such concepts, is not capable of any exact definition. This, however, does not mean that there is no agreement on the basic values which it represents. The term Rule of Law is used in contradistinction to 'rule of man' and 'rule according to law'. Even in the most autocratic forms of government there is some law according to which the powers of the government are exercised but it does not mean that there is the Rule of Law. Therefore, Rule of Law means that the law rules, which is based on the principles of freedom, equality, non-discrimination, fraternity, accountability and non-arbitrariness and is certain, regular and predictable, using the word 'law' in the sense of 'jus' and 'lex' both. In this sense 'the Rule of Law' is an ideal. It is a modern name for natural law. In history man has always appealed to something higher than that which is his own creation. In jurisprudence, Romans called it 'jusnatural'. Medievalists called it the 'Law of God', Hobbes, Locke and Rousseau called it 'social contract' or 'natural law' and the modern man calls it 'Rule of Law'.[9]

The term Rule of Law can be used in two senses:

(*i*) Formalistic sense; and
(*ii*) Ideological sense.

If used in the formalistic sense it refers to organised power as opposed to a rule by one man and if used in an ideological sense it refers to the regulation of the relationship of the citizens and the government and in this sense it becomes a concept of varied interest and contents.

In its ideological sense, the concept of Rule of Law represents an ethical code for the exercise of public power in any country. Strategies of this code may differ from society to society depending on the societal needs at any given time, but its basic postulates are universal covering all space and time. These postulates include equality, freedom and accountability. 'Equality' is not a mechanical and negative concept but has progressive and positive contents which oblige every government to create conditions social, economic and political where every individual has an equal opportunity to develop his personality to the fullest and to live with dignity. 'Freedom' postulates absence of every arbitrary action free speech, expression and association, personal liberty and many others. These basic rights of any society may be restricted only on the ground that the claims of these freedoms would be better served by such circumscription. The basic idea behind 'accountability' is that the rules with the Deference of the people, and therefore must be accountable to them in the ultimate analysis. Forms of accountability may differ, but the basic idea must remain the same that the holders of public power must be able publicly to justify the exercise of public power not only a legally valid but also socially just, proper and reasonable.[10]

(iii) Dicey's Rule of Law

Rule of law according to Dicey is one of the basic features of the English Constitutional system. Professor A.V. Dicey gave three meaning of the Rule of Law XI thus—

1. **Supremacy of the law:** It means, "the absolute supremacy or predominance of regular law as opposed to the influence of arbitrary power and excludes the existence of arbitrariness...... or even of wide discretionary authority on the part of the government."[11] In other words, a man may be punished for a breach of law, but he can be punished for nothing else.
2 **Equality before law:** The second meaning Dicey observed, not only that no man is above the law but that every man whatever be his rank or condition, is subject to the ordinary law of the realm and amenable to the Jurisdiction of the ordinary tribunals in England.
3. **The Constitution is the result of the ordinary law of the land:** It means that the source of the Right to individuals is not the written constitution but the rules as define and enforced by the Courts.

The first and the second aspects apply to Indian system but the third aspect of the Dicey rule of law does not apply to Indian system as the source of right of individuals in the Constitution of India.

The concept of rule of law, in modern age, does not oppose the practice of conferring discretionary powers upon the government but on the other hand emphasizes on spelling out the manner of their exercise. It also ensures that every man is bound by the ordinary laws of the land whether he be private citizen or a public officer; that private rights are safeguarded by the ordinary laws of the land. Thus the rule of law signifies that nobody is deprived of his rights and liberties by an administrative action; that the administrative authorities perform their functions according to law and not arbitrarily; that the laws of the land are not unconstitutional and oppressive; that the supremacy of courts is upheld and judicial control of administrative action is fully secured.

The **University of Chicago** held a conference subject on rule of law as understood in the west. These conferences attended by eleven countries like, United Kingdom, Germany, Italy, Canada, Sweden, Turkey, Brazil, Mexico, Israel, Poland and USSR. The Secretary of the Cailoguium described the broad areas of agreement as follows:[12]

(1) The Rule of Law is an expression of an endeavour to give reality to something which is not readily expressible; this difficulty is primarily due to identification of the rule of law with the concept of rights of man—all countries of the West recognize that the rule of law has a positive content, though that content is different in different countries. It is real and must be secured principlely, but not exclusively, by the ordinary courts.

(2) The Rule of Law is based upon the liberty of the individual and has as its object the harmonising of the opposing notions of individual liberty and public order. The notion of justice maintains a balance between these notions. Justice has a variable content and cannot be strictly defined, but at a given time a place there is an appropriate standard by which the balance between private interest and the common good can be maintained.

(3) There is an important difference between the concept of Rule of Law as the supremacy of law over the government and the concept of rule of law as the supremacy of law in society generally. The first concept is the only feature common to the West, connoting as it does the protection of the individual against arbitrary government—different techniques can be adopted to achieve the same end and the Rule of Law must not be conceived of as being linked to any particular technique. But it is fundamental that there must exist some technique for foreign the government to submit to the law; if such a technique does not exist, the government itself becomes the means whereby the law is achieved. This is the antithesis of the Rule of Law.

(4) Although much emphasis is placed upon the supremacy of the legislature in some countries of the

> West, the Rule of Law does not depend upon contemporary positive law—it may be expressed in positive law but essentially it consists of values and not institution; it cannot a climate of legality and legal order in which the nations of the west live and in which they wish to continue to live.

The concept of Rule of Law highly relevant to our context.

(iv) Rule of Law Promote the Right to Information

In a bid to enforce the rule of law in letter and spirit, the apex court of late is reiterating the twin principles of transparency and accountability in all state actions.[13] The culture of secrecy is the legacy inherited from the British rules and the same was initially made operational through Official Secrets Act of 1923. It is needless to emphasis that the veil of secrecy is incompatible with the rule of law and the basic postulates of participative democracy. Strong walls of secrecy, it may be asserted without any hesitation, have only generated corruption on a massive scale at all levels.[14]

In the case of ***S.P. Gupta* v. *Union of India***[15] the Supreme Court while advocating the need for openness in state actions in tune with the constitutional mandate or rules of law said : "Hidden government is the sworn enemy of the Rule of Law and an antithesis to the constitutional philosophy of good governance. For it is the veil of secrecy which lies at the bottom of oppression, corruption and abuse of power. Sweeping secrecy shrouds the evil actions of the state and is undemocratic as it evades public accountability. In a democratic polity wedded to rule of law transparency and accountability go together and they are mutually reinforcing. They are two sides of the same coin. Explaining the functional relationship between the two, it observed; "No democratic government can survive without accountability and the basic postulate of accountability is that the people should have information about the functioning of the government. It is only if people know how the government is functioning that they can fufil the role which democracy assigns to them and make democracy a really effective participatory democracy." Further, it then proceeded to say: "The concept of an open government is the direct emanation from the right to know which seems to be implicit in the right of free speech and expression guaranteed under Article 19(1)(a). Therefore, disclosure of information in regard to the functioning of the government must be the rule and secrecy, and exception, justified only when the strictest requirement of public interest so demands. Again in the same wave length, the apex court on the issue of participatory democracy held in another case ***Public Union for Civil Liberties* v. *Union of India.***[16] In this case Apex Court said that, "True democracy cannot exist unless all citizens have a right to participate in the affairs of the polity of the country. The right to participate in the affairs of the country is meaningless unless the citizens are well informed on all sides of the issues, in respect of which they are called upon to express their views. One sided information, disinformation, misinformation and non-information all equally create an uninformed citizenry which makes democracy a farce."[17]

Administrative law and the Rule of Law are not discrete series. Both aim at the "progressive diminution of arbitrariness and fostering a discipline of fairness and openness in the exercise of public power."[18] In modern times also there is a thinking that the growth of administrative powers, which was an inevitable consequence of planning and welfare activities of the State, has come in the way of rule of law. National planning has completely put into oblivion the ideals of personal freedom and liberty in several respects. There is greater degree of public control over so many areas which henceforth constituted the areas of operations of private rights. In carrying out the welfare activities of the State, the administration had to be armed with greater power and in this process a large measure of personal freedoms was bound to be eclipsed. If rule of law is intended to ensure personal freedom and rights and adequate safeguards against any encroachment on them, then the growth administrative law seemingly contradicts rule of law. But, in fact, the rule of law emphasises upon rule that the executive must act under the law and not by its own whins and fiat. The executive does not derive the powers out of its own accord but derives them from the law. The rule of law serves as the basis of judicial control over administrative action. Its principle concern like that of administrative law is to keep the executive and the operation of its powers within the limits of law so that it may not turn to be arbitrary. There is no incompatibility between the rule of law and administrative law. In reality, viewed as a system of control of administrative powers, it can be asserted that administrative law does not contradict but, on the other hand, promotes rule of law. Administrative law not unlike rule of law has not come to establish 'New Despotism' but to make it impossible. Like the rule of law it also ensures proper and orderly exercise of the administrative powers. Hence, the two are not opposed to each other but on the other hand go parallel with a common objective of achieving in orderly government[19] rule of law an effective role by emphasizing upon fair play and greater accountability of the administration. It lays greater emphasis upon the principles of natural justice and the rule of speaking order in administrative process in order to eliminate administrative arbitrariness.

In the case of ***Manika Gandhi* v. *Union of India*,**[20] the SC held that rule of law in every field of administrative functioning has assigned it a place of special significance in the Indian administrative law. The Supreme Court, in the process of interpretation of rule of law *vis-a-vis* operation of administrative powers, in several cases, emphasized upon the need of fair and just procedure, adequate safeguards against any executive encroachment on personal liberty, free legal aid to the poor and speedy trial in criminal cases as necessary adjuncts to rule of law.

In case of ***Bachan Singh* v. *State*,**[21] Learned Justice Bhagwati explains the significance of Rule of Law in the following words: *"The rule of law permeates the entire fabric of the Constitution and indeed forms one of its basic features. The rule of law excludes arbitrariness, its postulate in 'intelligence without passion' and reason free from desire. Wherever we find arbitrariness or unreasonableness there is denial of the rule of law. Law in the context of rule of law does not mean any law enacted by legislative authority, howsoever arbitrary, despotic it may be, otherwise even in dictatorship it would be possible to say that there is rule of law because every law made by the dictator, however arbitrary and unreasonable, has to be obeyed and every action has to be taken in conformity with such law in such a case too even where the political set-up is dictatorial, it is the law that governs the relationship between men and men and between men and State, but still it is not rule of law as understood in modern jurisprudence, because in jurisprudential terms, the law itself in such a case being an emanation from the absolute will of the dictator, it is in effect and substance the rule* *of man and not of law which prevails in such a situation. What is necessary element of rule of law is that the law must not be arbitrary or irrational and must satisfy the test of reason and the democratic form of polity seeks to ensure this element by making the framers of the law accountable to the people."*

Learned Justice Ramaswamy of the Supreme Court very aptly once remarked on the importance of rule of law in a planned society like India:

> *"In administration there is obvious need for individual action, there is call for speedy determination; there is necessity for direction, a large measure of freedom is, therefore, conferred upon government officials for carrying out administrative schemes. How far is this state of affairs compatible with the rules of law? It is true that national planning involves public control and direction of economic and social activities. National planning also involves control of basic industries, land ceilings, increased taxation, priorities, mobilisation of labour, control of imports and exports, slum clearance and so on. But the rule of law is one of the basic values in a democratic State. Unless there is rule of law, there is danger that the administration would become totalitarian. It is true that planning tends to eclipse the rule of law. There is concentration of power in the executive. The Legislature must increasingly delegate its power to administrative authorities. The Legislature is also compelled to confer judicial powers upon administrative authorities so that welfare projects may be implemented in an effective manner. The problem is now to reconcile national planning and administrative discretion with the greatest amount of legal safeguards. The development of a planned society necessarily means reorientation of the traditional legal approach by it does not mean the abrogation of the rule of law. In my opinion, rule of law is necessary if fundamental democratic values are to be preserved and if the democratic structure of the State is to be maintained."*

(b) Doctrine of Good Governance

(i) Meaning of Governance

The concept of "governance" is not new. It is as old as

human civilization. Simply put "governance" means : **the process of decision-making and the process by which decisions are implemented (or not implemented)**. Governance can be used in several contexts such as corporate governance, international governance, national governance and local governance. Since governance is the process of decision-making and the process by which decisions are implemented, an analysis of governance focuses on the formal and informal actors involved in decision-making and implementing the decisions made and the formal and informal structures that have been set in place to arrive at and implement the decision.

Government is one of the actors in governance. Other actors involved in governance vary depending on the level of government that is under discussion. In rural areas, for example, other actors may include influential landlords, associations of peasant farmers, cooperatives, NGOs, research institutions, religious leaders, finance institutions, political parties, the military, etc. The situation in urban areas is much more complex. At the national level, in addition to the above actors, media, lobbyists, international donors, multinational corporations, etc. may play a role in decision-making or influencing the decision-making process.

All actors other than government and the military are grouped together as part of the "civil society." In some countries in addition to the civil society, organized crime syndicates also influence decision-making, particularly in urban areas and at the national level.

Similarly, formal government structures are one means by which decisions are arrived at and implemented. At the national level, informal decision-making structures, such as "kitchen cabinets" or informal advisors may exist. In urban areas, organized crime syndicates such as the "land Mafia" may influence decision-making. In some rural areas locally powerful families may make or influence decision-making. Such informal decision-making is often the result of corrupt practices or leads to corrupt practices.

(ii) Meaning of Good Governance

According to a paper prepared by the Human Rights intentive good governance has 8 major facets. It is participatory, consensus oriented, accountable, transparent, responsive, effective and efficient, equitable and inclusive and follows the rule of law. It assures that corruption is minimized, the views of minorities are taken into account and that the voices of the most vulnerable in society are heard in decision-making. It is also responsive to the present and future needs of society.

FIGURE 1

Characteristics of Good Governance

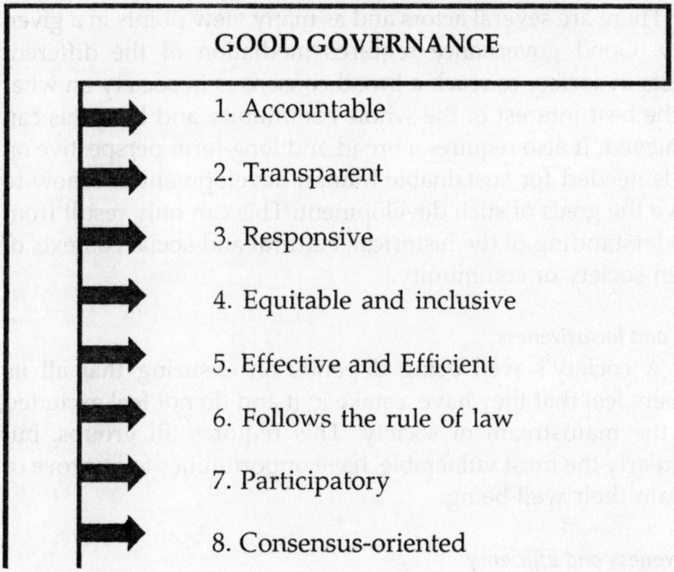

Participation

Participation by both men and women is a key cornerstone of good governance. Participation could be either direct or through legitimate intermediate institutions or representatives. It is important to point out that representative democracy does not necessarily mean that the concerns of the most vulnerable in society would be taken into consideration in decision-making. Participation needs to be informed and organized. This means freedom of association and expression on the one hand and an organized civil society on the other hand.

Rule of Law

Information is freely available and directly accessible to

those who will be affected by such decisions and their enforcement. It also means that enough information is provided and that it is provided in easily understandable forms and media.

Responsiveness

Good governance requires that institutions and processes try to serve all stakeholders within a reasonable timeframe.

Consensus-oriented

There are several actors and as many view points in a given society. Good governance requires mediation of the different interests in society to reach a broad consensus in society on what is in the best interest of the whole community and how this can be achieved. It also requires a broad and long-term perspective on what is needed for sustainable human development and how to achieve the goals of such development. This can only result from an understanding of the historical, cultural and social contexts of a given society or community.

Equity and Inclusiveness

A society's well being depends on ensuring that all its members feel that they have a stake in it and do not feel excluded from the mainstream of society. This requires all groups, but particularly the most vulnerable, have opportunities to improve or maintain their well-being.

Effectiveness and Efficiency

Good governance means that processes and institutions produce results that meet the needs of society while making the best use of resources at their disposal. The concept of efficiency in the context of good governance also covers the sustainable use of natural resources and the protection of the environment.

Accountability

Accountability is a key requirement of good governance. Not only governmental institutions but also the private sector and civil society organizations must be accountable to the public and to their institutional stakeholders. Who is accountable to whom varies depending on whether decisions or actions taken are internal or external to an organization or institution. In general an organization or an institution is accountable to those who will be affected by its decisions or actions. Accountability cannot be enforced without transparency and the rule of law.

(iii) Good Governance and Right to Information

The right to information is one of the methods by which success may be achieved in good governance.[22] The surprising response is a sequel to the rising tide of corruption; abdication of responsibility by the executive, both political and civil and prevalence of abuse of power on a large scale. Bound by the constitutional call of good governance, the court of law intervenes and ensure necessary correctives.[23]

"Good governance" means the efficient and effective administration in a democratic framework. It involves high level organization efficiency and effectiveness corresponding in a responsive way in order to attain the predetermined desirable goals of society. According to the World Bank document entitled 'Governance and Development (1991)', the parameters of good governance are as follow:

1. Legitimacy of the political system. This implies limited and democratic government.
2. Freedom of information and expression required for formulation of public policies, decision-making, monitoring and evaluation of government performance.
3. A sound administrative system leading to efficiency and effectiveness.
4. Cooperation between government and civil society organizations.
5. Freedom of association and participation by various social, economic, religious, cultural and professional groups in the process of governance.
6. An established legal framework based on the rule of law and independence of judiciary to protect human rights, secure social justice and guard against exploitation and abuse of power.
7. Bureaucratic accountability including transparency in administration.

In light of the above, if one were to venture a list of parameters that go into determination of the quality of governance, the major factors would include *limited Government, legitimacy of the Government, political and bureaucratic accountability, freedom of information and expression, transparency and cost effective administration, established legal framework based on rule of law for protecting the human life, securing social justice and checking abuse of power.*[24]

The basic premise behind the right to information is that, since Government is 'for the people'; it should be open and accountable and should have nothing to conceal from the people it purports to represent. In a responsible Government like ours where all the agents of the public must be responsible for their conduct, there could be no secrets. Information is an antidote to corruption, it limits abuse of discretion, protects civil liberties, it provides consumer information, it provides people's participation and brings awareness of laws and policies and is the elixir of the media.[25] It is true that good governance is a ideal which is difficult to achieve in its totality. The right to information promote the fair administration.

(iv) Administrative Efficiency and Right to Information

Although efficiency in the private sector may be judged in solely economic terms it cannot be so simply evaluated in the public sphere of Government. Unlike the business community, the purpose of Government is not to generate profits. Government has many duties in society including the allocation of scarce resources and the provision of social services such as health care, and its efficiency must be evaluated in broader, more distinct terms than profits and losses. Furthermore, Government is constrained by the public in terms of what is desired and what will be tolerated in ways that agents of the private sector are not. The Government is accountable to the people and, therefore, goals cannot be set by the Government alone; Government has to keep the citizens satisfied or at least pacified.[26]

There are three definitions of 'efficiency' in relation to Government;[27] *administrative efficiency, policy efficiency* and *service efficiency.*

Policy efficiency represents the idea of making the right political decisions. It involves the selection of appropriate programmes to achieve Government objectives.

Service efficiency is manifested in the effective provision of services to the public, responsive to public opinion and so on. Thus, the efficiency in Government must be measured in terms of all three facets of efficiency.

Administrative Efficiency

Administrative efficiency, the most important of the three, comprises of conducting the administration without unnecessary delays or ulterior or corrupt motives and giving reasons while passing various orders. It refers to the effective management of the political system. It encompasses good organization and efficient productivity. Where required or implied, principles of natural justice have to be observed.

It is common grievance of citizens that representations or statutory applications or appeals, are kept pending, for long periods, sometimes months or years, without disposal. Where the applicant is likely to benefit monetarily, such as where has to get money for services rendered under a contract or a refund of amounts payable to him by public authorities, there is a tendency to keep the matter pending for ulterior motives including corrupt motives. In some other cases, applications are simply disposed of as rejected or saying that the Government or the concerned authority "finds no reason" to accede to the request, etc. The avoidance of reasons is a device usually resorted to by officials who have no good reasons for denial of the relief.

(c) Doctrine of Public Accountability

(i) Meaning of Public Accountability

Doctrine of Public Accountability is one of the most important emerging facet of administrative law in recent times. The basic purpose of the emergence of the doctrine is to cheek the growing misuse of power by the administration and to provide speedy relief to the victims of such exercise of power. The doctrine is based on the premise that the power in the hands of administrative authorities is a public trust which must be exercised in the best interest of the people. Therefore, the trustee (public servant) who enriches himself by corrupt means holds the property acquired by him as a constructive trustee.[28]

Privy Council in ***A.G. of Hong Kong* v. *Reid***[29] as greatly widened the scope of this principle of jurisprudence in public law adjudication. Lord Templeman observed that engaging in bribery is an evil practice which threatens the foundations of any civilised society and that any benefit obtained by a fiduciary through the breach of duty belongs in equity to the beneficiary, is the basic norm subject to which all legal principles require to be interpreted. The Privy Council further observed that when bribe is accepted by a fiduciary in breach of his duty then he holds that bribe in trust for the person to whom the duty was owed. If the property representing the bribe decreases in value the fiduciary (public servant) must pay the difference between that value and the initial amount of the bribe because he should not have accepted the bribe and incurred the risk of loss. If the property increases in value, the fiduciary is not entitled to any surplus in sauces of the initial value of the bribe because he is not allowed by any means to make a profit out of a breach of a duty.

It was further held that a gift accepted by a person in fiduciary position as an incentive for breach of duty constituted a bribe and although in law it belonged to the fiduciary, in equity he not only becomes a debtor for the amount of the bribe to the person to whom the duty was owed but he also holds the bribe and any property acquired therewith on constructive trust for that person.[30]

In this pace-setting case the respondent, Reid who was Crown prosecutor in Hong Kong, took bribes as an inducement to suppress certain criminal prosecutions and with those monies acquired properties in New Zealand in his name, in the name of wife and his solicitor. The administration of Hong Kong claimed these properties on the ground that owners thereof are constructive trustees for the Crown. The Privy Council upheld the claim.

The Privy Council observed that if the theory constructive trust is not applied and properties attached when available, the danger is that properties may be sold and the proceeds whisked away to some 'numbered bank account'.

It was further observed that one can understand the immorality of the bankers who maintained numbered bank accounts but it is difficult to understand the amorality of the governments and their laws which sanction such practices—in effect encouraging them. The law laid down in this case equally applies to a situation even when fiduciary relationship does not exist.

The concept of constructive trust and equity to enforce public accountability as laid down in *Reid case* was followed by the Supreme Court in ***A.G. of India* v. *Amritlal Prajivandas***. The scope of public accountability has been further strengthened by developing such principles as "polluter must pay" in case of environmental pollution[31] and that every administrative authority shall be accountable for the proper and efficient discharge of its statutory duty.[32] ***Superintending Engineer, Public Health, Union Territory, Chandigarh* v. *Kuldeep Singh***[33] Supreme Court observed:

> "Every public servant is a trustee of the society and in all facets of public administration, every public servant has to exhibit honesty, integrity, sincerity and faithfulness in the implementation of the political, social, economic and constitutional polices to intergraded the nation, to achieve excellence and efficiency in public administration. A public servant entrusted with duty and power to implement constitutional policy............should exhibit transparency in implementation and should be accountable for due effectuation of constitutional goals."

(ii) Public Accountability and Right to Information

'Public Accountability' is a facet of administrative efficiency. Publicity of information serves as an instrument for the oversight of citizens. By the same token it suggests that law could become a means for fighting corruption. Therefore, a Government which produces a trustworthy flow of information creates greater certainty and transparency. This is especially appreciated by those who intend to invest in the Country. International experience shows that countries that allow citizens access to public information have seen a reduction in indicators of corruption and, consequently, substantial increases in administrative efficiency.[34]

'Public Accountability' is a part of governance. It is the Government that is accountable to the public for delivering a broad set of outcomes but more importantly it is the public service consisting of public servants that constitutes the delivery mechanism. Therefore, the accountability and governance arrangements between Government which acts as the principle and the public service which is its agent, impact on the Government's ability to deliver and on its accountability to the public. The challenge lies in ensuring that the public service is geared to meet the expectations of the Government of the day and that public service is neutral, whichever party is in power. When a Government department translates a Government's policy into programmes, the success of the translation is very much dependent on a clear understanding of and commitment to the outcomes that are sought. It is not surprising that the history of accountability and governance within the public service has shifted from measuring "inputs" to measuring "outputs", to matching outputs, and identify outcomes. The key which weakens accountability or the effectiveness of the Government or the public sector is the lack of information.[35] The right to information is necessary to promote a culture of accountability and to expose corruption and malpractice. Accessibility of information and release of facts pertaining to finance, proceedings and decisions of all the social actors whose activities have an impact on the public, is the guarantee that such actors will be accountable and will fufil their mandates. Accountability targets mismanagement, abuse of discretion, bribery, other forms of corruption and malpractices.[36]

5. RIGHT TO INFORMATION AND PRINCIPLE OF NATURAL JUSTICE

(A) Concept of Natural Justice

Natural Justice may mean simply "the natural sense of what is right and wrong" and even in its technical sense it is now often equated with 'fairness'. It has been said that romantic word "natural" adds nothing 'except perhaps a hint of nostalgia', and that 'justice is far from being a "natural" concept—the closer one goes to a state of nature, the less justice does one find. But in administrative law natural justice is a well-defined concept which comprises two fundamental rules of fair procedure: that a man may not be a judge in his own cause; and that a man's defence must always be fairly heard.[37] 'Principles of natural justice' is an expression used for describing the criteria of procedural fairness of the administrative process.[38] Famous Judge **Chinappa Reddy** observed in ***Swadeshi Cotton Mills* v. *Union of India*.**[39] Natural justice, like *ultra vires* and public policy, is a branch of the public law and is a formidable weapon, which can be wielded to secure justice to the citizen. While it may be used to protect certain fundamental liberties—civil and political rights—it may be used, as indeed it is used more often than not, to protect vested interests and to obstruct the path of progressive change.

(B) Basic Principle of Natural Justice

Two basic principles of the Natural Justice are:

(a) *Nemo Judex in Causa Sua*—which means that an adjudicator be disinterested and unbiased.
(b) *Audi Alteram Parten*—which means that the parties be given adequate notice and opportunity to be heard.

These two are required to make a fair action. They are applicable to quasi-judicial actions. Some times they are applicable even to purely administrative actions. The touchstone of applicability in the fairness of the action.[40]

(i) Nemo Judex in Causa Sua

These maxims means: A Judge should not hear matter in which he is personally interested. The rules requiring impartial adjudicators and fair hearings can be traced back to medieval precedents, and, indeed, they were not unknown in the ancient world. In their medieval guise they were regard as part of the immutable order of things, that in theory even the power of the legislature could not alter them. This theory lingered into the seventeenth and faintly even into the eighteenth century. It reached its high-water mark in *Dr Banham's* case (1610), where Chief Justice Coke went so far as to say that the court could declare an Act of Parliament void if it made a man judge in his own cause, or was otherwise 'against common right and reason'. This was one of his grounds for disallowing the claim of the College of Physicians to fine and imprison Dr. Bonham, a doctor of physics of Cambridge University, for practising in the City of London without the licence of the College of Physicians. The statute under which the College acted provided that fines should go half to the king and half to the College, so that the College had a financial interest in its own judgment and was judge in its own cause.[41]

It was further developed with a view to strengthening public confidence in the administration of justice and in conformity with the principle that justice should not only be done but must manifestly and undoubtedly seem to be done. It is important to note here that the disqualification on the ground of bias applies not only to quasi-judicial authorities but also to demonstrative authorities.[42]

Any administrative and Judicial decisions can be challenged on the ground of unreasonableness, arbitrariness, mala fide exercise of power or use or irrelevant factors or non-use of relevant factors. However, administrative decisions, which result in deprivation of a right or which adversely affect an interest, have to be in conformity with the principles of natural justice. Our Indian Supreme Court accept these principles of Natural Justice in various cases.

In the case of ***A.K. Kraipak* v. *Union of India***[43] our S.C. observed : "The real question is not whether he was biased. It is difficult to prove the state of mind of a person. Therefore, what we have to see is whether there is reasonable ground for believing that he was likely to have been biased....a mere suspicion of bias is not sufficient. There must be a reasonable likelihood of bias.

The Court held that there was in this case a reasonable likelihood that Nequishbund's presence would influence the selection board in his favour and against his rivals. Therefore, the selections were quashed."

In the case of ***Javid Russol* v. *State of Jammu & Kashmir***[44]. Justice **Chinappa Reddy** said that the principal of the medical college at Srinagar who was the member accused of bias had informed the selection committee at the very outset that his daughter was a candidate for admission, and that he would not have anything to do with the written test and would not present when she would be interviewed. The government had fixed the quorum of the selection committee consisting of the chairperson and any one member. Therefore, it was possible to have the quorum without the principal being on the committee.

The Learned Judge further said that, the procedure adopted by the Selection Committee and the member concerned was in accord with the quite well known and generally accepted procedure adopted by the Public Service Commissions everywhere. It is not unusual for candidates related to members of the Service Commission or other Selection Committee to seek employment. Whenever such a situation arise, the practice generally is for the member concerned to excuse himself when the particular candidate is interviewed.

The learned judge further observed that the marks obtained by her in the written test were not known when she was interviewed, 'and in fact...as a result of her performance at the interview, she lost rather than gained some place'. The learned judge has illustrated through this decision what is meant by reasonable likelihood of bias. This approach is intended to strike a balance between protecting confidence in impartial decision-making and discouraging fanciful and unmeritorious allegations of bias.[45]

In the case of ***Ashok Kumar Yadav v. State of Haryana***[46] Justice Bhagwati said, "It is one of the fundamental principles of our jurisprudence that no man can be a judge in his own case and that if there is a reasonable likelihood of bias it is in accordance with natural justice and commonsense that the justice so likely to be biased should be incapacitated from sitting. The question is not whether the judge is actually biased or in fact decides partially, but whether there is a real likelihood of bias. What is objectionable in such a case is not that the decision is actually tainted with bias but that the circumstances are such as to create a reasonable apprehension in the mind of others that there is a likelihood of bias affecting the decision. The basic principle underlying this rule is that justice must not only be done but must appear to be done and this rule has received wide recognition in several decisions of this Court. It is also important to note that this rule is not confined to cases where judicial power *stricto sensu* is exercised. It is appropriately extended to all cases where an independent mind has to be applied to arrive at a fair and just decision between the rival claims of parties.

(ii) ***Audi alteram partem***

'Hear the other side' it is fundamental to fair procedure that both sides should be heard: *audi alteram partem,* 'hear the other side'. This is the more far-reaching of the principles of natural

justice, since it can embrace almost every question of fair procedure, or due process, and its implications can be worked out in great detail. The right to a fair hearing has been used by the courts as a base on which to build a kind of code of fair administrative procedure, the first hearing in human history was given in the Garden of Eden.[47]

I remember to have heard it observed by a very learned man upon such an occasion, that even God himself did not pass sentence upon Adam, before he was called upon to make his defence. 'Adms, says God, where art thou? Hast thou not eaten of the tree, whereof commanded thee that thou shouldst not eat?' And the same question was put to Eve also.

This was in *'Bentley's* case, in which the University of Combridge had deprived that recalcitrant scholar of his degrees on account of his misconduct in insulting the Vice-Chancellor's court; but he was reinstated on a *mandamus* from the Court of the King's Bench, on the ground that deprivation was unjustifiable and that, in any case, he should have received notice so that he could make his defence, as required by 'the laws of God and man'. This is a nice example of the old conception of natural justice as divine and eternal law.[48]

The important aspect of hearing the other side are following:

(a) Notice
(b) Hearing
(c) Reasoned Decisions

(a) Notice

Notice means, what action is proposed and why it is proposed. The term 'Notice' originated from the Latin word *'Notitia'* which means 'being known'. In its popular sense it is equivalent to information, intelligence or knowledge. In legal sense it embraces a knowledge of circumstances that ought to induce suspicion or belief, as well as direct information of that fact.[49]

Natural justice demands that the person, who is to be directly affected by an administrative action, should be given prior adequate notice of what is proposed, so as to enable her to make a representation on her behalf, appear at the hearing or inquiry, if it is held, and meet effectively any points raised. Notice means communication of the charges. In the case of ***National Control Co-operative Bank Ltd.* v. *Ajay Kumar,***[50] the S.C. said, Where the required notice has not been issued and there has been failure to hear the party against whom adverse remarks are passed, the court held that the procedure is violative of the rules of natural justice. Further Supreme Court said in the case of ***Jauwad Ali* v. *State of U.P.,***[51] the petitioner belongs to the 'Sheikh' caste and said caste was recognized as backward caste. The petitioner applied for issuance of the caste certificate before appropriate authority, after having made necessary enquiry issued the caste certificate in favour of the petitioner at that time by the order of State respondent has cancelled the caste certificate of petitioner without giving him any opportunity of hearing. The Court observed that show cause notice must be given to the petitioner before the cancellation of caste certificate.

(b) Hearing

'Hearing' means giving an opportunity to a person against whom an adverse action is proposed to be taken to say why it should not be so taken. What does such an opportunity mean? It means that the person must be given a notice as to what is proposed to be done against her and why. Further, it should be possible for her to put forth her say either orally or in writing, she should be able to cross-examine the witnesses, if any, who might have testified against her, and should be able to contradict the allegations against her through such evidence as may be necessary.[52]

Venkatarma Aiyar once observed[53] Rules of natural justice require that a party should have the opportunity of adducing all relevant evidence on which he relies, that the evidence of the opponent should be taken in his presence, and that he should be given the opportunity of cross-examining the witnesses examined by that party, and that no materials should be relied on against him without his being given an opportunity of explaining them the requirement of hearing is an essential aspect of administrative and *quasi*-judicial proceedings. Any administrative order passed by the authority without reasonable opportunity of being heard is illegal and must be set aside. The requirement of an opportunity of hearing has two elements :

(a) The opportunity must be given; and
(b) The opportunity given must be adequate and reasonable.

Both these matters are justiciable. The opportunity of representing one case must be adequate, it implies a clear opportunity to be effected party at suitable stage. In ***Josoph Vilangaden*** v. ***Executive Engineer (PWD), Ernakullam,***[54] petitioner was a contractor and was blacklisted by an order of the Executive Engineer (PWD) whereby he was debarred from the privilege and advantage of entering into lawful relationship with the Government in future. The Executive Engineer (PWD) before cancelling the contract with petitioner and declaring him a defaulter gave him a show-cause notice, did not give a clear intimation to him that it was proposed to debar him from taking any contract with the department in future. The court held that the petitioner was not afforded and adequate opportunity to represent against the impugned action of the Executive Engineer. According to the view of the Court show-cause notice did not mean an opportunity of representation against the order of blacklisting.

(c) Reasoned Decisions

The principles of natural justice do not, as yet, include any general rule that reasons should be given for decisions. Nevertheless there is a strong case to be made for the giving of reasons as an essential element of administrative justice. The need for it has been sharply exposed by the expanding law of judicial review, now that so many decisions are liable to be quashed or appealed against on grounds of improper purpose, irrelevant considerations and errors of laws of various kinds. Unless the citizen can discover the reasoning behind the decision, he may be unable to tell whether it is reviewable or not, and so he may be deprived of the protection of the law. A right to reasons is therefore an indispensable part of a sound system of judicial review. Natural justice may provide the best opportunity for it, since the giving of reasons is required by the ordinary man's sense of justice. It is also a healthy discipline for all who exercise power over others. No single factor has inhibited the development of English administrative law as seriously as the absence of any general obligation upon public authorities to give reasons for their discision.[55] In this way reason for decisions is a part of Right to Information.

(C) Right to Hearing an Aspect of Right to Information

Hearing is a basic concept. The main object of hearing provided the information. Hearing is essential aspect of transparency in governance. It is now provided for in various statutes. Access to documents or information is an essential requisite of any open society. It also means right to information, which is implicit in the right to fair hearing.[56]

In the year 1984 very interesting question come up before the Supreme Court, the case in ***Maharashtra State Board of Higher secondary Eduction*** v. ***Paritosh.***[57] A regulation made by the Maharashtra State Board of Education provided that no candidate could claim or be entitled to revaluation of her answers, or disclosure, or inspection of her answer books, or other documents, as they were supposed to be confidential. The High Court of Bombay had struck down this provision as being unreasonable. The Supreme Court reversed the Bombay decision and upheld the regulation, thus holding valid such denial of opportunity for revaluation and inspection answer books. The Court rationalised that those were matters entirely within the autonomous sphere of the Board and it was the best judge of how examinations should be conducted and what procedures of verification and revaluation should be provided. Those were matters of policy, entrusted to the Board, which the courts would not go into. However, considering the fact that the Board's examination procedures cause serious doubts in the minds of candidates as well as their parents, such total exclusion of opportunity for inspection of answer books or revaluation might jeopardies the interests of young boys and girls. Further, such exclusion of access to answer books might further erode credibility or the examination system. While inspection of answer books might not be feasible, a provision for revaluation would go a long way in assuring the fears of examinees and their parents. Education boards and universities must amend their rules to bring in greater transparency in the examination system. It does not mean that a student should be given access to all the documents of a university or board. Access has to be selective. In a case of alleged use of malpractices in an examination, it was held that a delinquent student could not claim access to all university records. However, he should have been shown material as was the basis of allegation.

6. CONCLUSION

The Right to Information has been enacted for the sake of transparency in the works of administration and government under this Act we can ask for the audit and accounts of the expenditure of administration. Infact, these days corruption is a rampant phenomena in every walk of administration and government. By the enactment of Right to Information the common men have got an effective weapon to fight the corruption of administration and government. By this Act, at least accountability can be fixed at some level. It has helped a great deal for bringing transparency in administration and government.

Notes and References

1. I.P. Massey, Administrative Law, 7th Ed., p. 1.
2. S.P. Sathe, Administrative Law, 7th Ed., p. 4.
3. S.P. Sathe, Administrative Law, pp. 5-6.
4. *Ibid.*
5. (1994) 1 SCC 243.
6. S.P. Sathe, Administrative Law, pp. 5-6.
7. U.P.D. Keshari, Administrative Law.
8. *Ibid.*
9. I.P. Massey, Administrative Law, 7th Ed., pp. 25-26.
10. I.P. Massey, Administrative Law, 7th Ed., pp. 25-26.
11. A.V. Dicey, Law of Constitution, 10th Ed., p. 49.
12. Good Hard: The Rule of Law and Absolute Sovereignty.
13. Public Health Union Territory *v.* Kuldip Singh, 1972, 2 SC ale 138.
14. Burden of Corruption in daily life, *The Hindu*, Dated 27 December 2003, p. 15.
15. AIR 1982 SC 149.
16. 2003 (3) SC ale 263.
17. *Ibid.*
18. Harry *v.* Jones, 58 Col-LR 143.
19. *Ibid.*
20. AIR 1978 SC 597.
21. AIR 1980 SC, p. 556.
22. Justice Y.K. Sabharwal, Right to Information and Good Governance, Nayana Deep, p. 30.

23. Dr. K. Chandra Segarm and Dr. Ambedkar, Rule of Law and Right to Information, *Journal of Indian Legal Thought*, Vol. I, p. 187.
24. Mr. Prabha, Importance of Human Right to Information—A Key to Good Governance, In Chapter 27 of the Book, Good Governance in India.
25. *Ibid.*
26. Justice Y.K. Sabharwal, Right to Information and Good Governance, pp. 22-23.
27. http://imej.wfu.edu/articles/1999/1/02/demo/golossary/glossaryhtml/efficiency.html
28. I.P. Massey, Administrative Law, 7th Ed., pp. 372-73.
29. (1993) 3 WLR 1143.
30. I.P. Massey, Administrative Law, 7th Ed., pp. 372-73
31. Indian Council for Enviro-Legal Action *v.* Union of India (1996) 8 SCC 212.
32. Municipal Council, Ratlam *v.* Vardichand (1980) 4 SCC, p. 162.
33. (1997) 9 SCC, p. 199.
34. Justice Y.K. Sabharwal, Right to Information and Good Governance.
35. Governance and Accountability in the Public Sector Speech by Hon'ble Lianne Dalziel, 2003.
36. *Ibid.*
37. William Wade, Administrative Law, 8th edition, p. 434.
38. Dhakeswari Cotton Mills Ltd. *v.* CIT, West Bengal, AIR 1955 SC 65.
39. AIR 1981 SC 818.
40. S.P. Sathe, Administrative Law, 7 Ed., p. 191.
41. William Wade, Administrative Law, 8th Ed., p. 439.
42. S.P. Sathe, Administrative Law, 7th Ed., p. 191.
43. AIR 1970 SC 150.
44. (1984) 2 SCC 631.
45. William Wade, Administrative Law, 8th Ed., p. 459.
46. AIR 1987 SC 454 to 467.
47. William Wade, Administrative Law, 8th Ed., p. 469.
48. *Ibid.*
49. I.P. Massey, Administrative Law, 7th Ed., p. 223.
50. AIR 1954 SC 39.
51. AIR 2001 ALL 36.
52. S.P. Sathe, Administrative Law, 7th Ed., p. 191.
53. AIR 1957 SC 882 to 885.
54. AIR 1978 SC 930.
55. William Wade, Administrative Law, 8th Ed., p. 516.
56. S.P. Sathe, Administrative Law, p. 233.
57. AIR 1984 SC 1543.

CHAPTER

6

JUDICIAL APPROACH RELATING TO RIGHT TO INFORMATION

The Constitution, statute and Act are the compilation of words which are dead but the spirit and life is given to them by the way of judicial interpretation. It is said that the law must be living. Our Supreme Court has given life and dimension to our Constitution. There is no clear provision of Right to Information in our Constitution. The Supreme Court incorporated this concept in our Constitution as a fundamental right. This shows the spirit of the Supreme Court to keep pace with time.

In recent years, the Supreme Court has held that the Right to Information is a concomitant of the Right to Freedom of Speech and Expression as guaranteed by our Constitution as a fundamental right.

Judicial approach relating to Right to Information has changed from time to time. The flow chart on next page can show the different development stages of Right to Information.

The legal position with regard to the Right to Information has developed through several Supreme Court Judgements. The first step of the court pronounces Right to Information through Disclosure of Information. The government enjoys the privilege of withholding the disclosure of documents in courts if such disclosure of documents in courts if such disclosure is likely to

First Step = Disclosure of Information/Documents

⇩

Second Step = Right to Acquire and Disseminate Information

⇩

Third Step = Right to Know

⇩

Fourth Step = Right to Information

jeopardise public interest. In this area, the courts have succeeded in bringing claims for secrecy made by government under judicial scrutiny. Sections 122-27 of Indian Evidence Act, 1872 provide exceptions to the rule that all evidences must come before the court. Section 123 of the Evidence Act read as follows: ***"No one shall be permitted to give any evidence derived from unpublished official records relating to any affairs of State, except with the permission of the officer at the head of the department concerned who shall give or withhold such permission as he thinks fit."***

The section prohibits the disclosure of any evidence derived from unpublished official records relating to any affairs of State without the permission of the head of the department concerned, who has discretion to give or refuse such permission. Our Supreme Court has to decide whether the document relates to affairs of State. The most natural way to determine that would be to inspect to document but since Section 162 as interpreted by courts forbade such inspection, the Court had to look to other evidence to determine the nature of the document. According to Section 123 a claim for privilege must satisfy following conditions:

(i) The document must form part of the official records;
(ii) Such records must be unpublished;
(iii) The records must relate to affairs of the State; and
(iv) The officer at the head of the department must have withheld the permission.

A important judgement of Supreme Court, in the case of ***State of Punjab* v. *Sodhi Sukhdev Singh,***[1] the apex court delineated the scope of such a privilege. In order to determine whether a claim of privilege was legitimate or not, courts would have to examine whether the evidence in question related to any affairs of State. Learned Justice **Gajendragadkar** observed that Section 123 of the Evidence Act, 1872 was qualified by Section 162 of that Act which requited that a witness summoned to produce a document must bring it to the Court and then raise an objection against either its production or its admissibility. That section authorised the Court to decide the validity of such objections. While deciding upon the validity of the objection under Section 123, the Court could not permit any evidence about could be produce, which might help the Court in determining the validity of the objection. The Court observed that two questions were involved:

(i) whether the contents of the document pertained to the affairs of State; and
(ii) whether the production of such a document would harm public interest.

It was held that while the first question fell within the purview of judicial review, the second did not. The Court was competent, and indeed bound, to hold a preliminary inquiry and determine the validity of the objections to its production and that necessarily involved an inquiry into the question as to whether the evidence related to the affairs of State under Section 123. In this inquiry the Court had to determine the character or class of the document. If it came to the conclusion that the document did not relate to the affairs of State then it should reject the claim for privilege and direct its production. The Court, however, held that it injury to public interest. According to the learned judge, that clearly was a matter of policy on which the Court did not and should not generally express any opinion.

The legal discourse on the Right to Information started with petitions of the press to the Supreme Court for enforcement of certain logistical implications of the right to freedom of speech and expression such as challenging governmental orders for control of newsprint, bans on distributions of papers, etc. It was through these cases that the concept of the public right to know or Right to Information developed.

In the case of ***Sakal Newspaper Pvt. Ltd.*** **v.** ***Union of India.***[2] the Supreme Court for the first time said that readers had the right to read newspapers and this emanated from their right to know which was part of their right to freedom of speech and expression. This principle was even more clearly enunciated in ***Indian Express Newspaper Bombay Ltd.*** **v.** ***Union of India,***[3] the Court remarked, "The basic purpose of freedom of speech and expression is that all members should be able to form their beliefs and communicate them freely to others. In sum, the fundamental principle involved here in is the people's right to know."

In the case of ***Bennett Coleman and Co.*** **v.** ***Union of India,***[4] a leading newspaper publisher challenged the government's newsprint policy which put restrictions an acquisition, Sale and Consumption of newsprint. This was challenged as restricting the petitioner's right to freedom of speech and expression. The Court struck down the newsprint control order directly affected the petitioner's right to freely publish and circulate the paper.

In its decision favouring the petitioner the learned Judges also remarked, *"It is indisputable that by freedom of the press meant the right of all citizens to speak, publish and express their views"* and "Freedom of speech and expression includes within its compass the right of all citizens to read and be informed."

The dissenting judgement by Justice ***K.K. Mathew*** noted, *"The freedom of speech protects two kinds of interests. There is an individual interest, the need of men to express their opinion on matters vital to them and a social interest in the attainment of truth so that the country may not only accept the wisest course but carry it out in the wisest way. Now, in the method of political government, the point of ultimate interest is not in the words of the speakers but in the hearts of the hearers."*

The Right to Information got the legal support in 1975 in Supreme Court case of ***State of U.P.*** **v.** ***Raj Narain.***[5] A case in which the respondent had demanded information relating to the security expenses of the then Prime Minister of India, Indira Gandhi, the Court emphasised the importance of the public's right to know as a deterrent to oppression and corruption. In which **Mr. Justice Mathew** gave a landmark judgement, *"In a government of responsibility like ours, where all the agents of public must be responsible for their conduct, there can be but few secrets. The people of this country have a right to know, every public act, every thing that is done in a public way by the public functionaries. They are entitled to know, the particulars of every public transaction in all its bearing. Their right to know, which is derived form the concept of freedom of* *speech, though not absolute, is a factor, which should make one way when secrecy is claimed for transactions which can at any rate have no repression on public security."*

Supreme Court have derived the Right to Information from two distinct Constitutional sources, one is freedom of speech and expression guaranteed in Article 19(1)(a) and the other fundamental right that is right to life and personnel liberty guarantee under Article 21. Article 19(1)(a) of the Indian Constitution guarantees the fundamental right to free speech and expression, which by implication includes within it the right to access to information. Therefore, the Right to Information becomes a constitutional right being and aspect of the right to free speech and expression, which includes the right to receive and collect information.

Again full bench of Supreme Court ***In Re Mulgaoker's Case***[6] through **Justice V.R. Krishana Iyer and Kailasam, J.J.** said it is the right of every man in Parliament of out of its in the press or over the broadcast, to make fair comment even outspoken comment, on matters of public interest. Those who comment can deal faith fully with all that is done in a Court of Justice.

Further in the famous case of ***Maneka Gandhi* v. *Union of India***[7]. In this case learned **Justice P.N. Bhagwati** said, *"Democracy is based essentially on free debate an open discussion for, i.e., the only corrective of government action in a democratic set-up. In democracy means the governments of the people, by the people, it is obvious that every citizen must be entitled to participate in the democratic process and in order to enable him to intelligently his right to making a choice free and general discussion of public matters is absolutely essential."*

The legal basis of the right to information was strengthened further by series of new cases. In ***S.P. Gupta* v. *Union of India,***[8] the Court declared that *"disclosures of information in regard to the functioning of Government must be the rule, and secrecy an exception justified only where the strictest requirement of public interests so demands. The Court observed: "This is the new democratic culture of an open society towards which every liberal concept of an open government is the direct emanation from the right to know which seems to be implicit in the right of free speech and expression guaranteed under Article 19(1)(a). Therefore, disclosures of information in regard to the functioning of Government must be the rule, and secrecy an exception justified only where the strictest requirement of public interest so* *demands. The approach of the court must be to attenuate the area of secrecy as much as possible consistent with the requirement of public interests, bearing in mind all the time that disclosure also serves an important aspect of public interest."*

The Supreme Court in ***R.L.E.K. Dehradun* v. *State of U.P.*,**[9] stated that *"the question involving issues relating to environment and ecological balance, brings into sharp focus the conflict between development and conservation and serves to emphasis the need for reconciling the two in larger interest of the people residing within the area and the country. Therefore it cannot be said that action groups are trying to meddle in the affairs of Cantonment Board or are claiming any extralegal authority."* By this way the right to know has been reaffirmed in the context of environmental issues that have an impact upon people's very survival.

Article 21 of the Indian Constitution is the guarantee of the right to life and personal liberty, which includes the right to know about things that affect our lives.

In the case of ***Reliance Petrochemical Ltd.* v. *Proprietors of Indian Express Newspapers, Bombay Pvt. Ltd.***[10] The Supreme Court read in the Article 21 as broad right to include right to know with in its purview. The Supreme Court said that right to know is a basic ingredient of participatory democracy. In this case Supreme Court further observed, *"In view of transactional developments when distances are shrinking, international communities are coming together for cooperation in various spheres and they are moving towards global perspective in various fields including human rights, the expression "liberty" must receive an expanded meaning. The expression cannot be limited to mere absence necessary to receive information. Article 21 confers on all persons a right to know which includes a right to receive information. The ambit and scope of Article 21 is much wider as compared to Article 19(1)(a)."*

Another case, related environment awareness, has been decided by the Supreme Court comprising of ***Ranganath Mishra CJ, G.N. Ray and A.S. Anand JJ*** in ***M.C. Mehta* v. *Union of India*,**[11] the Court stated that: *"we are in a democratic polity, where dissemination of information is foundation of the system, Keeping the citizens informed is an obligation of the Government."* The Supreme Court, therefore accepted in principle the prayers made by the petitioner, for issuing appropriate directions to cinema exhibition halls to exhibits slides containing information and messages on environment free of cost, directions for the spread of information relating to environment in national and regional languages and for broadcasting thereof on the All India Radio and exposure thereof on the television with a view to educating the people of India.

In 1989 a writ petition involving ***Life Insurance Corporation of India* v. *Manubhai Shah,***[12] a noted consumer activist, and the Life Insurance Corporation of India, the court ruled that no official medium of information could transmit one set of views without also providing for the expression of alternative views, thus widening the range of opinions presented to the public. These and other similar cases effectively widened the scope of judicial protection for the right to information in India, and contributed to a greater interest in Freedom of Information legislation in India.

In a historic Judgement, the Supreme Court comprising of P.B. Sawant, S. Mohan and B.P. Jeevan Reddy J.J. In ***Secretary, Minister of Information and Broadcasting* v. *Cricket Association of West Bengal.***[13] The Court observed that, the Right to Circulate information is a part of right guaranteed under Article 19(1)(a). Right to Freedom of speech and expression also includes.

In the matter of ***T.N. Sheshan, CEC of India* v. *Union of India,***[14] the Supreme Court observed that the Preamble of our Constitution proclaims that we are in a Democratic Republic. Democracy being the basic structure of our constitutional set-up, there can be no two opinions that free and fair elections to our legislative bodies alone would guarantee the growth of healthy democracy in the country. Hence the right of a voter to know the bio-data of a candidate is the foundation of democracy.

Besides the government of India in 2002 became more sensitized on the right to information. The Representation of the People Act, 1951 was added with two new provisions, viz. Section 33A and Section 33B in this year. The Section 33A, i.e. right to information provides that besides other information a candidate has to furnish the information as to whether he is accused of any offence punishable with imprisonment for two years or more in a pending case and whether he has been convicted of an offence and sentenced to imprisonment for one year or more. The candidate or his propose shall also deliver to him an affidavit sworn by the candidate verifying the above information, etc.

The Section 33B, i.e. candidate to furnish information only

under the Act and the rules provides that no candidate shall be liable to disclose or furnish any such information which is not required to be disclosed. This provision later was declared by the Supreme Court as unconstitutional.

The legislators at the state and central level brought several legislations pertaining to Right to Information. The courts of law made interpretation of the statutes, keeping in view the spirit and objectives of such statutes and constitutional provisions of such statutes and constitutional on freedom of speech and expression while rendering judgments in cases.

The Supreme Court observed in ***People's Union for Civil Liberties* v. *Union of India***[15] that the foundation of a healthy democracy is to have well informed citizen voters. The reason to have right to information with regard to the antecedents of the candidate is that voter can judge and decide in whose favour he should cast his vote. It is voter's discretion whether to vote in favour of an illiterate or literate candidate. It is his choice whether to elect a candidate against whom criminal cases for serious or non-serious charges were filed but is acquitted or discharged. He is to consider whether his candidate mayor may not have sufficient assets so that he may not be tempted to indulge in unjustified means for accumulating wealth.

Justice Venkatarama in People's Union case held that for the first time the right to know about the candidate standing for election has been brought within the ambit of Article 19(1)(a) of the Constitution. There can be no doubt that by doing so, a new dimension has been given to the right embodied in Article 19(1)(a) through a creative approach dictated by the need to improve and refine the political process of election. The voters' right to know about the antecedents of the candidate contesting for election falls within the realm of freedom of speech and expression guaranteed by Article 19(1)(a) and can be justified on good and substantial grounds.

From the Supreme Court point of view it is clear that the court took into consideration every aspect of voters' right to know. According to the Supreme Court the Democratic Republic is part of the basic structure of the Constitution. Free and fair elections are must for it. The citizen voters should be well informed about all aspects of a candidate for having healthy democracy. So the foundation of healthy democracy is to have well-informed citizen-voters. The reason to have right to information with regard to the antecedents of the candidate is that voter can judge and decide in whose favour he should cast his vote.

A landmark judgment in ***Union of India* v. *Association for Democratic Reforms***[16] which can be termed as an important judicial benchmark in the field of electional reforms. In that judgment, the Court declared that where law is silent, Article 324 is a reservoir of power for the Commission and the same can be used for free and fair election; that the Commission can fill in the vacuum till there is a legislation on the subject to meet the particular situation or contingency; to maintain purity of election and to bring transparency in the process of election, the Commission can ask the candidate about the expenditure incurred by the political parties. The Court further held that the elector has right to know full particulars of a candidate who is to represent him in legislature and that under Article 19(1)(a) voter's right of speech and expression in case of election would include casting of votes. The Supreme Court further consideration by a larger Bench in the light of the judgments of this Court whereby the elector's right to be informed about the assets and antecedents of the persons seeking election to the legislature has been duly recognized.

Further the Supreme Court said, in this case the right to get information in democracy is recognised all throughout and it is natural right flowing from the concept of democracy. The public interests in freedom of discussion stems form the requirement that members of a democratic society should be sufficiently informed.

The Right to Information being part of the Right to freedom of speech was recognised in several other decisions. In ***PUCL* v. *Union of India,***[17] the Supreme Court held section 33B of the Representation of the People (Amendment) Act, 2002 invalid on the ground that it violated people's right to know the antecedents of candidates who contests elections to the legislature. Section 33A of the impugned Act specified the information, which a person had to give in her nomination application. Information regarding previous convictions in criminal cases for offences punishable by more than two years imprisonment and pending cases in which charge had been framed had to be provided at the time of filing nomination papers. Section 33B said that notwithstanding any judgment of any Court, the candidate would not have to give any other information. This was clearly in contrast with the decision of the Supreme Court, which made giving of information regarding assets and liabilities and educational qualification by the candidate obligatory as being in fulfilment of the voter's right to information. The Supreme Court therefore held it to be void. This was further reaffirmation of the peoples' right to information.

In case of ***Dinesh Trivedi, M.P.* v. *Union of India,***[18] the Supreme Court held that freedom of speech and expression includes right of citizens to know about the affairs of government. In this case petitioners have urged to direct the Union Government to make public the annexures memorial and written evidence that were placed before the **N.H. Vohara Committee**[19] and also urged to direct the Union Government to present an effective package of the follow-up measures taken with regard to the Report. Lastly a declaration to the effect that Section 5 of the Official Secrets Act, 1923 is over-broad, unreasonable and unconstitutional and ought to be supplanted by the formulation of a Freedom of Information Policy, was also urged. While petition opinion Court issued notice to the Union of India and directed that an authenticated version of the Report of the Vohara Committee[20] be placed before it, and Union of India was also required to apprise the Court of the follow-up measures in initiated pursuant to the Report. The Supreme Court observed: "*In modern constitutional democracies, it is axiomatic that* citizens have a Right to Know about the affairs of the government which, having been elected by them, seeks to formulate sound policies of governance aimed at their welfare. However, like all other rights, even this right has recognized limitations, it is by no means absolute.[21]

The Supreme Court further observed: "To ensure the continued participation of the people in the democratic process, they must be kept informed of the vital decisions taken by the government and the basis thereof. Democracy, therefore, expects openness and openness is a concomitant of a free society.

Thus the Supreme Court expanded the scope of the Right to Information by the way of Judicial activation. In this case Supreme Court issued the directives to Election Commission of India regarding voters' right to know the antecedents of the election candidates.

In the case of ***Research Foundation for Science Technology and Natural Resource Policy* v. *Union of India,***[22] the Right to Information and community participation for protection of environment and human health is also a right which flows from Article 21.

In the case of ***Hemani Malhotra* v. *High Court of Delhi.***[23] In this case Right to Information played the important role. The petitioners claim that they filed an application under Right to Information Act before the Public Information Officer of High Court of Delhi on April 28, 2007 seeking information about the result, etc. of Delhi Higher Judicial Service Examination, 2006. According to the petitioners the Public Information Officer of the High Court did not supply most of the information demanded by them on the pretext of confidentiality, but in reply dated June 20, 2007 only a part of the information was given to the petitioner in that out of 750 marks for which written test was conducted, she had secured 141 marks and 363 marks out of 750 marks of which *viva-voce* test was conducted. The petitioner in Writ Petition Civil No. 491 of 2007 was informed by intimation dated June 20, 2007 that she had obtained 153.50 marks out or 250 marks for which written test was conducted and 316 marks out of 750 marks for which viva-voce test was conducted.

Right to Information had played a major role for **Hemani Malhotra** case. She asked for her marks obtained Delhi Higher Judicial Service Examination 2006. After getting the response she filed a writ petition in Supreme Court for her result. Finally, she got herself selected by Supreme Court in Delhi Higher Judicial Service Examination, 2006. This is supported to be a classical example of good use of Right to Information.

In the case of ***The CPIO Supreme Court of India* v. *Subhash Chandra Agrawal and ANR,***[24] in an important judgement, the Delhi High Court upheld the Chief Information Commission's order stating that the Chief Justice of India's office is a public authority and is under the purview of the Right to Information Act.

Learned Justice S. Ravindra Bhatt said that a person can seek information about declaration of assets by Supreme Court judges. This comes under the Act.

"The Chief Justice of India is a public authority under the Right to Information Act and the Chief Justice of India holds the information pertaining to assets declaration in his capacity as Chief Justice. That

office is a public authority under the Act and is covered by its provisions."

Further Justice S. Ravindra Bhatt said:

> *"Declaration of assets by Supreme Court judges is an information under Section 2(f) of the Right to Information Act. The information nation pertaining to declaration given to the Chief Justice of India and the contents of such declaration are information and subject to provisions of the Right to Information Act"*, Bhatt said. Judges are accountable but they are also subjective to some constraints, Bhatt said, adding: "The dignity of the judges adds value to the democracy. Judges are under public attack and revealing of assets and other information may increase the reputation of the judges." "Chief Public Information Officer of the Supreme Court shall release the information about the declaration of the assets to the petitioner within four weeks of time," he said. The judge also said judges should declare their assets. The court refused to comment on the recent development of declaration of assets by judges of various state high courts. The Delhi High Court on May 4, 2009 had reserved its order on the Supreme Court plea challenging Chief Information Commissioner's order that judges declare their assets. Solicitor General **G.E. Vahanvati** contended before Justice Bhatt that disclosure of information on personal assets by judges will affect the independence of the judicial system.

The historic judgment came on an appeal filed by the Supreme Court against a Central Information Commission order on January 6, 2009 this year, asking it to provide information in possession of the Chief Justice of India.

Upholding the CIC ruling, the high court asked the apex court to provide information to a Delhi-based Right to Information activist, **Subhash Chandra Agarwal**, within four weeks on whether the Supreme Court judges were declaring their assets to the CJI.

The Supreme Court registry is likely to challenge the judgment soon. The High Court verdict contradicts CJI **K.G. Balakrishnan's** recent views that his office was not covered by the information law, since it was *"privy to highly privileged communication."* With judges of the Supreme Court and four high courts deciding to declare their assets and put the details on websites of respective courts, the high court judgment now shifts focus on other information considered to confidential till now.

SC Agarwal's lawyer **Prashant Bhushan** said the verdict makes it clear that the CJI's office will now have to provide information to Right to Information applicants. "It is clear from the judgment that the Supreme Court and the CJI's office will have to claim exemption under the relevant sections of Right to Information Act, in case they wish to withhold any information," he said. The top court has been reluctant to provide information on judges' appointments and any disciplinary action against them so far.[25]

CONCLUSION

The above discussion shows that the logic and spirit of Right to Information has been established by our Supreme Court and High Court by different judicial discussions.

There is also a view that the Constitution should be amended to make room for the Right to Information. According to a leading lawyer **F.S. Nariman** the right to privacy and freedom of information are not provided or guaranteed by the constitution or laws... In the end both the right and the freedom being unwritten are the ultimate case and at the mercy of the Supreme Court. So, instead of leaving it to the vagaries of judicial discretion and pronouncements, it is better to make it a constitutional right which is always considered better and stronger than any statutory right.

There are also authorities like **Justice H.R. Khanna** and **Soli Sorabjee**, who favour statutory amendments and a fresh enactment for this purpose. **Justice H.R. Khanna** favour omnibus amendments of The Official Secrets Act, 1923, The Commission of Enquiry Act, 1952, and The Contempt of Courts Act, 1971. **Soli Sorabjee** is of view that since the right to information has been accorded a Constitutional status by the judgements of the Supreme Court, an amendment can do no more than expressly declare it a fundamental right. It is not the function of the Constitution to spell out the details, modalities and procedures for working out and implementing this right in its various facets, for that purpose, legislation provided for freedom of information is necessary.

The above mentioned discussion has an elaborate detail of judicial view towards Right to Information. Infact, it was the judiciary which threw light on Right to Information in earlier phase and made way for this right in its present form by its different judicial pronouncement and personal inclination.

Notes and References

1. AIR 1961 SC 493.
2. AIR 1962 SC 305.
3. AIR 1986 SC 515.
4. AIR 1973 SC 783.
5. AIR 1975 SC 865.
6. (1978) 3 SCC 339.
7. AIR 1978 SC 597.
8. AIR 1982 SC 149.
9. AIR 1985 SC 652.
10. (1988) 4 SCC 592 SCC.
11. AIR, 1992 SC 382 at 384.
12. AIR 1993 SC 171.
13. (1995) 2 SCC 161.
14. (1995) 4 SCC 611.
15. AIR 1998 SC 889.
16. AIR 2002 SC 2112.
17. (2003) 4 SCC 399.
18. (1997) 4 SCC 306.
19. N.H. Vohara Committee Report.
20. *Ibid.*
21. (1997) 4 SCC 306 at 313.
22. MANU/SC/7894/2007
23. MANU/SC/1844/2008
24. *The Times of India*, dt. 3 September 2009 and Judgement Pronounced on 2-9-2009.
25. *The Hindustan Times*, 3 September 2009, p. 1.

CHAPTER

7

NEW HORIZONS OF RIGHT TO INFORMATION

I. INTRODUCTION

The Right to Information is relatively a new concept as regards the enactment point of view in India. By the virtue of progressive, liberal and contemporary interpretation of constitution our Supreme Court had already made the right to know as an integral part of Part III of the Constitution. Fundamental Right, right to know with the passage of time has evolved in Right to Information and now-a-days we have an enactment for Right to Information.

But again the Right to Information is not confined only to the ambit of the Act; it is ever growing and expanding itself to touch the different walks of life and society, to help the masses in fighting corruption and non-transparency.

A number of case studies is used to illustrate the new horizons of Right to Information for all Sections of society. New Horizons of Right to Information can be classified under the following categories:

2. NEW HORIZONS OF RIGHT TO INFORMATION

(i) Right to Information includes, Right to Educate, to Inform and to Entertain

We adopted the Sovereign, Socialistic, Secular pattern of Society, as is evident from the preamble to the Constitution of India, which reads as under:

> "WE THE PEOPLE OF INDIA, having solemnly resolved to constitute India into a **SOVEREIGN SOCIALIST SECULAR DEMOCRATIC REPUBLIC** and to secure all its citizens;
>
> **JUSTICE**, social, economic and political;
>
> **LIBERTY** of thought, expression, belief, faith and worship;
>
> **EQUALITY** of status and of opportunity and to promote among them all;
>
> **FRATERNITY** assuring the dignity of the individual and the unity and integrity of the Nation;
>
> *IN OUR CONSTITUENT ASSEMBLY this twenty-sixth day or November, 1949, DO HEREBY ADOPT, ENACT AND GIVE TO OURSELVES THIS CONSTITUTION."*

Moreover, there are fundamental rights in the Constitution of India have been grouped under six heads as under :

(i) Right to equality comprising Articles 14 to 18, the most important of which is Article 14 guaranteeing right to equality;

(ii) Right to freedom comprising Articles 19 to 22 which guarantee several freedoms, the most important of which is Article 19 concerning the freedom of speech and expression;

(iii) Right against exploitation under Articles 23 and 24;

(iv) Right to freedom of religion guaranteed by Articles 25 to 28;

(v) Cultural and educational rights guaranteed by Articles 29 and 30; and

(vi) Right to Constitutional remedies under Articles 32 to 35.

Our Supreme Court has expanded the reach and ambit of the Fundamental Right rather than to attenuate their meaning and content by a process of *judicial construction.*[1] Article 19 of the Constitution of India guaranteed fundamental right of freedom of speech and expression, which right includes the right to information. Article 19(1)(a) of the Constitution of India is reproduced below:

"Protection of certain right regarding freedom of speech, etc.— (1) All citizens shall have the right,—

(a) to freedom of speech and expression;

(2) Nothing in sub-clause (a) of clause (1) shall affect the operation of any existing law, or prevent the State from making any law, in so far as such law imposes reasonable restrictions on the exercise of the right conferred by the said sub-clause in the interests of the sovereignty and integrity of India, the security of the State, friendly relations with foreign states, public order, decency or morality or in relation to contempt of court, defamation or incitement to and offence."

When we come to the interpretation of Article 19(1)(a) and (2) of the Constitution *vis-a-vis* right to information, the Supreme Court of India has held down that right to information is a fundamental right under Article 19(1)(a) of the Constitution. Right to Information is a facet of the freedom of "speech and expression" as contained in Article 19(1)(a) of the Constitution of India, Right to Information, thus, indisputably is a fundamental right. The right to impart and receive information is a species of the right of freedom of speech and expression guaranteed by Article 19(1)(a) of the Constitution. A citizen has a fundamental right to use the best means of imparting and receiving information and as such to have an access to telecasting for the purpose.[2]

In ***Secretary, Ministry of Information and Broadcasting, Govt. of India* v. *Cricket Association of Bengal,***[3] Hon'ble Supreme Court held that the right to freedom of speech and expression includes right to educate, to inform and to entertain, Supreme Court further said :

"The democracy cannot exist unless all citizens have a right to participate in the affairs of the polity of the country. The right

to participate in the affairs of the country is meaningless unless the citizens are well informed on all sides of the issues, in respect of which they are called upon to express their views. One-sided information, dis-information, mis-information and non-information all equally create an uninformed citizenry which makes democracy a farce when medium of information is monopolized either by a partisan central authority or by private individuals or oligarchy organization. This is particularly so in a country like ours where about 65 per sent of the population is illiterate and hardly 1½ per cent of the population has an access to the print media which is not subject to precensorship...."

(ii) Right to Information is the Best Weapon of Consumer

The right to information leads to open and transparent government in a welfare democratic nation. It leads citizens to make informed choices about purchase of consumer goods and services which finally lead to higher consumer satisfaction. ***Mahatma Gandhi**, the father of Nation, has rightly pointed out as published in **'Harijan'**[4]*, that business, ethics, honesty and truthfulness should go together in the following words:

"It is wrong to think that business is incompatible with ethics. I know that it is perfectly possible to carry business profitably and yet honestly and truthfully. The plea that business and ethics never agree is advanced only by those who are actuated by nothing higher than narrow self-interest. He, who will serve his own ends, will do so by all kinds of questionable means, but he, who will earn to serve the community, will never sacrifice truth or honesty. You must bear in mind that you have the right to earn as much as you like, but not the right to spend as much as you like. Anything that remains, after the needs of a decent living are satisfied, belongs to the community."

As per ***the resolution of the United Nations General Assembly,***[5] the following guidelines were adopted for consumer protection:

(a) there should be access of the consumers to information needed to make choices;
(b) there should be physical safety to the consumers;

(c) there should be protection of economic interests of the consumers;
(d) there should be measures to enable the consumers to obtain redress;
(e) there should be satisfactory production and performance standards;
(f) there should be adequate business practices;
(g) there should be system of distribution of essential goods; and
(h) there should be international co-operation in the field of consumer protection.

To protect consumers from the exploitation of traders and from adulterated and sub-standard goods and for the better protection of the interests of consumers, the **Consumer Protection Act, 1986** has been enacted, which seeks, *inter alia,* to promote and protect the right of the consumers, such as,—

(a) the right to be protected against the marketing of goods (and services) which are hazardous to life and property;
(b) *the right to be informed about the quality, quantity, potency, purity, standard and price of goods or services,* as the case may be, so as to protect the consumers against unfair trade practices;
(c) the right to be assured, wherever possible, access to a variety of goods and services at competitive prices;
(d) the right to be heard and to be assured that consumer's interests will receive due consideration at appropriate fora;
(e) the right to seek redressal against unfair trade practices (or restrictive trade practices) or unscrupulous exploitation of consumers; and
(f) the right to consumer education.

If public awareness is created regarding the Right to Information Act, it is sure that the consumer would become the sovereign and would get maximum satisfaction.

There can be no difference of opinion that every consumer must have access to market information including a right to be informed about the quality, quantity, potency, purity, standard and price of goods or services, as the case may be, so as to protect the consumer against unfair trade practices.

(iii) Right to Information and Elections

*The **Preamble of our Constitution proclaims*** that we are Democratic Republic. Democracy being the basic feature of our constitutional set-up, there can be no two opinions that free and fair elections to our legislative bodies along would guarantee the growth of a healthy democracy in the country. In order to ensure the purity of the election process it was thought by our Constitution-makers that the responsibility to hold free and fair election in the country should be entrusted to an independent body which would be insulated from political and executive interference.[6]

'Right to information' is a part of fundamental right of 'freedom of speech and expression' enshrined in Article 19 of the Constitution of India. The 'right to information *vis-a-vis* elections' has been highlighted in the speech of the then *Prime Minister of India,* referred to in *B.R. Kapoor's* case cited in *People's Union of Civil Liberties (PUCL)* v. *Union of India,* as under:

> ".......Mr. Diwan in course of his arguments had raised some submissions on the subject—"*Criminalisation of Politics and participation of criminals in the electoral process as candidates*" and in that connection, he had brought to our notice the order of the Election Commission of India dated 28-8-1997. .... "*Whether Accountability*" published in the Pioneer, *Shri Atal Bihari Vajpayee* had called for a national debate on all the possible alternatives for systematic changes to cleanse our democratic governing system of its present mess. He has expressed his dissatisfaction that neither Parliament nor the State Vidhan Sabhas are doing, with any degree of competence or commitment, what they are primarily meant to do, legislative function. According to him, barring exceptions, those who get elected to these democratic institutions are neither trained, formally or informally, *in law-making* nor do they seem to have an inclination to develop the necessary knowledge and competence in their profession. He has further indicated that those individuals in society who are generally

interested in serving the electorate and performing legislative functions are finding it increasingly difficult to succeed in today's electoral system and the electoral system has been almost totally subverted by money power, muscle power, and vote bank considerations of castes and communities. *Shri Vajpayee* also had indicated that the corruption in the governing structures has, therefore, corroded the very core of elective democracy. According to him, the certainty of scope of corruption in the governing structure has heightened opportunism and unscrupulousness among political parties, causing them to marry and divorce one another at will, seeks opportunistic alliance and coalitions often without the popular mandate. Yet they capture and survive in power due to inherent systematic flows. He further stated that casteism, corruption and politicization have eroded the integrity and efficacy of our civil service structure also. The manifestos, policies, programmes of the political parties have lost meaning in the present system of government due to lack of accountability."

True democracy cannot exist unless all citizens have a right to participate in the affairs of the polity of the country. The right to participate in the affairs of the country is meaningless unless the citizens are well informed on all sides of the issues, in respect of which they are called upon to express their views. *One-sided information, disinformation, misinformation and non-information all equally create an uniformed citizenry which makes democracy a farce.*[7]

The legal and constitutional position regarding powers of the Election Commission and transparency in the process of elections as well as right of citizens (voters) to get information have been laid down by the Supreme Court of India, on March 13, 2003[8] directed the Election Commission to make it mandatory for contesting candidates to disclose their antes and in an affidavit along with nomination form, so that the voter may think over and make a right choice. This was recogized as part of right to freedom of speech and expression under Article 19(1)(a), which is held to be basic structure of constitution and hence inviolable, i.e., the parliament's plenary poser to amend will not extend to tamper with it. The Supreme Court of India makes important guidelines of election is as under:

(1) To maintain the purity of elections and in particular to bring transparency in the process of election, the Commission can ask the candidates about the expenditure incurred by the political parties and *this transparency in the process of election would include transparency of a candidate who seeks election or re-election.* In a democracy, the electoral process has a strategic role. The little man of this country would have basic elementary right to know full particulars of a candidate who is to represent him in Parliament where laws to bind his liberty and property may be enacted.

(2) The *right to get information in democracy is recognized all throughout* and it is a natural right following from the concept of democracy. At this stage, we would refer to Article 19(1) and (2) of the International Covenant of Civil and Political Rights, which is as under." (i) Everyone shall have the right to hold opinions without interference, and (ii) Everyone shall have the right to freedom of expression; this right shall include freedom to seek, receive and impart information and ideas of all kinds, regardless of frontiers, either orally, in writing or in print, in the form of art, or through any other media of his choice.

(3) On cumulative reading of a plethora of decisions of the Court it is clear that if the field meant for legislature and executive is left unoccupied detrimental to the public interest, this Court would have ample jurisdiction under Article 32 read with Articles 141 and 142 of the Constitution to issue necessary directions to the executive to sub-serve public interest.

(4) In our Indian Constitution, Article 19(1)(a) provides for freedom of speech and expression. Voter's speech or expression in case of election would include casting of vote; that is to say, voter speaks out or express by casting vote. For this purpose, *information about the candidate to be selected is a must. Voter's (little-citizen's) right to know antecedents including criminal past of his*

> *candidate contesting election for MP or MLA is much more fundamental and basic for survival of democracy.* The little man may think over before making his choice of electing *law-breakers* as *law-makers*9.

The Right to Information provided for by the Parliament under section 33 of the Representation of the People (3rd Amendment) Act, 2002 in regard to the pending criminal cases and past involvement in such cases is reasonably adequate and safeguard the right to information vested in the voter/citizen. However, there is no good reason for excluding the pending cases in which cognizance has been taken by Court from the ambit of disclosure. The provisions made in section 75A regarding declaration of assets and liabilities of the elected candidates to the Speaker or the Chairman of the House has failed to effectuate the right to information and the freedom of expression of voters/citizens. Having accepted the need to insist on disclosure of assets and liabilities of the elected candidate together with those of spouse or dependent children, the Parliament ought to have made a provision for furnishing this information at the time of filing the nomination. Failure to do so has resulted in the violation of guarantee under Article 19(1)(a) of the Constitution of India.[10]

(iv) Right to Information Protect our Environment

> क्षिति जल पावक गगन समीरा। पंच रचित अति अधम सरीरा।।[11]

Every human being consists of five elements - earth, air, water, fire and sky. *Earth is the mother* and we belong to the earth but earth does not belong to any human being. *Earth, water and air help to* grow crops, plants and trees. The forests are our friends because they protect the environment and after consuming carbon-dioxide give us oxygen, without which it is impossible to survive. *The fire is sacred,* being a source of energy. *Air helps us* to breath without which human beings cannot survive even for a few minutes. Similarly, *water,* drinking of which is an essential for every living creature. Therefore, we must remember that if we cause any harm to *any one of these basic elements,* it is going to harm us because human being is not supreme but these basic elements constituting every human being are supreme and we should protect, preserve and improve these basic elements as trustees for coming generations.

Article 48A of the Constitution of India embodies the Directive Principle for the protection and improvement of environment and safeguarding of forests and wild life in the following words:

> *"The State shall endeavour to protect and improve the environment and to safeguard the forests and wild life of the country."*

The Supreme Court in ***R.L.E.K. Dehradun* v. *State of U.P.*,**[12] it was stated that *"the question involving issues relating to environment and ecological balance, brings into sharp focus the conflict between development and conservation and serves to emphasis the need for reconciling the two in larger interest of the people residing within the area and the country. Therefore, it cannot be said that action groups are trying to meddle in the affairs of Cantonment Board or are claiming any extralegal authority."* The right to know has been reaffirmed in the context of environmental issues that have an impact upon people's very survival.

Another case, which is related to environment awareness, has been decided by the Bench of the Supreme Court comprising of **Ranganath Mishra, CJ, G.N. Ray and A.S. Anand, JJ** in ***M.C. Mehta* v. *Union of India***[13] the Court stated that: *"we are in a democratic polity, where dissemination of information is foundation of the system. Keeping the citizens informed is an obligation of the Government."*

The Supreme Court, therefore accepted on principle the prayers made by the petitioner, for issuing appropriate directions to cinema exhibition halls to exhibits slides containing information and messages on environment free of cost, directions for the spread of information relating to environment in national and regional languages and for broadcasting thereof on the All India Radio and exposure thereof on the television with a view to educating the people of India.

(v) Right to Information and Arrested Person

Arrest means apprehension of a person, this puts a Bar on free movement of a person. Article 22(1) of the Constitution of

India guarantees to every person, in the event of his arrest, the fundamental right of being informed of the grounds of arrest, as soon as possible, the Article is reproduced below:

No person who is arrested shall be detained in custody without being informed, as soon as may be, of the grounds for such arrest nor shall be denied the right to consult, and to be defended by, a legal practitioner of his choice.

* * * * *

Further Article 22(5) read as follows:

When any person is detained in pursuance of an order made under any law providing for preventive detention, the authority making the order shall, as soon as may be, communicate to such person the grounds on which the order has been made and shall afford him the earliest opportunity of making a representation against the order.

The two requirements of clause (1) of Article 22 of the Constitution of India are meant to afford the earliest opportunity to the arrested person to remove any mistake, misapprehension or misunderstanding in the minds of the arresting authority and, also to know exactly what the accusation against him is, so that he can exercise the second right, namely, of consulting a legal practitioner of his choice and to be defended by him.[14]

In the historical judgement of ***D.K. Basu* v. *State of West Bengal*,**[15] the Supreme Court of India laid down the following requirements to be followed in all cases of arrest or detention till legal provisions are made in that behalf as preventive measures:

(1) The police personnel carrying out the arrest and handling the interrogation of the arrestee should bear accurate, visible and clear identification and name tags with their designations. The particulars of all such police personnel who handle interrogation of the arrestee must be recorded in a register.

(2) That the police officer carrying out the arrest of the arrestee shall prepare a memo of arrest at the time of arrest and such memo shall be attested by at least one witness, who may either be a member of the family of the arrestee or a respectable person of the locality from where the arrest is made. It shall also be

countersigned by the arrestee and shall contain the time and date of arrest.

(3) A person who has arrested or detained and is being held in custody in a police station or interrogation centre or other lockup, shall be entitled to have one friend or relative or other person known to him or having interest in his welfare, *being informed*, as soon as practicable, that he has been arrested and is being detained at the particular place, unless the attesting witness of the memo of arrest is himself such a friend or a relative of the arrestee.

(4) The time, place of arrest and venue of custody of an arrestee must be notified by the police where the next friend or relative of the arrestee lives outside the district or town through the Legal Aid Organisation in the District and the police station of the area concerned telegraphically within a period of 8 to 12 hours after the arrest.

(5) The person arrested must be made aware of *this right to have someone informed of his arrest or detention* as soon as he is put under arrest or is detained.

(6) An entry must be made in the diary at the place of detention regarding the arrest of the person which shall also *disclose the name of the next friend of the person who has been informed of the arrest* and the names and particulars of the police officials in whose custody the arrestee is.

(7) The arrestee should, where he so requests, be also examined at the time of his arrest and major and minor injuries, if any present on his/her body, must be recorded at that time. The "Inspection Memo" must be signed both by the arrestee and that the police officer effecting the arrest and its copy provided to the arrestee.

(8) The arrestee should be subjected to medical examination by a trained doctor every 48 hours during his detention in custody by a doctor on the panel of approved doctors appointed by Director, Health Services of the State or Union Territory concerned. Director, Health Services should prepare such a panel for all tehsils and districts as well.

(9) Copies of all documents including the memo of arrest, referred to above, should be sent to the *Illaqa* Magistrate for his record.

(10) The arrestee may be permitted to meet his lawyer during interrogation, though not throughout the interrogation.

(11) *A police control room* should be provided at all district and State headquarters, where *information regarding the arrest and the place of custody of the arrestee shall be communicated by the Officer causing the arrest, within 12 hours* of effecting the arrest and at the police control room it should be displayed on a conspicuous notice board.

It is great on the part of government that the legislature has incorporated these above mentioned suggestions.

(vi) Right to Information and Corruption

Transparency International has published an annual **Corruption Perceptions Index (CPI)** ordering the countries of the world according to "the degree to which corruption is perceived to exist among public officials and politicians." The organization defines corruption as "the abuse of entrusted power for private gain."

India has the dubious tag of being the Eighty-fifth most corrupt nation in recently 2008 complied list of 180 countries around the world. This is consistent with most people's everyday experiences; corruption in India is rampant, from the common clerk to the highest offices of the country. Big scams—(for example, regarding defence deals, fodder procurement, and sugar prices) have frequently made the headlines. Coupled with the tardiness of the judicial system, these sachems have done serious harm to the economy. Although media attention tends to focus on mega scam, small-scale corruption is widespread and affects the everyday lives ordinary people, for whom it has become a routine social and financial burden. People even have to pay bribes to access basic information, such as their own electricity bills.

The 'Right to Information *vis-a-vis* Corruption' has been highlighted in the speech of the then ***Prime Minister of India***, referred to in ***B.R. Kapoor's*** case cited in ***People's Union for Civil Liberties (PUCL)* v. *Union of India***,[16] as under:

In this eminent counsel Mr. Diwan in course of his argument cited the lines once said in the speech of then Prime Minister of India Mr. Atal Bihari Bajpayee. Shri Vajpayee also had indicated that the corruption in the governing structure has, therefore, corroded the very core of elective democracy. According to him, the certainty of scope of corruption in the governing structure has heightened opportunism and unscrupulousness among political parties, causing them to marry and divorce one another at will, seek opportunistic alliance and coalitions often without the popular mandate. Yet they capture and survive in power due to inherent systematic flows. He further stated that casteism, corruption and politicization have eroded the integrity and efficacy of our civil service structure also. The manifestos, policies, programmes of the political parties have lost meaning in the present system of government due to lack of accountability."

Information is a key of transparency which is not important for development and effective functioning of a democratic government. The Right to Information is thus a patent tool for countering corruption and for exposing corrupt officials.

(vii) Right to Information and e-Governance

The electronification of documents delivers benefits directly to the eligible persons and the services that are essential for the poor are easier to manage through E-governance if these are designed in a way that poor and illiterate rustic may also participate in the same. Now, the question is what we mean by term 'E-governance'. Electronic governance popularly known as E-governance can be defined as "delivery of government services and information to general public using electronic means." E-governance is the buzzard of the new millennium, the benefit of which is that it shall make the life of the citizens hassle free. To harness the benefits of Information and Communication Technology for effective and transparent functioning of the administration is one of the most important areas of the Information Technology policy of the government because it makes routine transaction faster, smoother and transparent. Thus, E-governance has become the keyword in every department of the government today with tremendous potential to improve efficiency, access, transparency and accountability as we all know that it enhance transparency and accountability while reducing neptunium and corruption besides increasing productivity in the administration.[17]

The aim of E-governance is to make the interaction of the citizens with the government offices hassle free and to share information in a free and transparent manner. It further makes the right to information a meaningful reality. In a democracy, people govern themselves and they cannot govern themselves properly unless they are aware of social, political, economic and other issues confronting them. To enable them to make a proper judgement on those issues, they must have the benefit of a range of opinions on those issues. This plurality of opinions, views and ideas is indispensable for enabling them to make an informed judgment on those issues, to know what is their true interest, to make them responsible citizens to safeguard their rights as also the interest of society and State. All the constitutional courts of leading democracies have recognized and reiterated this aspect. In ***Union of India*** v. ***Association for Democratice Reforms***[18], the Supreme Court observed that the citizens of India have a right to know every public act, everything that is done in public interest by the public functionaries. Public education is essential for functioning of the process of popular government and to assist the discovery of truth and strengthening the capacity of an individual in participating in the decision-making process. The right to get information in a democracy is recognized all throughout and it is a natural right flowing from the concept of democracy.

The concept of E-governance to promote efficient delivery of government services by means of reliable electronic records is recognized even in the Preamble to the Information Technology Act, 2000, which provides as under:

> "An Act to provide legal recognition for transactions carried out by means of electronic data interchange and other means of electronic communication, commonly referred to as "electronic commerce", which involve the use of alternatives to paper-based methods of communication and storage of information, *to facilitate electronic filing of documents with the Government agencies* and further to amend the Indian Penal Code, the Indian Evidence Act, 1872, the Banker's Book Evidence Act, 1891 and the Reserve Bank of India Act, 1934 and for matters connected therewith or incidental thereto."

Thus, e-governance and right to information are interrelated and are two sides of the same coin. With the enactment of the Information Technology Act, 2000 more and more transparency is expected in government functioning by keeping people aware of the State's plan, policies, objectives and achievements.[19]

(viii) Right to Information and Judiciary

The main objective of the Right to Information Act, 2005 is promoting transparency and credibility in governance. Section 4 of the Right to Information Act, 2005 provide access to its documents, proceedings. The Right to Information Act defines word public authority. According to Section 2(h) of the Act. Public authority as "any and every body constituted under constitution or any law of the government on the basis of these definition judiciary also within its purview.[20] But judiciary is seeking to effectively remove itself from the purview of the Right to Information Act. Chief Justice of India **K.G. Balakrishnan** had recently said his office was not covered by the Right to Information Act, 2005. Further the Supreme Court has said that the Chief Information Commissioner can not direct it to disclose any information and it recommended amending the Act. Further that any information interdicted by the Chief Justice of India on the ground of independence of the Judiciary will not be provided.

In the case of ***Indira Jaising* v. *Registrar General, Supreme Court of India,***[21] an inquiry report was made by the committee to the CJI, in respect of alleged involvement of sitting judges of the High Court of Karnataka in certain incidents. The petitioner sought the publication of the inquiry. The Supreme Court held that it is not appropriate for the petitioner to approach the Supreme Court for relief or direction for release of the report, for what the CJI has done is only to get information from peer judge of those who are accused and the report made to the CJI is wholly confidential. It is purely preliminary in nature, *ad-hoc* and not final.

The Court further held that in a democratic framework free flow of information to the citizens is necessary for proper functioning, particularly in matters which form part of public record. The right to information is, however, not absolute. There are several areas where such information need not to be furnished. Even the Freedom of Information Act, 2002 does not say in absolute terms that information gathered at any level, in any manner and for any purpose shall be disclosed to the public. The inquiry ordered and the report made to the CJI being confidential and discreet is only for the purpose of his information and not for the purpose of disclosure to any other person. The Court thus rejected the contention to release the said report. The Court, however, made it clear that if the petitioner can substantiate that any criminal offence has been committed by any of the judges mentioned in the course of the petition, appropriate complaint can be lodged before a competent authority for taking action by complying with requirements of law.

In view of the Supreme Court Bar in retaliation to the declaration made by the Chief Justice of India, made a rigorous demand for bringing even the Supreme Court within the purview of the Right to Information Act, 2005.[22] It is relevant to extract the 1997 Resolution, as well as the Judicial Conference of 1999's resolution, followed by material provisions of the Act, which are reproduced below.[23]

The 1997 Resolution

"RESOLUTION

The following two Resolutions have been ADOPTED in the Full Court Meeting of the Supreme Court of India on May 7, 1997:

RESOLVED that an in-house procedure should be devised by the Hon'ble Chief Justice of India to take suitable remedial action against Judges who by their acts of omission or commission do not follow the universally accepted values of judicial life including those indicated in the "Restatement of Values of Judicial Life."

RESOLVED FURTHER THAT every Judge should make a declaration of all his/her assets in the form of real estate or investments (held by him/her in his/her own name or in the name of his/her spouse or any person dependent on him/her) within a reasonable time of assuming office and in the case of sitting Judges within a reasonable time of adoption of this Resolution and thereafter whenever any acquisition of a substantial nature is made, it shall be disclosed within a reasonable time. The declaration so made should be to the Chief Justice of the Court. The Chief Justice should make a similar declaration for the purpose of the record. The declaration made by the Judges or the Chief Justice, as the case may be, shall be confidential."

The 1999 Judicial Conference Resolution

"RESTATEMENT OF VALUES OF JUDICIAL LIFE (CODE OF CONDUCT) ADOPTED IN THE CHIEF JUSTICES' CONFERENCE IN DECEMBER 1999.

The Conference of Chief Justices of all High Courts was held on 3rd and 4th December, 1999 in the Supreme Court premises. During the said Conference, the Chief Justices unanimously resolved to adopt the "Restatement of Values of Judicial Life" (Code of Conduct).

WHEREAS by a Resolution passed in the Chief Justices' Conference held at New Delhi on September 18-19, 1992, it was resolved that it is desirable to restate the pre-existing and universally accepted norms, guidelines and conventions reflecting the high values of judicial life to be followed by Judges during their tenure of office;

AND WHEREAS the Chief Justice of India was further requested by that Resolution to constitute a Committee for preparing the draft restatement to be circulated to the Chief Justices of the High Courts for discussion with their colleagues, which was duly circulated on 21.11.1993;

AND WHEREAS suggestions have been received from the Chief Justices of the High Courts after discussion with their colleagues;

AND WHEREAS a Committee has been reconstituted by the Chief Justice of India on April 7, 1997, to finalize the 'Restatement of Values of Judicial Life' after taking note of the draft Restatement of Values of Judicial Life prepared by a Committee appointed pursuant to the Resolution passed in the Chief Justices' Conference, 1992 and placed before the Chief Justices' Conference in 1993;

AND WHEREAS such a Committee constituted by the Chief Justice of India has prepared a draft restatement after taking into consideration the views received from various High Courts to the draft which was circulated to them;

NOW THEREFORE, on a consideration of the views of the High Courts on the draft, the restatement of the pre-existing and universally accepted norms, guidelines and conventions called the 'RESTATEMENT OF VALUES OF JUDICIAL LIFE' to serve as a guide to be observed by Judges, essential for an independent, strong and respected judiciary, indispensable in the impartial administration of justice, as redrafted, has been considered in the Full Court Meeting of the Supreme Court of India on May 7, 1997 and has been ADOPTED for due observance.

RESTATEMENT OF VALUES OF JUDICIAL LIFE

(1) Justice must not merely be done but it must also be seen to be done. The behaviour and conduct of members of the higher judiciary must reaffirm the people's faith in the impartiality of the judiciary. Accordingly, any act of a Judge of the Supreme Court or a High Court, whether in official or personal capacity, which erodes the credibility of this perception has to be avoided.

(2) A Judge should not contest the election to any office of a Club, society or other association; further he shall not hold such elective office except in a society or association connected with the law.

(3) Close association with individual members of the Bar, particularly those who practice in the same court, shall be eschewed.

(4) A Judge should not permit any member of his immediate family, such as spouse, son, daughter, son-in-law or daughter-in-law or any other close relative, if a member of the Bar, to appear before him or even be associated in any manner with a cause to be dealt with by him.

(5) No member of his family, who is a member of the Bar, shall be permitted to use the residence in which the Judge actually resides or other facilities for professional work.

(6) A Judge should practice a degree of aloofness consistent with the dignity of his office.

(7) A Judge shall not hear and decide a matter in which a member of his family, a close relation or a friend is concerned.

(8) A Judge shall not enter into public debate or express his views in public on political matters or on matters that are pending or are likely to arise for judicial determination.

(9) A Judge is expected to let his judgments speak for themselves; he shall not give interview to the media.

(10) A Judge shall not accept gifts or hospitality except from his family, close relations and friends.

(11) A Judge shall not hear and decide a matter in which a company in which he holds shares is concerned unless he has disclosed his interest and no objection to his hearing and deciding the matter is raised.

(12) A Judge shall not speculate in shares, stocks or the like.

(13) A Judge should not engage directly or indirectly in trade or business, either by himself or in association with any other person. (Publication of a legal treatise or any activity in the nature of a hobby shall not be construed as trade or business).

(14) A Judge should not ask for, accept contributions or otherwise actively associate himself with the raising of any fund for any purpose.

(15) A Judge should not seek any financial benefit in the form of a perquisite or privilege attached to his office unless it is clearly available. Any doubt in this behalf must be got resolved and clarified through the Chief Justice.

(16) Every Judge must at all times be conscious that he is under the public gaze and there should be no act or omission by him which is unbecoming of the high office he occupies and the public esteem in which that office is held.

These are only the "Restatement of the Values of Judicial Life" and are not meant to be exhaustive but only illustrative of what is expected of a Judge.

Even the public opinion is towards more transparency in judiciary. The Right to Information Act if implemented will provide right to information for judicial as well as administrative functions of the Courts, and will enhance judicial accountability in the system. Taking a cue from the Supreme Court, must High Courts have not even appointed Public Information Officers under the Act till now and many High Courts have framed rules contrary to the Act. The Delhi High Court being one of them.[24]

In a major boost for transparency in higher judiciary, the Delhi High Court ruled that the case of ***CPIO Supreme Court* v. *S.C. Agrawal and Others***[25] Justice **S. Ravindra Bhatt** said Chief Justice of India was not outside the purview of the Right to Information Act, 2005. *"The CJI is a public authority under the Right to Information Act and he holds the information pertaining to asset declarations in his capacity as Chief Justice. CJI's office is covered under the provisions of the Act."* The High Court rejected the Supreme Court argument that the information on judges' assets provided to the CJI was "confidential", which could not be revealed.

In this case Delhi High Court cited Dr. Aharon Barack, former Chief Justice of Israel, in his acclaimed work *"Judges in a Democracy"* underlines that transient "popular" notions of justice can never be the basis of a proper verdict. He summarizes this paradox as follows:

> *...An essential condition for realizing the judicial role is public confidence in the judge. This means confidence in judicial independence, fairness and impartiality. It means public confidence in the ethical standards of the judge. It means public confidence that judges are not interested parties to the legal struggle and that they are not fighting for their own power but to protect the constitution and democracy. It means that public confidence that the judge does not express his own personal views but rather the fundamental beliefs of the nation...This fact means that the public recognizes the legitimacy of judicial decisions, even if it disagrees with their content.*

The precondition of 'public confidence' runs the risk of being misunderstood. The need to ensure public confidence does not mean the need to ensure popularity. Public confidence does not mean following popular trends or public opinion polls. Public confidence does not mean accountability to the public in the way the executive and the legislature are accountable. Public confidence does not mean pleasing the public; public confidence does not mean ruling contrary to the law or contrary to the judge's conscience to bring about a result that the public desires.

On the contrary, public confidence means ruling according to the law and according to the judge's conscience, whatever the attitude of the public may be..."

(ix) Right to Information is the Boon for the Poors

The Right to Information has strengthened the voice of the voiceless individuals of our society. It has built up a solid platform for the citizens especially the marginalized sections of our society. Now, ordinary citizens, traditionally governed by the public functionaries, have been raising their voices against the oppressive, suppressive and exploitative attitudes of the public officials.[26]

The Right to Information is not a mere 'information bank', rather it has facilitated the individuals to share a 'common platform' and fight for a 'common cause'. Moreover, the Act can also be used in tackling the social issues that create hurdles in the process of rural development. According to Shri V.P. Singh, the former Prime Minister of India, the Right to Information Act could be used by the civil society organizations as well as the people's movements in stamping poverty out from rural as well as urban landscapes. While releasing a copy of the Citizens' Report on Millennium Development Goals at the People's Summit against Poverty, he mentioned "the Right to Information Act will remain on paper unless used by the poor." In fact, the Act is an innovative attempt to deal with various issues that surround the socio-economic development of the rural poor. Right to Information has almost become a nationwide revolution whereby a plethora of organization and alert citizens are making their efforts to unearth corruption, expose scams, inform the public and institute responsiveness and probity in administration.[27]

(x) Right to Information in Case of Food and Drugs

Section 23 r/w Rule 32 of the Prevention of Food Adulteration Act, 1954 confers on consumers of food products a right to be informed whether or not the article of food is vegetarian or non-vegetarian. As regards drugs and cosmetics, necessary amendments have not been made in the relevant statute.

In ***Ozir Husain* v. *Union of India*,**[28] a Division Bench of Delhi High Court observed that it is the Fundamental Right of the consumers to know whether the food products, cosmetics and drugs are of non-vegetarian or vegetarian origin, as otherwise it will violate their Fundamental Right under Articles 19(1)(a), 21 and 25 of the Constitution. The packages of non-vegetarian products should bear a symbol giving their non-vegetarian origin; and a package of a vegetarian product should also bear a symbol. To enable a person to practice the beliefs and opinions, which he hold, in a meaningful manner, it is essential for him to receive the relevant information; otherwise he may be prevented from acting in consonance with his beliefs and opinions. In case a vegetarian consumer does not know the ingredients of the drugs or food products which he/she wishes to buy, it will be difficult for him/her to practice vegetarianism. Moreover, reading Article 19(1)(a) along with International Covenant of Civil and Political Rights, it must be recognized that right to freedom of speech and expression includes freedom to seek, receive and impart information and also a right to know the ingredients or the constituents of drugs and food products. However, as far as life saving drugs are concerned a limited exception will apply because a patient, who is suffering from serious ailment, which can be fatal if a life saving drug is not administered to him, need not be informed in his own interest as to whether or not the drug contains part of any animal as it is conducive to the preservation of life and, therefore, in tune with Article 21 of the Constitution.

Thus, the High Court issued certain directions about declarations and different colored symbols to be displayed on packages of drugs and cosmetics regarding their vegetarian or non-vegetarian origin, till amendments are made in the Act.

(xi) Right to Information is a Best Instrument to Control the Public Authority

In our present democratic framework, free flow of the information for the citizens suffers from several bottlenecks including the existing legal framework, lack of infrastructure at the grass-root levels and an attitude and tendency of maintaining secrecy in the day-to-day governmental functioning to remove these unreasonable restrictions. The Right to Information Act, 2005 has been enacted by the Parliament. The Act provides for freedom to every citizen to secure access to information under the control of public authorities consistent with public interest, in order to promote openness, transparency and accountability in administration and in relations to matter connected therewith or incidental thereto. The Act is in accordance with both Article 19 of the Constitution as well as Article 19 of the Universal Declaration of Human Right, 1948. The Act enables the citizens to have an access to information on a statutory basis.

3. CONCLUSION

With the passage of time there was an increment in the demand of this right. Today the scope of Right to Information is very wide. Now we are using this in any sphere of society for getting the information. Our Supreme Court has also elaborated the scope of Right to Information by its judicial decision. Right to Information for consumers, Right to Information for Voters, shows the dynamic trends of Right to Information. This shows that the nature of Right to Information has become multi-dimensional.

NOTES AND REFERENCES

1. Manika Gandhi *v.* Union of India, AIR 1978 SC 597.
2. AIR 1995 SC 1236.
3. *Ibid.*
4. Dated 4th May, 1935.
5. Dated 16th April, 1985.
6. Report of National Commission for review of the working of the Constitution, para 4.14.1, p. 89.
7. Secretary, Minister of Information and Broad Casting *v.* Cricket Association of of Bengal, AIR 1995 SC 1236.
8. (2003) 3 SCC 93.
9. Union of India Association Democratic Reforms, AIR 2002 SC 2112.
10. People's Union for Civil Liberties (PUCL) *v.* Union of India, AIR 2003 SC 2363.
11. Ram Charitra Manas, Kishkindha Kand, Geeta Press, Hindi Ed., p. 302.
12. AIR 1985 SC 652.
13. AIR 1992 SC 382 at 384.
14. Madhu Limaye (in re:) AIR 1969 SC 1014.
15. AIR 1997 SC 610.
16. AIR 2003 SC 2363.
17. Dr. J.N. Barowalia, Right to Information Act, 2005, p. 188.
18. (2002) 5 SCC 294.
19. Praveen Dalal and Shruti Gupta, Bring Transparency through Electronic Governance (2003) ACE(J).

20. *Amar Ujala*, 27 November 2008.
21. (2002) 5 ACE 552.
22. SC Bar to vote on putting judiciary under RTI purview, *Times of India*, January 27, 2007.
23. The CPIO SC *v.* SC, Agrawal Law Resource, India, pp. 9-11.
24. Prashant Bhusan, "Judicial Accountability or Illusion", *EPW*, Commentary, November 25, 2006.
25. The CPIO Supreme Court *v.* S.C. Agrawal and ANR.
26. RTI : Decentralization and procedural semolification, *Social Action*, Vol. 56, December 2006, p. 390.
27. *Ibid*.
28. AIR 2003 Del 103.

CHAPTER

8

CONCLUSION AND SUGGESTIONS

Today's Information is power, Information is knowledge. Knowledge was synonymous with power and the power includes liberty. Equal access to knowledge has been an important issue in the struggle for social and economic equality. Until the end of the second world war, struggle for access to knowledge has been universal. In the present time 'knowledge' has become the most valuable resource. It is the possession of knowledge that makes a society or a nation advanced, strong and secure. Right to Information is increasingly being recognized as a necessary condition to achieve accountable, transparent and participatory governance and people-centered development. Access to information is often called, and rightly so, as the "Oxygen for a democratic society." In a foreword by the Director General of UNESCO to the Mac Bride Report titled "Many Voices, One World", the distinguished statement emphasizes that communication is at the heart of all social intercourse. Why, because in the words of the Director General, "It is essential that all men and women, in all social and cultural environments, should be given the opportunity of joining in the process of collective thinking thus initiated, for new ideas must be developed and more positive measures must be taken to shake-off the prevailing inertia. With the coming of a new world communication order, each people must be able to learn from the others, while at the same time conveying to them its own understanding of its own condition and its own view of world affairs. Mankind will then have made a decisive step forward on the path to freedom democracy and fellowship."

A report prepared for the Government of India noted—

> *"It is now widely recognized that openness and accessibility of people to information about the government's functioning is a vital component of democracy."*

The demand for Right to Information is the outcome of arbitrariness and corruption of that remained in practice for a very long time agencies of the State. The Right to Information is essentially a citizen's fundamental right. The nature of Right to Information has been very interesting. It is supposed that not only today but in primitive human society too, there was Right to Information according to that age. Though at different stages of civilization its nature has changed. It has been there in one or the other form be it in the form of declaration or holy sermons. The above mentioned contents have elaborate discussion regarding this where it can be found that there are numerous instances of Right to Information in different texts.

The present scenario is witness to the fact that Right to Information has become a global phenomenon. It has covered a long distance since its inception at international level. Right to Information is a necessary prerequisite for a successful democracy.

In the present time, most of the countries have their own Right to Information. In our country we have a specific law, namely, Right to Information Act, 2005. The need for the legal status of the Right to Information is a cause and concern today. India observed the judicial pronouncements and democratic need of such right during the past years. The Law Commission of India's 179th Report and Reports of number of Committees and Councils working on this subject sensitized the government of India to enact a specific law on the right to information. In May 2005 the Right to Information Act was passed by the Indian Parliament. The Act in its Preamble says to provide for the setting up of the practical regime of Right to Information for all citizens to secure access to information under the control of public authorities in order to promote transparency and accountabilities in the working of every public authority. The whole Act is in right of democratic approach of participating government. The Act has made provisions for constitution of Central Information Commissions and State Information Commissions for the respective States as the appellate authorities. On the perusal of the whole of the Act, it is inferred that the statutory provisions made for the Right to Information and all citizens possess such right.

Other than this law other enactment also protect the Right to Information. There is a great deal of contribution of our constitution in protecting information Right. Now-a-days we can find that it has been tried to take this Right to Information law at grass-root level for help and protection of general public. In the democratic form of government there is the participation of public in government. Because of this form of government is supposed to be a good form of government. The democracy gets its strength from people, and flow of information in democracy makes this participation more strange. Through Right to Information public participation has increased in day-to-day functioning of government and administration. In today's changing scenario this Right to Information has proved to be a milestone. At the lowest level of democracy, i.e., Gram Panchayat, too, this Right to Information is very useful and effective. A very common application of this Act is seen in the form that the public is asking the authorities for the accounts and other things of development projects initiated by government.

Today the scope of Right to Information is very wide. Now we are using this in any sphere of society for getting the information. Our Supreme Court has also elaborated the scope of Right to Information by its judicial decisions. Right to Information for consumers, Right to Information for Voters, shows the dynamic trends of Right to Information. Today the nature of Right to Information has become multi-dimensional. Transparency, accountability and good governance in a democracy cannot be ensured without an effective Right to Information. The United Nations High Commissioner for Human Rights has outlined the essential attributes of governance as follows:

Transparency : people should know what the government is doing,

Responsibility : the manner in which authority should be exercised,
Accountability : decision-makers should be accountable to people,
Participation : people should be able to participate in decision-making, and
Responsiveness: to the needs and legitimate aspirations of the people.

These are not merely attributes that should characterise democratic governance. They are also indicative of the duties that public functionaries are required to perform.

Our country was a colony of British Empire. The British ruled here for a long time. So, it is required to know whether at the time of British rule there was Right to Information? By a thorough study of the then prevailing laws it is clear that Right to Information was almost absent at that time confidential information relating to government could not be obtained . There was an Official Secrets Act, 1923, which was great barrier in the way of Right to Information. During the colonial rule every leader like, M.K. Gandhi, Tilak and Nehru was against the Official Secrets Act, 1923.

We got independence on 15th August, 1947 and on 26th November 1949 we enacted, adopted and gave to ourselves our Constitution. Constitution does not specifically provide for the right to information as a fundamental right though the constitutional philosophy amply supports it. Preamble of the Constitution constitutes India into a democracy and secures for its people, justice—social, economic and political, liberty of thought, expression and belief. This justifies the conclusion that the Indian Constitution is drawn upon the idea of open government. In the same manner freedom of thought and expression, right to life and personal liberty would become redundant if information is not freely available. In India right to information is a direct consequence of people movement for reaching socio-economic justice to the deprived sections of the society whose entitlements under rural development schemes were being deprived due to lack of information on developmental projects.

The biggest obstacles to seeking public Information came from the colonial legacy, namely, the Official Secrets Act, 1923, which legitimized secrecy in governance, Section 123 of the

Indian Evidence Act, 1872, which prohibited the use of unpublished official information as evidence without prior permission of the relevant head of Department, and section 11 of the Central Civil Service Conduct Rule, 1964, which prohibit public servants from communicating any official information without authorization.

In India Right to Information emerged from the demand of people from remote villagers. The movement Right to Information promotes many social activities and organizations. The second Administrative reforms commission headed by Verrappa Moily has recommended that the Official Secrets Act, 1923, be repealed saying it is incongruous with the regime of transparency in a democratic society. The Right to Information can purvey new life for democracy and developmental process; after all, it is the precondition for just development and good governance. Despite a guaranteed right to information under Article 19(1)(a) of our Constitution why do we need a separate Act? It is largely due to lack of a culture and environment where right, freedom and democratic ways of life are respected.

Taking serious note of this overarching regime of opacity the planning commission of India has made transparency a central obligation to be honoured by the development administration. The Commission recognizes that the task of the development administration will become easy if it takes steps to make information available to people as a matter of right. Three things are noteworthy in this prescription for curing the evils of secrecy—

> ...that information should be made available to people—implying both voluntary and reactive disclosure of information.
>
> ...that it should be given as a matter of right—implying an obligation placed upon the officers and the presupposition of a grievance redressal mechanism to challenge unreasonable denial of access to information, and
>
> ...that steps should be taken—implying institutional changes that are required to change or replace the regime of secrecy with one of openness.

Jeremy Bentham very aptly asserts that secrecy is an

instrument of conspiracy.....ought not, therefore, be the system of a regular government.

In these contexts the statement of HD Shourie is more relevant. According to H.D. Shourie, "while it made sense for the British to ensure secrecy in administrative matters when they were ruling a colony, secrecy doesn't serve any purpose today. The government is still functioning in secrecy and people cannot approach government officials directly."

He warned that the secrecy breeds corruption and information on policy matters should be passed on to the public. The official secrets Act represents the culture of secrecy imbibed by the Indians even after the independence. Though the British changed secrecy law to reduce the rigor of culture of secrecy in administration, the Indian Government is reluctant to bring in those changes.

It is true that the Right to Information aims at inculcating transparency and accountability in administration. For the effective implementation of Right to Information certain suggestions are being given, which are as under:

1. Indian Constitution must be amended to include the Right to Information, as one of the fundamental right and judicial interpretation must always not be sought for obtaining this right. Inclusion of this right in Part III of our Constitution in Article 19 by amendment in the Constitution this Right must be included in Article 19(1)(a) conspicuously. This would help the citizens to access the information as a fundamental right.
2. The enactment must be simultaneously accompanied by awareness. Thus, systematic awareness campaigns must be conducted across the country in order to inform and educate people about the existence, objectives, benefits and vitality of the Right to Information Act, 2005.
3. The procedure can be made simpler. Individual can deposit the application in the local Panchayat office or any level of the three-tier Panchayati Raj system. It should be the duty of the office-bearers of such offices to channelize and send the application to the appropriate department. This will reduce the

possibility of innocent villagers/individuals being cheated, harassed, misguided and buffaloed by the government officials. The steps involved in accessing information should be simple and straightforward.

4. Per-printed application forms should be available in all local languages.
5. Sanctions should penalize the institutions that have failed to respond to requests for information. In case of non-compliance on the part of concerned government officials, the penalty is 250 rupees per day which will not exceed Rs. 25000. These penalties are not sufficient. However, the said penalty, instead of being monetary, can be 'procedural' in nature. For example, the defaulting official can be given 'show cause' notice, followed by suspension from the job, after it is proved.
6. Right to Information training programmes should be conducted for the government officials. They should not treat clients and people with suspicion. It is a part of their job to help and inform the public. The functioning of the Act depends much on the cooperation of the officials. It is not enough that there is an Act, it should be respected by both the parties officials and the public.
7. Public bodies should be required and facilitated to maintain proper and timely records. There must be proper maintenance of records that too in electronic form. So, as to make them easily accusable for every one.
8. Sufficient funds should be allocated to implement of Right to Information legislation. This includes allocation of funds to each public body specifically for record-keeping and responding to Right to Information requests, as well as to designated Right to Information bodies.
9. Ideally people should be able to make requests for information free of charge. If fees are necessary the fees charged may only be for the actual costs incurred by the public authority, such as the cost-price of photocopying the document requested. Right to

Information laws should establish that information may be viewed free of charge, it is also the norm that where information is delivered electronically, such as by e-mail, it be free of charge.

10. These too should be kept simple and information about them should be readily available. Ideally, there should be internal appellate mechanisms within each public body. If these do not provide satisfaction, people should have the option of taking appeals to independent external bodies.
11. Time limit should be kept to minimum. There should be a strict time limit imposed on the time taken to respond to requests. The limit should be reasonable and should not jeopardize a person's rights. There should also be fast track procedures to access urgent information.
12. The Right to Information Act, 2005 provides a number of exemptions. According to Section 8 dealing with exemptions, each of which widens the exemptions under the Act. Firstly, the amendment to the provisions to clause (1) of Section 8, now restricts access of Cabinet papers to only the actual decisions and reasons thereof, after the decision, rather than to all the papers. This is also unreasonable. In a democracy where the Cabinet is just the representative of the people, who are the real masters, there is no justification for excluding all Cabinet papers from public view.

13 Right to Information law is not only a tool to uncover corruption; it can also prevent it by highlighting poor administration regarding how public funds are spent. Right to Information can also help improve internal efficiency and information management in administrations unused to such levels of accountability, even from internal supervision organs.

14. An information bank should be established for the effective implementation of Right to Information Act, 2005. So that any person seeking any information may receive the required information immediately and without any difficulty from there through an

application. This will conceal the identity of the person seeking information and it will be helpful to persons seeking the same information in future. It will save both time and the wastage of money. This model can be seen through a model chart as follows.

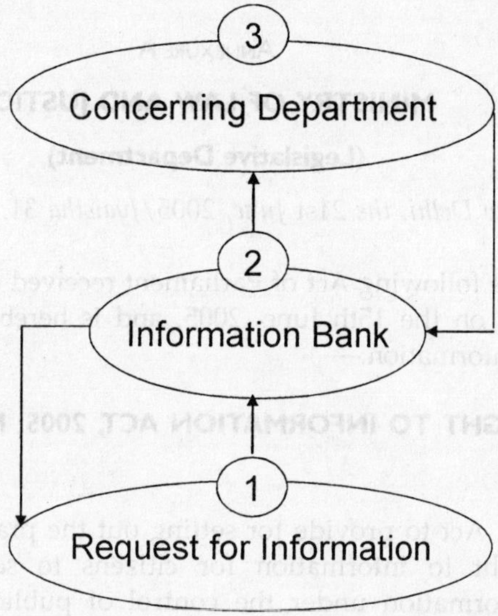

15. The Bureaucrat must not be appointed at the post of information commissioner. Because of this there is seen a lack in effectiveness of Right to Information Act, 2005.
16. Sections 124 and 125 of India Evidence Act must be amended to make adjustment with the new climate of the demand of right free access and information.

Right to Information is a very strong tool in the hand of Indian citizens. It is generally considered that information is the basis for knowledge which is thought-provoking. Right to Information is basic Human Right. It is essential not only for society but also for the individual. The Right to Information promotes, transparency, empowers the citizen; reduces corruption; increases efficiency; makes officials accountable, and puts an end to their indifference, arrogance and corruption.

ANNEXURE A

MINISTRY OF LAW AND JUSTICE

(Legislative Department)

New Delhi, the 21st *June,* 2005/*Jyaistha* 31, 1927 (*Saka*)

The following Act of Parliament received the assent of the President on the 15th June, 2005, and is hereby published for general information:—

THE RIGHT TO INFORMATION ACT, 2005, No. 22 of 2005

[15th June, 2005.]

An Act to provide for setting out the practical regime of right to information for citizens to secure access to information under the control of public authorities, in order to promote transparency and accountability in the working of every public authority, the constitution of a Central Information Commission and State Information Commissions and for matters connected therewith or incidental thereto.

WHEREAS the Constitution of India has established democratic Republic;

AND WHEREAS democracy requires an informed citizenry and transparency of information which are vital to its functioning and also to contain corruption and to hold Governments and their instrumentalities accountable to the governed;

AND WHEREAS revelation of information in actual practice is likely to conflict with other public interests including efficient operations of the Governments, optimum use of limited fiscal resources and the preservation of confidentiality of sensitive information;

AND WHEREAS it is necessary to harmonise these conflicting interests while preserving the paramountcy of the democratic ideal;

NOW, THEREFORE, it is expedient to provide for furnishing certain information to citizens who desire to have it.

BE it enacted by Parliament in the Fifty-sixth Year of the Republic of India as follows:—

CHAPTER I
Preliminary

1. Short title, extent and commencement.—(*1*) This Act may be called the Right to Information Act, 2005.

(*2*) It extends to the whole of India except the State of Jammu and Kashmir.

(*3*) The provisions of sub-section (*1*) of section 4, sub-sections (*1*) and (*2*) of section 5, sections 12, 13, 15,16, 24, 27 and 28 shall come into force at once, and the remaining provisions of this Act shall come into force on the one hundred and twentieth day of its enactment.

2. Definitions.—In this Act, unless the context otherwise requires,—

(*a*) "appropriate Government" means in relation to a public authority which is established, constituted, owned, controlled or substantially financed by funds provided directly or indirectly—

(*i*) by the Central Government or the Union territory administration, the Central Government;

(*ii*) by the State Government, the State Government;

(*b*) "Central Information Commission" means the Central Information Commission constituted under sub-section (*1*) of section 12;

(*c*) "Central Public Information Officer" means the Central Public Information Officer designated under sub-section (*1*) and includes a Central Assistant Public Information Officer designated as such under sub-section (2) of section 5;

(*d*) "Chief Information Commissioner" and "Information Commissioner" mean the Chief Information Commissioner and Information Commissioner appointed under sub-section (*3*) of section 12;

(*e*) "competent authority" means—

- (*i*) the Speaker in the case of the House of the People or the Legislative Assembly of a State or a Union territory having such Assembly and the Chairman in the case of the Council of States or Legislative Council of a State;
- (*ii*) the Chief Justice of India in the case of the Supreme Court;
- (*iii*) the Chief Justice of the High Court in the case of a High Court;
- (*iv*) the President or the Governor, as the case may be, in the case of other authorities established or constituted by or under the Constitution;
- (*v*) the administrator appointed under Article 239 of the Constitution;

(*f*) "information" means any material in any form, including records, documents, memos, e-mails, opinions, advices, press releases, circulars, orders, logbooks, contracts, reports, papers, samples, models, data material held in any electronic form and information relating to any private body which can be accessed by a public authority under any other law for the time being in force;

(*g*) "prescribed" means prescribed by rules made under this Act by the appropriate Government or the competent authority, as the case may be;

(*h*) "public authority" means any authority or body or institution of self-government established or constituted—

- (*a*) by or under the Constitution;
- (*b*) by any other law made by Parliament;
- (*c*) by any other law made by State Legislature;
- (*d*) by notification issued or order made by the appropriate Government,

and includes any—

- (*i*) body owned, controlled or substantially financed;
- (*ii*) non-Government organisation substantially financed;

directly or indirectly by funds provided by the appropriate Government;

(*i*) "record" includes—

(*a*) any document, manuscript and file;

(*b*) any microfilm, microfiche and facsimile copy of a document;

(*c*) any reproduction of image or images embodied in such microfilm (whether enlarged or not); and

(*d*) any other material produced by a computer or any other device;

(*j*) "right to information" means the right to information accessible under this Act which is held by or under the control of any public authority and includes the right to—

(*i*) inspection of work, documents, records;

(*ii*) taking notes, extracts or certified copies of documents or records;

(*iii*) taking certified samples of material; and

(*iv*) obtaining information in the form of diskettes, floppies, tapes, video cassettes or in any other electronic mode or through printouts where such information is stored in a computer or in any other device;

(*k*) "State Information Commission" means the State Information Commission constituted under sub-section (*1*) of section 15;

(*l*) "State Chief Information Commissioner" and "State Information Commissioner" mean the State Chief Information Commissioner and the State Information Commissioner appointed under sub-section (*3*) of section 15;

(*m*) "State Public Information Officer" means the State Public Information Officer designated under sub-section (*1*) and includes a State Assistant Public Information Officer designated as such under sub-section (*2*) of section 5;

(*n*) "third party" means a person other than the citizen making a request for information and includes a public authority.

CHAPTER II
Right to Information and Obligations of Public Authorities

3. Right to information.—Subject to the provisions of this Act, all citizens shall have the right to information. Right to information

4. (*1*) Every public authority shall—

(*a*) maintain all its records duly catalogued and indexed in a manner and the form which facilitates the right to information under this Act and ensure that all records that are appropriate to be computerised are, within a reasonable time and subject to availability of resources, computerised and connected through a network all over the country on different systems so that access to such records is facilitated;

(*b*) publish within one hundred and twenty days from the enactment of this Act,—

(*i*) the particulars of its organisation, functions and duties;

(*ii*) the powers and duties of its officers and employees;

(*iii*) the procedure followed in the decision-making process, including channels of supervision and accountability;

(*iv*) the norms set by it for the discharge of its functions;

(*v*) the rules, regulations, instructions, manuals and records, held by it or under its control or used by its employees for discharging its functions;

(*vi*) a statement of the categories of documents that are held by it or under its control;

(*vii*) the particulars of any arrangement that exists for consultation with, or representation by, the members of the public in relation to the formulation of its policy or implementation thereof;

(*viii*) a statement of the boards, councils, committees and other bodies consisting of two or more persons constituted as its part or for the purpose of its advice, and as to whether meetings of those boards, councils, committees and other bodies are open to the public, or the minutes of such meetings are accessible for public;

(ix) a directory of its officers and employees;

(x) the monthly remuneration received by each of its officers and employees, including the system of compensation as provided in its regulations;

(xi) the budget allocated to each of its agency, indicating the particulars of all plans, proposed expenditures and reports on disbursements made;

(xii) the manner of execution of subsidy programmes, including the amounts allocated and the details of beneficiaries of such programmes;

(xiii) particulars of recipients of concessions, permits or authorisations granted by it;

(xiv) details in respect of the information, available to or held by it, reduced in an electronic form;

(xv) the particulars of facilities available to citizens for obtaining information, including the working hours of a library or reading room, if maintained for public use;

(xvi) the names, designations and other particulars of the Public Information Officers;

(xvii) such other information as may be prescribed; and thereafter update these publications every year;

(*c*) publish all relevant facts while formulating important policies or announcing the decisions which affect public;

(*d*) provide reasons for its administrative or quasi-judicial decisions to affected persons.

(2) It shall be a constant endeavour of every public authority to take steps in accordance with the requirements of clause (*b*) of sub-section (*1*) to provide as much information *suo motu* to the public at regular intervals through various means of communications, including internet, so that the public have minimum resort to the use of this Act to obtain information.

(3) For the purposes of sub-section (*1*), every information

shall be disseminated widely and in such form and manner which is easily accessible to the public.

(*4*) All materials shall be disseminated taking into consideration the cost effectiveness, local language and the most effective method of communication in that local area and the information should be easily accessible, to the extent possible in electronic format with the Central Public Information Officer or State Public Information Officer, as the case may be, available free or at such cost of the medium or the print cost price as may be prescribed.

Explanation.—For the purposes of sub-sections (*3*) and (*4*), "disseminated" means making known or communicated the information to the public through notice boards, newspapers, public announcements, media broadcasts, the internet or any other means, including inspection of offices of any public authority.

5. Designation of Public Information Officers.—(*1*) Every public authority shall, within one hundred days of the enactment of this Act, designate as many officers as the Central Public Information Officers or State Public Information Officers, as the case may be, in all administrative units or offices under it as may be necessary to provide information to persons requesting for the information under this Act.

(2) Without prejudice to the provisions of sub-section (*1*), every public authority shall designate an officer, within one hundred days of the enactment of this Act, at each sub-divisional level or other sub-district level as a Central Assistant Public Information Officer or a State Assistant Public Information Officer, as the case may be, to receive the applications for information or appeals under this Act for forwarding the same forthwith to the Central Public Information Officer or the State Public Information Officer or senior officer specified under sub-section (*1*) of section 19 or the Central Information Commission or the State Information Commission, as the case may be:

Provided that where an application for information or appeal is given to a Central Assistant Public Information Officer or a State Assistant Public Information Officer, as the case may be, a period of five days shall be added in computing the period for response specified under sub-section (*1*) of section 7.

(3) Every Central Public Information Officer or State Public

Information Officer, as the case may be, shall deal with requests from persons seeking information and render reasonable assistance to the persons seeking such information.

(*4*) The Central Public Information Officer or State Public Information Officer, as the case may be, may seek the assistance of any other officer as he or she considers it necessary for the proper discharge of his or her duties.

(*5*) Any officer, whose assistance has been sought under sub-section (*4*), shall render all assistance to the Central Public Information Officer or State Public Information Officer, as the case may be, seeking his or her assistance and for the purposes of any contravention of the provisions of this Act, such other officer shall be treated as a Central Public Information Officer or State Public Information Officer, as the case may be.

6. Request for obtaining information.—(*1*) A person, who desires to obtain any information under this Act, shall make a request in writing or through electronic means in English or Hindi or in the official language of the area in which the application is being made, accompanying such fee as may be prescribed, to—

(*a*) the Central Public Information Officer or State Public Information Officer, as the case may be, of the concerned public authority; and

(*b*) the Central Assistant Public Information Officer or State Assistant Public Information Officer, as the case may be,

specifying the particulars of the information sought by him or her:

Provided that where such request cannot be made in writing, the Central Public Information Officer or State Public Information Officer, as the case may be, shall render all reasonable assistance to the person making the request orally to reduce the same in writing.

(*2*) An applicant making request for information shall not be required to give any reason for requesting the information or any other personal details except those that may be necessary for contacting him.

(*3*) Where an application is made to a public authority requesting for an information,—

(*i*) which is held by another public authority; or

(*ii*) the subject matter of which is more closely connected with the functions of another public authority,

the public authority, to which such application is made, shall transfer the application or such part of it as may be appropriate to that other public authority and inform the applicant immediately about such transfer:

Provided that the transfer of an application pursuant to this sub-section shall be made as soon as practicable but in no case later than five days from the date of receipt of the application.

7. Disposal of request.—(*1*) Subject to the proviso to sub-section (2) of section 5 or the proviso to sub-section (3) of section 6, the Central Public Information Officer or State Public Information Officer, as the case may be, on receipt of a request under section 6 shall, as expeditiously as possible, and in any case within thirty days of the receipt of the request, either provide the information on payment of such fee as may be prescribed or reject the request for any of the reasons specified in sections 8 and 9:

Provided that where the information sought for concerns the life or liberty of a person, the same shall be provided within forty-eight hours of the receipt of the request.

(2) If the Central Public Information Officer or State Public Information Officer, as the case may be, fails to give decision on the request for information within the period specified under sub-section (*1*), the Central Public Information Officer or State Public Information Officer, as the case may be, shall be deemed to have refused the request.

(*3*) Where a decision is taken to provide the information on payment of any further fee representing the cost of providing the information, the Central Public Information Officer or State Public Information Officer, as the case may be, shall send an intimation to the person making the request, giving—

(*a*) the details of further fees representing the cost of

providing the information as determined by him, together with the calculations made to arrive at the amount in accordance with fee prescribed under sub-section (*1*), requesting him to deposit that fees, and the period intervening between the despatch of the said intimation and payment of fees shall be excluded for the purpose of calculating the period of thirty days referred to in that sub-section; and

(*b*) information concerning his or her right with respect to review the decision as to the amount of fees charged or the form of access provided, including the particulars of the appellate authority, time limit, process and any other forms.

(*4*) Where access to the record or a part thereof is required to be provided under this Act and the person to whom access is to be provided is sensorially disabled, the Central Public Information Officer or State Public Information Officer, as the case may be, shall provide assistance to enable access to the information, including providing such assistance as may be appropriate for the inspection.

(*5*) Where access to information is to be provided in the printed or in any electronic format, the applicant shall, subject to the provisions of sub-section (*6*), pay such fee as may be prescribed:

Provided that the fee prescribed under sub-section (*1*) of section 6 and sub-sections (*1*) and (*5*) of section 7 shall be reasonable and no such fee shall be charged from the persons who are of below poverty line as may be determined by the appropriate Government.

(*6*) Notwithstanding anything contained in sub-section (*5*), the person making request for the information shall be provided the information free of charge where a public authority fails to comply with the time limits specified in sub-section (*1*).

(*7*) Before taking any decision under sub-section (*1*), the Central Public Information Officer or State Public Information Officer, as the case may be, shall take into consideration the representation made by a third party under section 11.

(*8*) Where a request has been rejected under sub-section (*1*), the Central Public Information Officer or State Public Information Officer, as the case may be, shall communicate to the person making the request,—

(*i*) the reasons for such rejection;

(*ii*) the period within which an appeal against such rejection may be preferred; and

(*iii*) the particulars of the appellate authority.

(*9*) An information shall ordinarily be provided in the form in which it is sought unless it would disproportionately divert the resources of the public authority or would be detrimental to the safety or preservation of the record in question.

8. Exemption from disclosure of information.—(*1*) Notwithstanding anything contained in this Act, there shall be no obligation to give any citizen,—

(*a*) information, disclosure of which would prejudicially affect the sovereignty and integrity of India, the security, strategic, scientific or economic interests of the State, relation with foreign State or lead to incitement of an offence;

(*b*) information which has been expressly forbidden to be published by any court of law or tribunal or the disclosure of which may constitute contempt of court;

(*c*) information, the disclosure of which would cause a breach of privilege of Parliament or the State Legislature;

(*d*) information including commercial confidence, trade secrets or intellectual property, the disclosure of which would harm the competitive position of a third party, unless the competent authority is satisfied that larger public interest warrants the disclosure of such information;

(*e*) information available to a person in his fiduciary relationship, unless the competent authority is satisfied that the larger public interest warrants the disclosure of such information;

(*f*) information received in confidence from foreign Government;

(*g*) information, the disclosure of which would endanger the life or physical safety of any person or identify the source of information or assistance given in confidence for law enforcement or security purposes;

(*h*) information which would impede the process of investigation or apprehension or prosecution of offenders; and

(*i*) cabinet papers including records of deliberations of the Council of Ministers, Secretaries and other officers:

Provided that the decisions of Council of Ministers, the reasons thereof, and the material on the basis of which the decisions were taken shall be made public after the decision has been taken, and the matter is complete, or over:

Provided further that those matters which come under the exemptions specified in this section shall not be disclosed;

(*j*) information which relates to personal information the disclosure of which has no relationship to any public activity or interest, or which would cause unwarranted invasion of the privacy of the individual unless the Central Public Information Officer or the State Public Information Officer or the appellate authority, as the case may be, is satisfied that the larger public interest justifies the disclosure of such information:

Provided that the information which cannot be denied to the Parliament or a State Legislature shall not be denied to any person.

(2) Notwithstanding anything in the Official Secrets Act, 1923 nor any of the exemptions permissible in accordance with sub-section (*1*), a public authority may allow access to information, if public interest in disclosure outweighs the harm to the protected interests.

(3) Subject to the provisions of clauses (*a*), (*c*) and (*i*) of sub-

section (*1*), any information relating to any occurrence, event or matter which has taken place, occurred or happened twenty years before the date on which any request is made under section 6 shall be provided to any person making a request under that section:

Provided that where any question arises as to the date from which the said period of twenty years has to be computed, the decision of the Central Government shall be final, subject to the usual appeals provided for in this Act.

9. Grounds for rejection to access in certain cases.—Without prejudice to the provisions of section 8, a Central Public Information Officer or a State Public Information Officer, as the case may be, may reject a request for information where such a request for providing access would involve an infringement of copyright subsisting in a person other than the State.

10. Severability.—(*1*) Where a request for access to information is rejected on the ground that it is in relation to information which is exempt from disclosure, then, notwithstanding anything contained in this Act, access may be provided to that part of the record which does not contain any information which is exempt from disclosure under this Act and which can reasonably be severed from any part that contains exempt information.

(2) Where access is granted to a part of the record under sub-section (*1*), the Central Public Information Officer or State Public Information Officer, as the case may be, shall give a notice to the applicant, informing—

(*a*) that only part of the record requested, after severance of the record containing information which is exempt from disclosure, is being provided;

(*b*) the reasons for the decision, including any findings on any material question of fact, referring to the material on which those findings were based;

(*c*) the name and designation of the person giving the decision;

(*d*) the details of the fees calculated by him or her and the amount of fee which the applicant is required to deposit; and (*e*) his or her rights with respect to review of the decision regarding non-disclosure of part of the information, the amount of fee charged or the form of access provided, including the particulars of the senior officer specified under sub-section (*1*) of section 19 or the Central Information Commission or the State Information Commission, as the case may be, time limit, process and any other form of access.

11. Third party information.—(*1*) Where a Central Public Information Officer or a State Public Information Officer, as the case may be, intends to disclose any information or record, or part thereof on a request made under this Act, which relates to or has been supplied by a third party and has been treated as confidential by that third party, the Central Public Information Officer or State Public Information Officer, as the case may be, shall, within five days from the receipt of the request, give a written notice to such third party of the request and of the fact that the Central Public Information Officer or State Public Information Officer, as the case may be, intends to disclose the information or record, or part thereof, and invite the third party to make a submission in writing or orally, regarding whether the information should be disclosed, and such submission of the third party shall be kept in view while taking a decision about disclosure of information:

Provided that except in the case of trade or commercial secrets protected by law, disclosure may be allowed if the public interest in disclosure outweighs in importance any possible harm or injury to the interests of such third party.

(*2*) Where a notice is served by the Central Public Information Officer or State Public Information Officer, as the case may be, under sub-section (*1*) to a third party in respect of any information or record or part thereof, the third party shall, within ten days from the date of receipt of such notice, be given the opportunity to make representation against the proposed disclosure.

(*3*) Notwithstanding anything contained in section 7, the Central Public Information Officer or State Public Information

Officer, as the case may be, shall, within forty days after receipt of the request under section 6, if the third party has been given an opportunity to make representation under sub-section (2), make a decision as to whether or not to disclose the information or record or part thereof and give in writing the notice of his decision to the third party.

(*4*) A notice given under sub-section (*3*) shall include a statement that the third party to whom the notice is given is entitled to prefer an appeal under section 19 against the decision.

CHAPTER III
The Central Information Commission

12. Constitution of Central Information Commission.—(*1*) The Central Government shall, by notification in the Official Gazette, constitute a body to be known as the Central Information Commission to exercise the powers conferred on, and to perform the functions assigned to, it under this Act.

(*2*) The Central Information Commission shall consist of—

(*a*) the Chief Information Commissioner; and

(*b*) such number of Central Information Commissioners, not exceeding ten, as may be deemed necessary.

(*3*) The Chief Information Commissioner and Information Commissioners shall be appointed by the President on the recommendation of a committee consisting of—

(*i*) the Prime Minister, who shall be the Chairperson of the committee;

(*ii*) the Leader of Opposition in the Lok Sabha; and

(*iii*) a Union Cabinet Minister to be nominated by the Prime Minister.

Explanation.—For the purposes of removal of doubts, it is hereby declared that where the Leader of Opposition in the House of the People has not been recognised as such, the Leader of the single largest group in opposition of the Government in the House of the People shall be deemed to be the Leader of Opposition.

(*4*) The general superintendence, direction and

management of the affairs of the Central Information Commission shall vest in the Chief Information Commissioner who shall be assisted by the Information Commissioners and may exercise all such powers and do all such acts and things which may be exercised or done by the Central Information Commission autonomously without being subjected to directions by any other authority under this Act.

(*5*) The Chief Information Commissioner and Information Commissioners shall be persons of eminence in public life with wide knowledge and experience in law, science and technology, social service, management, journalism, mass media or administration and governance.

(*6*) The Chief Information Commissioner or an Information Commissioner shall not be a Member of Parliament or Member of the Legislature of any State or Union territory, as the case may be, or hold any other office of profit or connected with any political party or carrying on any business or pursuing any profession.

(*7*) The headquarters of the Central Information Commission shall be at Delhi and the Central Information Commission may, with the previous approval of the Central Government, establish offices at other places in India.

13. Term of office and conditions of service.—(*1*) The Chief Information Commissioner shall hold office for a term of five years from the date on which he enters upon his office and shall not be eligible for reappointment:

> Provided that no Chief Information Commissioner shall hold office as such after he has attained the age of sixty-five years.

(2) Every Information Commissioner shall hold office for a term of five years from the date on which he enters upon his office or till he attains the age of sixty-five years, whichever is earlier, and shall not be eligible for reappointment as such Information Commissioner:

> Provided that every Information Commissioner shall, on vacating his office under this sub-section be eligible for appointment as the Chief Information Commissioner in the manner specified in sub-section (3) of section 12:

Provided further that where the Information Commissioner is appointed as the Chief Information Commissioner, his term of office shall not be more than five years in aggregate as the Information Commissioner and the Chief Information Commissioner.

(3) The Chief Information Commissioner or an Information Commissioner shall before he enters upon his office make and subscribe before the President or some other person appointed by him in that behalf, an oath or affirmation according to the form set out for the purpose in the First Schedule.

(4) The Chief Information Commissioner or an Information Commissioner may, at any time, by writing under his hand addressed to the President, resign from his office:

Provided that the Chief Information Commissioner or an Information Commissioner may be removed in the manner specified under section 14.

(5) The salaries and allowances payable to and other terms and conditions of service of—

(*a*) the Chief Information Commissioner shall be the same as that of the Chief Election Commissioner; and

(*b*) an Information Commissioner shall be the same as that of an Election Commissioner:

Provided that if the Chief Information Commissioner or an Information Commissioner, at the time of his appointment is, in receipt of a pension, other than a disability or wound pension, in respect of any previous service under the Government of India or under the Government of a State, his salary in respect of the service as the Chief Information Commissioner or an Information Commissioner shall be reduced by the amount of that pension including any portion of pension which was commuted and pension equivalent of other forms of retirement benefits excluding pension equivalent of retirement gratuity:

Provided further that if the Chief Information Commissioner or an Information Commissioner if, at the time of his appointment is, in receipt of retirement benefits in respect of any previous service rendered in a Corporation established by or under any Central Act or State Act or a Government company owned or controlled by the Central Government or the State Government, his salary in respect of the service as the Chief Information Commissioner or an Information Commissioner shall be reduced by the amount of pension equivalent to the retirement benefits:

Provided also that the salaries, allowances and other conditions of service of the Chief Information Commissioner and the Information Commissioners shall not be varied to their disadvantage after their appointment.

(*6*) The Central Government shall provide the Chief Information Commissioner and the Information Commissioners with such officers and employees as may be necessary for the efficient performance of their functions under this Act, and the salaries and allowances payable to and the terms and conditions of service of the officers and other employees appointed for the purpose of this Act shall be such as may be prescribed.

14. Removal of Chief Information Commissioner or Information Commissioner.—(*1*) Subject to the provisions of sub-section (*3*), the Chief Information Commissioner or any Information Commissioner shall be removed from his office only by order of the President on the ground of proved misbehaviour or incapacity after the Supreme Court, on a reference made to it by the President, has, on inquiry, reported that the Chief Information Commissioner or any Information Commissioner, as the case may be, ought on such ground be removed.

(*2*) The President may suspend from office, and if deem necessary prohibit also from attending the office during inquiry, the Chief Information Commissioner or Information Commissioner in respect of whom a reference has been made to the Supreme Court under sub-section (*1*) until the President has passed orders on receipt of the report of the Supreme Court on such reference.

(*3*) Notwithstanding anything contained in sub-section (*1*), the President may by order remove from office the Chief Information Commissioner or any Information Commissioner if the Chief Information Commissioner or a Information Commissioner, as the case may be,—

(*a*) is adjudged an insolvent; or

(*b*) has been convicted of an offence which, in the opinion of the President, involves moral turpitude; or

(*c*) engages during his term of office in any paid employment outside the duties of his office; or

(*d*) is, in the opinion of the President, unfit to continue in office by reason of infirmity of mind or body; or

(*e*) has acquired such financial or other interest as is likely to affect prejudicially his functions as the Chief Information Commissioner or a Information Commissioner.

(4) If the Chief Information Commissioner or a Information Commissioner in any way, concerned or interested in any contract or agreement made by or on behalf of the Government of India or participates in any way in the profit thereof or in any benefit or emolument arising therefrom otherwise than as a member and in common with the other members of an incorporated company, he shall, for the purposes of sub-section (*1*), be deemed to be guilty of misbehaviour.

CHAPTER IV

The State Information Commission

15. Constitution of State Information Commission.—(*1*) Every State Government shall, by notification in the Official Gazette, constitute a body to be known as the .... (name of the State) Information Commission to exercise the powers conferred on, and to perform the functions assigned to, it under this Act.

(2) The State Information Commission shall consist of—

(*a*) the State Chief Information Commissioner, and

(*b*) such number of State Information Commissioners, not exceeding ten, as may be deemed necessary.

(3) The State Chief Information Commissioner and the State Information Commissioners shall be appointed by the Governor

on the recommendation of a committee consisting of—

(i) the Chief Minister, who shall be the Chairperson of the committee;

(ii) the Leader of Opposition in the Legislative Assembly; and

(iii) a Cabinet Minister to be nominated by the Chief Minister.

Explanation.—For the purposes of removal of doubts, it is hereby declared that where the Leader of Opposition in the Legislative Assembly has not been recognised as such, the Leader of the single largest group in opposition of the Government in the Legislative Assembly shall be deemed to be the Leader of Opposition.

(*4*) The general superintendence, direction and management of the affairs of the State Information Commission shall vest in the State Chief Information Commissioner who shall be assisted by the State Information Commissioners and may exercise all such powers and do all such acts and things which may be exercised or done by the State Information Commission autonomously without being subjected to directions by any other authority under this Act.

(*5*) The State Chief Information Commissioner and the State Information Commissioners shall be persons of eminence in public life with wide knowledge and experience in law, science and technology, social service, management, journalism, mass media or administration and governance.

(*6*) The State Chief Information Commissioner or a State Information Commissioner shall not be a Member of Parliament or Member of the Legislature of any State or Union territory, as the case may be, or hold any other office of profit or connected with any political party or carrying on any business or pursuing any profession.

(*7*) The headquarters of the State Information Commission shall be at such place in the State as the State Government may, by notification in the Official Gazette, specify and the State Information Commission may, with the previous approval of the State Government, establish offices at other places in the State.

16. Term of office and conditions of service.—(*1*) The State

Chief Information Commissioner shall hold office for a term of five years from the date on which he enters upon his office and shall not be eligible for reappointment:

Provided that no State Chief Information Commissioner shall hold office as such after he has attained the age of sixty-five years.

(2) Every State Information Commissioner shall hold office for a term of five years from the date on which he enters upon his office or till he attains the age of sixty-five years, whichever is earlier, and shall not be eligible for reappointment as such State Information Commissioner:

Provided that every State Information Commissioner shall, on vacating his office under this sub-section, be eligible for appointment as the State Chief Information Commissioner in the manner specified in sub-section (3) of section 15: Provided further that where the State Information Commissioner is appointed as the State Chief Information Commissioner, his term of office shall not be more than five years in aggregate as the State Information Commissioner and the State Chief Information Commissioner.

(3) The State Chief Information Commissioner or a State Information Commissioner, shall before he enters upon his office make and subscribe before the Governor or some other person appointed by him in that behalf, an oath or affirmation according to the form set out for the purpose in the First Schedule.

(4) The State Chief Information Commissioner or a State Information Commissioner may, at any time, by writing under his hand addressed to the Governor, resign from his office:

Provided that the State Chief Information Commissioner or a State Information Commissioner may be removed in the manner specified under section 17.

(5) The salaries and allowances payable to and other terms and conditions of service of—

(*a*) the State Chief Information Commissioner shall be the same as that of an Election Commissioner; and

(*b*) the State Information Commissioner shall be the same as that of the Chief Secretary to the State Government:

Provided that if the State Chief Information Commissioner or a State Information Commissioner, at the time of his appointment is, in receipt of a pension, other than a disability or wound pension, in respect of any previous service under the Government of India or under the Government of a State, his salary in respect of the service as the State Chief Information Commissioner or a State Information Commissioner shall be reduced by the amount of that pension including any portion of pension which was commuted and pension equivalent of other forms of retirement benefits excluding pension equivalent of retirement gratuity:

Provided further that where the State Chief Information Commissioner or a State Information Commissioner if, at the time of his appointment is, in receipt of retirement benefits in respect of any previous service rendered in a Corporation established by or under any Central Act or State Act or a Government company owned or controlled by the Central Government or the State Government, his salary in respect of the service as the State Chief Information Commissioner or the State Information Commissioner shall be reduced by the amount of pension equivalent to the retirement benefits:

Provided also that the salaries, allowances and other conditions of service of the State Chief Information Commissioner and the State Information Commissioners shall not be varied to their disadvantage after their appointment.

(*6*) The State Government shall provide the State Chief Information Commissioner and the State Information Commissioners with such officers and employees as may be necessary for the efficient performance of their functions under this Act, and the salaries and allowances payable to and the terms and conditions of service of the officers and other employees appointed for the purpose of this Act shall be such as may be prescribed.

17. Removal of State Chief Information Commissioner or State Information Commissioner.—(*1*) Subject to the provisions of sub-section (*3*), the State Chief Information Commissioner or a State Information Commissioner shall be removed from his office only by order of the Governor on the ground of proved misbehaviour or incapacity after the Supreme Court, on a reference made to it by the Governor, has on inquiry, reported that the State Chief Information Commissioner or a State Information Commissioner, as the case may be, ought on such ground be removed.

(*2*) The Governor may suspend from office, and if deem necessary prohibit also from attending the office during inquiry, the State Chief Information Commissioner or a State Information Commissioner in respect of whom a reference has been made to the Supreme Court under sub-section (*1*) until the Governor has passed orders on receipt of the report of the Supreme Court on such reference.

(*3*) Notwithstanding anything contained in sub-section (*1*), the Governor may by order remove from office the State Chief Information Commissioner or a State Information Commissioner if a State Chief Information Commissioner or a State Information Commissioner, as the case may be,—

(*a*) is adjudged an insolvent; or

(*b*) has been convicted of an offence which, in the opinion of the Governor, involves moral turpitude; or

(*c*) engages during his term of office in any paid employment outside the duties of his office; or

(*d*) is, in the opinion of the Governor, unfit to continue in office by reason of infirmity of mind or body; or

(*e*) has acquired such financial or other interest as is likely to affect prejudicially his functions as the State Chief Information Commissioner or a State Information Commissioner.

(*4*) If the State Chief Information Commissioner or a State Information Commissioner in any way, concerned or interested in any contract or agreement made by or on behalf of the

Government of the State or participates in any way in the profit thereof or in any benefit or emoluments arising therefrom otherwise than as a member and in common with the other members of an incorporated company, he shall, for the purposes of sub-section (*1*), be deemed to be guilty of misbehaviour.

CHAPTER V
Powers and Functions of the Information Commissions, Appeal and Penalties

18. **Powers and functions of Information Commissions.**—(*1*) Subject to the provisions of this Act, it shall be the duty of the Central Information Commission or State Information Commission, as the case may be, to receive and inquire into a complaint from any person,—

(*a*) who has been unable to submit a request to a Central Public Information Officer or State Public Information Officer, as the case may be, either by reason that no such officer has been appointed under this Act, or because the Central Assistant Public Information Officer or State Assistant Public Information Officer, as the case may be, has refused to accept his or her application for information or appeal under this Act for forwarding the same to the Central Public Information Officer or State Public Information Officer or senior officer specified in sub-section (*1*) of section 19 or the Central Information Commission or the State Information Commission, as the case may be;

(*b*) who has been refused access to any information requested under this Act;

(*c*) who has not been given a response to a request for information or access to information within the time limit specified under this Act;

(*d*) who has been required to pay an amount of fee which he or she considers unreasonable;

(*e*) who believes that he or she has been given incomplete, misleading or false information under this Act; and

(*f*) in respect of any other matter relating to requesting or obtaining access to records under this Act.

(2) Where the Central Information Commission or State Information Commission, as the case may be, is satisfied that there are reasonable grounds to inquire into the matter, it may initiate an inquiry in respect thereof.

(3) The Central Information Commission or State Information Commission, as the case may be, shall, while inquiring into any matter under this section, have the same powers as are vested in a civil court while trying a suit under the Code of Civil Procedure, 1908, in respect of the following matters, namely:—

(a) summoning and enforcing the attendance of persons and compel them to give oral or written evidence on oath and to produce the documents or things;

(b) requiring the discovery and inspection of documents;

(c) receiving evidence on affidavit;

(d) requisitioning any public record or copies thereof from any court or office;

(e) issuing summons for examination of witnesses or documents; and

(f) any other matter which may be prescribed.

(4) Notwithstanding anything inconsistent contained in any other Act of Parliament or State Legislature, as the case may be, the Central Information Commission or the State Information Commission, as the case may be, may, during the inquiry of any complaint under this Act, examine any record to which this Act applies which is under the control of the public authority, and no such record may be withheld from it on any grounds.

19. **Appeal.**—*(1)* Any person who, does not receive a decision within the time specified in sub-section *(1)* or clause *(a)* of sub-section *(3)* of section 7, or is aggrieved by a decision of the Central Public Information Officer or State Public Information Officer, as the case may be, may within thirty days from the expiry of such period or from the receipt of such a decision prefer an appeal to such officer who is senior in rank to the Central Public Information Officer or State Public Information Officer as the case may be, in each public authority:

Provided that such officer may admit the appeal after the

expiry of the period of thirty days if he or she is satisfied that the appellant was prevented by sufficient cause from filing the appeal in time.

(2) Where an appeal is preferred against an order made by a Central Public Information Officer or a State Public Information Officer, as the case may be, under section 11 to disclose third party information, the appeal by the concerned third party shall be made within thirty days from the date of the order.

(3) A second appeal against the decision under sub-section (*1*) shall lie within ninety days from the date on which the decision should have been made or was actually received, with the Central Information Commission or the State Information Commission:

Provided that the Central Information Commission or the State Information Commission, as the case may be, may admit the appeal after the expiry of the period of ninety days if it is satisfied that the appellant was prevented by sufficient cause from filing the appeal in time.

(*4*) If the decision of the Central Public Information Officer or State Public Information Officer, as the case may be, against which an appeal is preferred relates to information of a third party, the Central Information Commission or State Information Commission, as the case may be, shall give a reasonable opportunity of being heard to that third party.

(*5*) In any appeal proceedings, the onus to prove that a denial of a request was justified shall be on the Central Public Information Officer or State Public Information Officer, as the case may be, who denied the request.

(*6*) An appeal under sub-section (*1*) or sub-section (2) shall be disposed of within thirty days of the receipt of the appeal or within such extended period not exceeding a total of forty-five days from the date of filing thereof, as the case may be, for reasons to be recorded in writing.

(*7*) The decision of the Central Information Commission or State Information Commission, as the case may be, shall be binding.

(*8*) In its decision, the Central Information Commission or

State Information Commission, as the case may be, has the power to—

(*a*) require the public authority to take any such steps as may be necessary to secure compliance with the provisions of this Act, including—

(*i*) by providing access to information, if so requested, in a particular form;

(*ii*) by appointing a Central Public Information Officer or State Public Information Officer, as the case may be;

(*iii*) by publishing certain information or categories of information;

(*iv*) by making necessary changes to its practices in relation to the maintenance, management and destruction of records;

(*v*) by enhancing the provision of training on the right to information for its officials;

(*vi*) by providing it with an annual report in compliance with clause (*b*) of sub-section (*1*) of section 4;

(*b*) require the public authority to compensate the complainant for any loss or other detriment suffered;

(*c*) impose any of the penalties provided under this Act;

(*d*) reject the application.

(*9*) The Central Information Commission or State Information Commission, as the case may be, shall give notice of its decision, including any right of appeal, to the complainant and the public authority.

(*10*) The Central Information Commission or State Information Commission, as the case may be, shall decide the appeal in accordance with such procedure as may be prescribed.

20. Penalties.—(*1*) Where the Central Information Commission or the State Information Commission, as the case may be, at the time of deciding any complaint or appeal is of the opinion that the Central Public Information Officer or the State Public Information Officer, as the case may be, has, without any reasonable cause, refused to receive an application for information or has not furnished information within the time specified under sub-section (*1*) of section 7 or malafidely denied the request for information or knowingly given incorrect, incomplete or misleading information or destroyed information which was the subject of the request or obstructed in any manner in furnishing the information, it shall impose a penalty of two hundred and fifty rupees each day till application is received or information is furnished, so however, the total amount of such penalty shall not exceed twenty-five thousand rupees:

Provided that the Central Public Information Officer or the State Public Information Officer, as the case may be, shall be given a reasonable opportunity of being heard before any penalty is imposed on him:

Provided further that the burden of proving that he acted reasonably and diligently shall be on the Central Public Information Officer or the State Public Information Officer, as the case may be.

(2) Where the Central Information Commission or the State Information Commission, as the case may be, at the time of deciding any complaint or appeal is of the opinion that the Central Public Information Officer or the State Public Information Officer, as the case may be, has, without any reasonable cause and persistently, failed to receive an application for information or has not furnished information within the time specified under sub-section (*1*) of section 7 or malafidely denied the request for information or knowingly given incorrect, incomplete or misleading information or destroyed information which was the subject of the request or obstructed in any manner in furnishing the information, it shall recommend for disciplinary action against the Central Public Information Officer or the State Public Information Officer, as the case may be, under the service rules applicable to him.

CHAPTER VI
Miscellaneous

21. Protection of action taken in good faith.—No suit, prosecution or other legal proceeding shall lie against any person for anything which is in good faith done or intended to be done under this Act or any rule made thereunder.

22. Act to have overriding effect.—The provisions of this Act shall have effect notwithstanding anything inconsistent therewith contained in the Official Secrets Act, 1923, and any other law for the time being in force or in any instrument having effect by virtue of any law other than this Act.

23. Bar of jurisdiction of courts.—No court shall entertain any suit, application or other proceeding in respect of any order made under this Act and no such order shall be called in question otherwise than by way of an appeal under this Act.

24. Act not to apply to certain organisations.—(*1*) Nothing contained in this Act shall apply to the intelligence and security organisations specified in the Second Schedule, being organisations established by the Central Government or any information furnished by such organisations to that Government:

Provided that the information pertaining to the allegations of corruption and human rights violations shall not be excluded under this sub-section:

Provided further that in the case of information sought for is in respect of allegations of violation of human rights, the information shall only be provided after the approval of the Central Information Commission, and notwithstanding anything contained in section 7, such information shall be provided within forty-five days from the date of the receipt of request.

(2) The Central Government may, by notification in the Official Gazette, amend the Schedule by including therein any other intelligence or security organisation established by that Government or omitting therefrom any organisation already specified therein and on the publication of such notification, such organisation shall be deemed to be included in or, as the case may be, omitted from the Schedule.

(3) Every notification issued under sub-section (2) shall be laid before each House of Parliament.

(4) Nothing contained in this Act shall apply to such intelligence and security organisation being organisations established by the State Government, as that Government may, from time to time, by notification in the Official Gazette, specify:

Provided that the information pertaining to the allegations of corruption and human rights violations shall not be excluded under this sub-section:

Provided further that in the case of information sought for is in respect of allegations of violation of human rights, the information shall only be provided after the approval of the State Information Commission and, notwithstanding anything contained in section 7, such information shall be provided within forty-five days from the date of the receipt of request.

(*5*) Every notification issued under sub-section (*4*) shall be laid before the State Legislature.

25. Monitoring and Reporting.—(*1*) The Central Information Commission or State Information Commission, as the case may be, shall, as soon as practicable after the end of each year, prepare a report on the implementation of the provisions of this Act during that year and forward a copy thereof to the appropriate Government.

(2) Each Ministry or Department shall, in relation to the public authorities within their jurisdiction, collect and provide such information to the Central Information Commission or State Information Commission, as the case may be, as is required to prepare the report under this section and comply with the requirements concerning the furnishing of that information and keeping of records for the purposes of this section.

(3) Each report shall state in respect of the year to which the report relates,—

(*a*) the number of requests made to each public authority;

(*b*) the number of decisions where applicants were not entitled to access to the documents pursuant to the requests, the provisions of this Act under which these decisions were made and the number of times such provisions were invoked;

(*c*) the number of appeals referred to the Central Information Commission or State Information Commission, as the case may be, for review, the nature of the appeals and the outcome of the appeals;

(*d*) particulars of any disciplinary action taken against any officer in respect of the administration of this Act;

(*e*) the amount of charges collected by each public authority under this Act;

(*f*) any facts which indicate an effort by the public authorities to administer and implement the spirit and intention of this Act;

(*g*) recommendations for reform, including recommendations in respect of the particular public authorities, for the development, improvement, modernisation, reform or amendment to this Act or other legislation or common law or any other matter relevant for operationalising the right to access information.

(*4*) The Central Government or the State Government, as the case may be, may, as soon as practicable after the end of each year, cause a copy of the report of the Central Information Commission or the State Information Commission, as the case may be, referred to in sub-section (*1*) to be laid before each House of Parliament or, as the case may be, before each House of the State Legislature, where there are two Houses, and where there is one House of the State Legislature before that House.

(*5*) If it appears to the Central Information Commission or State Information Commission, as the case may be, that the practice of a public authority in relation to the exercise of its functions under this Act does not conform with the provisions or spirit of this Act, it may give to the authority a recommendation specifying the steps which ought in its opinion to be taken for promoting such conformity.

26. Appropriate Government to prepare programmes.—(*1*) The appropriate Government may, to the extent of availability of financial and other resources,—

(*a*) develop and organise educational programmes to advance the understanding of the public, in particular of disadvantaged communities as to how to exercise the rights contemplated under this Act;

(*b*) encourage public authorities to participate in the development and organisation of programmes referred to in clause (*a*) and to undertake such programmes themselves;

(*c*) promote timely and effective dissemination of accurate information by public authorities about their activities; and

(*d*) train Central Public Information Officers or State Public Information Officers, as the case may be, of public authorities and produce relevant training materials for use by the public authorities themselves.

(2) The appropriate Government shall, within eighteen months from the commencement of this Act, compile in its official language a guide containing such information, in an easily comprehensible form and manner, as may reasonably be required by a person who wishes to exercise any right specified in this Act.

(3) The appropriate Government shall, if necessary, update and publish the guidelines referred to in sub-section (2) at regular intervals which shall, in particular and without prejudice to the generality of sub-section (2), include—

(*a*) the objects of this Act;

(*b*) the postal and street address, the phone and fax number and, if available, electronic mail address of the Central Public Information Officer or State Public Information Officer, as the case may be, of every public authority appointed under sub-section (*1*) of section 5;

(*c*) the manner and the form in which request for access to an information shall be made to a Central Public Information Officer or State Public Information Officer, as the case may be;

(*d*) the assistance available from and the duties of the Central Public Information Officer or State Public Information Officer, as the case may be, of a public authority under this Act;

(*e*) the assistance available from the Central Information Commission or State Information Commission, as the case may be;

(*f*) all remedies in law available regarding an act or failure to act in respect of a right or duty conferred or imposed by this Act including the manner of filing an appeal to the Commission;

(*g*) the provisions providing for the voluntary disclosure of categories of records in accordance with section 4;

(*h*) the notices regarding fees to be paid in relation to requests for access to an information; and

(*i*) any additional regulations or circulars made or issued in relation to obtaining access to an information in accordance with this Act.

(*4*) The appropriate Government must, if necessary, update and publish the guidelines at regular intervals.

27. Power to make rules by appropriate Government.—(*1*) The appropriate Government may, by notification in the Official Gazette, make rules to carry out the provisions of this Act.

(2) In particular, and without prejudice to the generality of the foregoing power, such rules may provide for all or any of the following matters, namely:—

(*a*) the cost of the medium or print cost price of the materials to be disseminated under sub-section (*4*) of section 4;

(*b*) the fee payable under sub-section (*1*) of section 6;

(*c*) the fee payable under sub-sections (*1*) and (*5*) of section 7;

(*d*) the salaries and allowances payable to and the terms and conditions of service of the officers and other employees under sub-section (*6*) of section 13 and sub-section (*6*) of section 16;

(*e*) the procedure to be adopted by the Central Information Commission or State Information Commission, as the case may be, in deciding the appeals under sub-section (*10*) of section 19; and

(*f*) any other matter which is required to be, or may be, prescribed.

28. Power to make rules by competent authority.—(*1*) The competent authority may, by notification in the Official Gazette, make rules to carry out the provisions of this Act.

(2) In particular, and without prejudice to the generality of the foregoing power, such rules may provide for all or any of the following matters, namely:—

(*i*) the cost of the medium or print cost price of the materials to be disseminated under sub-section (*4*) of section 4;

(*ii*) the fee payable under sub-section (*1*) of section 6;

(*iii*) the fee payable under sub-section (*1*) of section 7; and

(*iv*) any other matter which is required to be, or may be, prescribed

29. Laying of rules.—(*1*) Every rule made by the Central Government under this Act shall be laid, as soon as may be after it is made, before each House of Parliament, while it is in session, for a total period of thirty days which may be comprised in one session or in two or more successive sessions, and if, before the expiry of the session immediately following the session or the successive sessions aforesaid, both Houses agree in making any modification in the rule or both Houses agree that the rule should not be made, the rule shall thereafter have effect only in such modified form or be of no effect, as the case may be; so, however, that any such modification or annulment shall be without prejudice to the validity of anything previously done under that rule.

(2) Every rule made under this Act by a State Government shall be laid, as soon as may be after it is notified, before the State Legislature.

30. Power to remove difficulties.—(*1*) If any difficulty arises in giving effect to the provisions of this Act, the Central Government may, by order published in the Official Gazette, make such provisions not inconsistent with the provisions of this Act as appear to it to be necessary or expedient for removal of the difficulty:

Provided that no such order shall be made after the expiry of a period of two years from the date of the commencement of this Act.

(2) Every order made under this section shall, as soon as may be after it is made, be laid before each House of Parliament.

31. Repeal .—The Freedom of Information Act, 2002 is hereby repealed.

THE FIRST SCHEDULE
[*See* Sections 13(3) and 16(3)]

Form of oath or affirmation to be made by the Chief Information Commissioner/the Information Commissioner/the State Chief Information Commissioner/the State Information Commissioner:

> "I, ..., having been appointed Chief Information Commissioner/Information Commissioner/State Chief Information Commissioner/State Information Commissioner swear in the name of God
>
> solemnly affirm
>
> that I will bear true faith and allegiance to the Constitution of India as by law established, that I will uphold the sovereignty and integrity of India, that I will duly and faithfully and to the best of my ability, knowledge and judgment perform the duties of my office without fear or favour, affection or ill-will and that I will uphold the Constitution and the laws.."

THE SECOND SCHEDULE
(*See* Section 24)

Intelligence and security organisation established by the Central Government

1. Intelligence Bureau.
2. Research and Analysis Wing of the Cabinet Secretariat.
3. Directorate of Revenue Intelligence.
4. Central Economic Intelligence Bureau.
5. Directorate of Enforcement.
6. Narcotics Control Bureau.
7. Aviation Research Centre.
8. Special Frontier Force.
9. Border Security Force.
10. Central Reserve Police Force.
11. Indo-Tibetan Border Police.
12. Central Industrial Security Force.

13. National Security Guards.
14. Assam Rifles.
15. Special Service Bureau
16. Special Branch (CID), Andaman and Nicobar.
17. The Crime Branch-C.I.D.-CB, Dadra and Nagar Haveli.
18. Special Branch, Lakshadweep Police.

T.K. VISWANATHAN,
Secy. to the Govt. of India.

Printed by the Manager, Government of India Press, Minto Road, New Delhi and Published by the Controller of Publications, Delhi, 2005.
MGIPMRND—1359GI(S3)—22-06-2005.

ANNEXURE B

REPORT OF NATIONAL COMMISSION TO REVIEW THE WORKING OF THE CONSTITUTION, 2002*

**Vide* the Report of NCRWC under the Chairmanship of Justice M.N. Venkatachaliah, dated March 31, 2002. (relevant provisions)

C. FUNDAMENTAL RIGHTS

Background and Approach

Constitutional guarantees for the human rights of our people were one of the persistent demands of our leaders throughout the freedom struggle. By the year 1949, when the Constituent Assembly had completed the drafting of the Fundamental Rights Chapter, it has before it the 'Universal Declaration of Human Rights, 1948.

The International Covenant on Civil and Political Rights, 1966 (ICCPR) broadly referred to the inherent right to life and liberty and the right against arbitrary deprivation of those rights and its various aspects (Articles 6 to 14); privacy, family, etc. (Article 17); freedom of conscience and religion (Article 18); freedom of expression and information (Article 19); Right of peaceful assembly (Article 21); freedom of association (Article 22); rights of minorities (Article 27);, etc. The International Covenant on Economic, Social and Cultural Rights, 1966 (ICESCR) broadly referred to the "right to work" and its various aspects (Articles 6 and 7); right to form trade unions for promotion of economic or social interests and the right to strike (Article 8); right to social security and social insurance (Article 9); family, marriage, children and mothers' rights (Article 10); adequate standard of living, right to food, clothing and housing, freedom from hunger (Article 11); physical and mental health (Article 12); education

(Article 13); compulsory primary education (Article 14) and cultural (Article 15). The treaty obligations under the covenant enjoined the State Parties to ensure these rights without discrimination and "to take steps" to promote them "to the maximum of its available resources", with a view to achieving "progressively" the full realizations of these rights. The Directive Principles of State Policy in Part IV of the Constitution are indeed the precursor to economic, social and cultural rights specified in the ICESCR.

During the last three decades, a vast number of human rights have found place in new constitutions and bills of rights of more than eighty countries and of supra-national entities. Countries which enacted these new constitutions have had the benefit of all the developments in the human rights jurisprudence which have taken place since 1950. Also, our Supreme Court has by judicial interpretation expanded the scope of the fundamental rights, particularly in relation to Article 21, and this has included more civil and political rights which were not explicit in Part III.

A new development is that of the principle of 'basic structure' of the Constitution enunciated by the Supreme Court in 1973 in *Kesavananda Bharati* v. *State of Kerala*. As to what are these basic features, the debate still continues. The Supreme Court has also held that the scope of certain fundamental rights could be adjudged by reading into them or reading them not only in the light of the Directive Principles of State Policy but also international covenants of conventions which were in harmony with the Fundamental Rights.

The Commission feels that after fifty years, time in ripe to review and enlarge suitably the contents of some of the Fundamental Rights, particularly those Fundamental Rights which have been judicially deduced.

Freedom of Press and Freedom of Information

Article 19(1)(a) refers to 'freedom of speech and expression'. It is proposed that the article must expressly include the freedom on the press and other media, the freedom to hold opinion and to seek, receive and impart information and ideas. It is also proposed to amend Article (19)(2) by adding a further restriction on disclosure of information received in confidence except if required in public interest.

The Commission recommends that Article 19(1)(a) and (2) be amended to read as follows:

> "*Art. 19(1)*: All citizens shall have the right—(a) to freedom of speech and expression which shall include the freedom of the press and other media, the freedom to hold opinions and to seek, receive and impart information and ideas."
> *19(2)*: "Nothing in sub-clause (a) of clause (1) shall affect the operation of any existing law, or prevent the State from making any law, in so far as such law imposes reasonable restrictions on the exercise of the right conferred by the said sub-clause in the interests of the sovereignty and integrity of India, the security of the State, friendly relations with foreign States, public order, decency or morality, or in relation to contempt of court, defamation or incitement to an offence, or preventing the disclosure of information received in confidence except when required in public interest."

A mere legislation by the Parliament by amending the Contempt of Courts Act, 1971 alone may not suffice because the power of the Supreme Court and the High Courts to punish for contempt is recognized in the Constitution. Therefore, the Commission recommends that an appropriate proviso to Article 19(2) of the Constitution may be added as under:

"Provided that, in matters of contempt, it shall be open to the Court to permit a defence of justification by truth on satisfaction as to the bonafides of the plea and it being in public interest."

Right to Privacy

The Supreme Court has included:

'Right to Privacy' in the Right to 'Life' under Article 21.

It is, therefore, proposed that a new article, namely, Article 21-B, should be inserted on the following lines:

"*21-B.* (1) Every person has a right to respect for his private and family life, his home and his correspondence.

(2) Nothing in clause (1) shall prevent the State from making any law imposing reasonable restrictions on the exercise of the right conferred by clause (1), in the interests of security of the State, public safety or for the prevention of disorder or crime, or for the protection of health or morals, or for the protection of the rights and freedoms of others.

Justiciability and Enforceability

The judiciary is not suited, according to several writers to enforce some of the ICESCR rights, where the resources of the nation are involved and a question of priority arises, the remedy cannot be judicial. However, the concept here is not "justiciability" at the instance of individuals in courts of law, but the concept is one of "enforceability" which means that the State must "recognize", and "take steps", by adopting "legislative" or other measures for the "full realizations" and "to the maximum of the State's available resources, both "individually and through international assistance and co-operation." These are the words actually used by the ICESCR and have been the subject matter of voluminous literature. These rights are described as "entitlements" of the people and give rise to "obligations", minimum core "obligations" as stated in Para 10 of the General Comment No. 3 of 1990 of the U.N. Committee of Economic, Social and Cultural Rights.

It is felt that an appropriate mechanism must be devised to oblige the State to take action step by step and progressively for the realizations of these rights to the maximum within the resources of the State.

The Commission recommends that the heading of Part IV of the Constitution should be amended to read as "DIRECTIVE PRINCIPLES OF STATE POLICY AND ACTION."

The Right to Information

Major assumption behind a new style of governance is the citizen's access to information. Much of the common man's distress and helplessness could be traced to his lack of access to information and lack of knowledge of decision-making processes. He remains ignorant and unaware of the processes which vitally affect his interest. Government procedures and regulations shrouded in a veil of secrecy do not allow the clients to know their cases are being handled. They shy away from questioning officers handing their cases because of the latter's snobbish attitude and bow-wow style. Right to Information should be guaranteed and needs to be given real substance. In this regard, government must assume a major responsibility and mobilize skills to ensure flow of information to citizens. The traditional insistence on secrecy should be discarded. In fact, we should have an oath of transparency in place of an oath of secrecy. Administration should become transparent and participatory. Right to Information can usher in many benefits, such as speedy disposal of cases, minimizing manipulative and dilatory tactics of the babudom, and, last but most importantly, putting a considerable check on graft and corruption.

Freedom of Information Bill, 2000

The object of the Freedom of Information Bill, 2000 now pending before Parliament is to promote transparency in government activity. The public has a right to know what decisions are being taken and why. Dissemination of information about policies and actions in the public realm leads to a more accountable government. This deserves full support. The Commission recommends that the Union Government should take steps to move the Parliament for early enactment of the Freedom of Information Legislation. It will be a major step forward in strengthening the values of a free and democratic society.

FUNDAMENTAL RIGHTS, DIRECTIVE PRINCIPLES AND FUNDAMENTAL DUTIES

Fundamental Rights

(1) In Article 12 of the Constitution, the following Explanation should be added:—

'*Explanation.*—In this Article, the expression "other authorities" shall include any person in relation to such of its functions which are of a public nature. [Para 3.5]

* * * * * *

(3) Article 19(1)(a) and (2) should be amended to read as follows:

"*Art. 19(1)*: All citizens shall have the right—

(a) to freedom of speech and expression which shall include the freedom of the press and other media, the freedom to hold opinions and to seek, receive and impart information and ideas."

19(2): "Nothing is sub-clause (a) of clause (1) shall affect the operation of any existing law, or prevent the State from making any law, in so far as such law imposes reasonable restrictions on the exercise of the right conferred by the said sub-clause in the interests of the sovereignty and intergrity of India, the security of the State, friendly relations with foreign States, public order, decency or morality, or in relation to contempt of court, defamation or incitement to an offence, or in relation to contempt of court, defamation or incitement to an offence, or preventing the disclosure of information received in confidence except when required in public interest." [Para 3.8.1]

* * * * * *

(8) A new article, namely Article 21-B, should be inserted on the following lines:

"21-B. (1) Every person has a right to respect for his private and family life, his home and his correspondence.

* * * * * *

179TH REPORT OF LAW COMMISSION OF INDIA ON PUBLIC INTEREST DISCLOSURE AND PROTECTION OF INFORMER, 2001*

(RELEVANT PROVISIONS)

* * * * * *

FREEDOM OF SPEECH, RIGHT TO KNOW AND RIGHT TO PRIVACY

Before discussing the proposals for a Bill enabling public servants to provide information about corruption or mal-administration in their department, it is necessary to refer to the Constitutional provisions relating to Freedom of Speech, Right to Know and the Right to Privacy.

Freedom of speech and expression is guaranteed by sub-clause (a) of Article 19(1) of the Constitution of India. This right is, however, subject to Article 19(2) which permits law to be made for the purpose of imposing reasonable restrictions in the interest of the sovereignty and integrity of India, the security of State, friendly relations with foreign States, public order, decency or morality or in relation to contempt of court, defamation or incitement to an offence.

In this context, we may point out that Art. 19(a) of the Universal Declaration of Human Rights and Art. 19(2) of the Covenant of Civil and Political Rights and Art. 10 of the European Convention of Human Rights and Fundamental Freedoms expressly refer to the:

> "freedom to seek, receive and impart information and ideas of all kinds, regardless of frontiers, either orally, in writing or in print, in the form of art, or through any other media of his choice"

and this right is, however, subject to restrictions that may be imposed by law, (a) for respecting the rights or reputations of others or (b) for the protection of national security or of public order or of public health and morals.

The First Amendment to the American Constitution also refers to the Right of Free Speech. The American Supreme Court has held in one of the most celebrated judgments in *New York Times* v. *Sullivan*, (1964) 376 US 254 that the 'central meaning' of the First Amendment was the:

> "profound national commitment to the principle that debate on public issues should be uninhibited, robust and wide open and that it may well include vehement, caustic and sometimes unpleasantly sharp attacks on government and public servants."

The above case involved the right of the public official to seek damages for libel and the court held:

> "The constitutional guarantees require ..... a federal rule that prohibits a public official from recovering damages for

a defamatory falsehood relating to his official conduct unless he proves that the statement was made with 'actual malice'—that is, with knowledge that it was false or with reckless regard of whether it was false or not."

The word 'Public official' would include an elected representative, an appointed official and all governmental employees, even those located near the bottom of any organization provided they are government officials 'who have or appear to have substantial responsibility or control the conduct of governmental affairs'. *Rosenblatt* v. *Baer*, (1966) 383 US 75. In principle, not every person in government is a 'public official'. His position must be one which could invite the public scrutiny and discussion occasioned by the particular charges in controversy. Again, in relation to what is 'official conduct' of the public servant, the law has been laid down expansively. In *Garrison* v. *Louisiane*, (1954) 379 US 64, the Supreme Court held that allegations of 'laziness, inefficiency and obstruction directed against local criminal court judges were relevant to official conduct such judges'. Allegations could be 'anything which might touch on an official's fitness for office' and they would be relevant.

Our Supreme Court had occasion to deal with the exposure of the conduct of government through the media or otherwise. In one of the earliest cases in *S. Rangarajan* v. *P. Jagjivan Ram*, 1989 (2) SCC 574, the Supreme Court held that criticism of government policies was not prohibited though there should be a proper balance between freedom of expression and social interests. But courts cannot simply balance the two interests as if they are of equal weight. The Court's commitment to freedom of expression demands that it cannot be suppressed unless the situations created by allowing the freedom are pressing and the community interest will be endangered. The anticipated damage should not be remote, or conjectural or farfetched. It should have proximate and have a direct nexus with the expression.

In *Life Insurance Corporation* v. *Manubhai D. Shah*, (1992) 3 SCC 637, the Supreme Court held that there is nothing wrong in requesting the publication of the respondent's rejoinder in the Life Insurance Corporation's (LIC) inhouse journal though the rejoinder referred to the discriminatory practices of the

Corporation which were adversely affecting the interests of a large number of policy-holders. This was because; the statute required the Corporation to function in the best interests of the community. The Court observed that the 'community is, therefore, entitled to know whether or not this requirement of the statute is being satisfied in the functioning of the LIC. The LIC was bound to publish the rejoinder of the organization be it, in its inhouse journal, so that the readers who read the magazine obtained a complete picture of the corporation and not a one sided one. The LIC's refusal to publish the rejoinder was therefore violative of the right of the community to know the internal functioning of the Corporation.

The legal foundation for exposure of corruption, misconduct or maladministration by public servant was laid down by the Supreme Court in *R. Rajagopal* v. *State of Tamil Nadu*, (1994) 6 SCC 632. The case involved the publication of serious misconduct of public servants by a convict who was serialkiller. The case squarely deals with the right to know and the limits of privacy of public servants. The Supreme Court referred to the judgments of the American Court in *New York Times* v. *Sullivan*, already referred to and another judgment of the House of Lords in England reported in *Derbyshire* v. *Times Newspaper Ltd.*, 1993 (2) WLR 449. The Supreme Court held that while decency and defamation were two of the grounds referred to in Clause (2) of Art. 19, still any publication against any person will not be objectionable if such publication was based on 'public record'. In addition, in the case of 'public official', the right to privacy or for the matter, the remedy of action for damages is simply not available with respect to their acts and conduct relevant to the discharge of their official duties. This is so even where the publication is based upon facts and statements which are not true, unless the public official establishes that the publication was made with reckless disregard for truth. In such a case, it would, however, be enough for the person who published the news to prove that he reacted after a reasonable verification of the facts. It is not necessary for him to prove that what he has published is true. Of course, where the publication is proved to be false and actuated by malice or personal animosity, the public official enjoys the same protection in respect of his privacy as any other citizen (The judiciary and Parliament and legislatures are not subject to these principles and enjoy greater immunity). The above principle does not, however, mean that the press is not bound by the Official Secrets Act, 1923 or any similar enactment.

The above declaration of law by the Supreme Court is of fundamental importance on the subject of exposure of corrupt officials. If the law permits furnishing of information regarding corruption, past, present or impending and gives protection to the information from reprisals, unless the disclosure is proved to be malicious, such a law can play a very useful role.

Recently, the Supreme Court has traced the origins of the community's 'right to know' from his right to freedom of speech and expression. The Court observed in *Dinesh Trivedi* v. *Union of India*, 1997 (4) SCC 306 that in modern constitutional democracies, it is axiomatic that citizens have a right to know about the affairs of the government which, having been elected by them, seeks to formulate sound policies of government which, having been elected by them, seeks to formulate sound policies fo governance aimed at their welfare. To ensure that the continued participation of the people in the democratic process, he must be kept informed of the vital decisions taken by the government and the basis thereof. The Court was dealing with the Vohra Committee Report and stated that though it was not advisable to make public the basis on which certain conclusions were arrived at in the Report, the conclusion reached in the Report should be examined by a new body or institution or a special committee to be appointed by the President of India on the advice of the Prime Minister and after consideration with the Speaker of the Lok Sabha.

It is therefore clear that the Supreme Court has accepted that the right to know is part of the fundamental right of freedom of speech and expression guaranteed under Art. 19(1)(a). Of course, it will be subject to the reasonable restrictions, as may be imposed by law under Article 19(2).

It is now recognized that while a public servant may be subject to a duty of confidentiality, this duty does not extend to remaining silent regarding corruption of other public servants. Society is entitled to know and public interest is better served more if corruption or maladministration is exposed. The Whistleblower laws are based upon this principle.

In the light of the above judgment of the American and English Courts and our Supreme Court, on the question as to the scope of 'free speech', the Commission is of the view that a statute enabling complaints to be made by public servants, or persons or NGO's against other public servants and the grant of protection to such complainants is perfectly valid and will not offend the right to privacy emanating from sub-clause (a) of clause (1) of Art. 19. The right to privacy has to be adequately balanced against the right to know. Both these rights emanate from same sub-clause in Art. 19.

THE PUBLIC INTEREST DISCLOSURE (PROTECTION OF INFORMERS) BILL, 2002*

A Bill to encourage disclosure of information relating to the conduct of any public servant involving the commission of any offence under the Prevention of Corruption Act, 1988 or any other law for the time being in force, abuse of official position or maladministration, to protect the persons making such disclosures and for matters connected therewith or incidental thereto.

Be it enacted in Parliament in the Fifty-third Year of Republic of India as follows:

1. Short title and extent.—(1) This Act may be called as the Public Interest Disclosure (Protection of Informers) Act, 2002.

(2) It extends to the whole of India and applies also to public servants outside India.

2. Definitions.—In this Act unless the context otherwise requires—

(a) "action" means action taken by way decision, recommendation or finding or any other proceeding and includes to act and all other expressions connoting action or act shall be construed accordingly;

(b) "Competent Authority" in relation to,—

(i) a Minister, means any Authority notified by the President in this behalf;

(ii) any other public servant, means the Central Vigilance Commission constituted under the Central Vigilance Commission Ordinance, 1999 which ceased to operate, and continued under the Government of India in the Ministry of Personnel, Public Grievances and Pensions

(Department of Personal and Training) Resolution No. 371/20/99-AVD-III dated the 4th April, 1999;

(c) "disclosure" means a disclosure of information that the person making the disclosure reasonably believes, that it tends to show discussable conduct;

(d) "discussible conduct" means such conduct as a public servant may engage in or has engaged or is engaging, or proposes to engage in, which amounts to,—

(i) abuse or misuse of power or discretion vested in him; or

(ii) an attempt to commit or the commission of an offence under the Prevention of Corruption Act, 1988, the Indian Penal Code, 1860 or any other law for the time being in force; or

(iii) mal-administration;

(e) "mal-administration" includes any action taken or purporting to have been taken or being taken or proposed to be taken in the exercise of administrative or statutory power or discretion,—

(i) where such action is unreasonable, unjust, oppressive or discriminatory;

(ii) where there has been negligence or undue delay in taking such action;

(iii) where there has been reckless, excessive or unauthorized use of power in taking such action;

(iv) where such action amounts to breach of trust;

(v) where such action involves the conduct of a public servant which would result in wastage of public funds or causes loss or prejudice to the State or is prejudicial to public interest in any manner; or

(vi) where such action is outside the authority of law or amounts to violation of systems and procedures.

(f) "Minister" means a member of the Council of the Ministers for the Union and includes the Minister of State and Deputy Minister but does not include the Prime Minister;

(g) "prescribed" means prescribed by rules made under this Act;

(h) "public servant" denotes a person falling under any of the descriptions hereinafter following, namely:

(i) every Minister;

(ii) every officer who is appointed to a public service or post in connection with the affairs of the Union;

(iii) every person in the service or pay of,—

(A) any local authority in any Union territory, (which is notified by the Central Government in this behalf in the Official Gazette);

(B) any corporation (not being a local authority) established by or under a Central Act and owned or controlled by the Central Government;

(C) any Government company within the meaning of section 617 of the Companies Act, 1956, in which not less than fifty-one per cent of the paid up share capital is held by the Central Government, or any company which is a subsidiary of a company in which not less than fifty-one per cent of the paid up share capital is held by the Central Government.

(D) any cooperative society receiving any financial aid from the Central Government; or

(E) any society registered under the Societies Registration Act, 1860, which is subject to the control of the Central Government and which is notified by that Government in this behalf in the Official Gazette;

(i) "victimisation" with all its grammatical variations, in relation to a public servant other than a Minister, shall include—

(A) suspension pending inquiry, transfer, dilution or withdrawal of duties, powers and responsibilities, recording adverse entries in the service records, issue of memos, verbal abuse, all classes of major or minor punishment specified in the disciplinary rules, orders or regulations applicable to such public servant and such other type of harassment;

(B) any of the acts referred to in sub-clause (A) whether committed by the person against whom a disclosure is made or by any other person or public authority at his instance.

3. Requirements of a Public Interest Disclosure.—(1) Any disclosure of information revealing a discussable conduct shall be a public interest disclosure for the purposes of this Act.

(2) Notwithstanding anything contained in the Official Secrets Act, 1923, any public servant other than those referred to clauses (a) to (d) of Article 33 of the Constitution or any other person including any non-governmental organization, may make a public interest disclosure to the Competent Authority.

(3) Every disclosure shall be made in good faith and the person making it shall solemnly affirm that he reasonably believes that the information disclosed and any allegation contained therein is substantially true.

(4) Every disclosure shall be in writing and shall contain as full particulars as possible and shall be accompanied by supporting documents or other material.

(5) The Competent Authority may, if it deems fit call for further information or particulars form the person making the disclosure.

(6) The Competent Authority shall not entertain a disclosure under sub-section (1) unless the indemnity of the person making it is disclosed in the disclosure.

4. Procedure on receipt of Public Interest Disclosure.—(1) On receipt of a public interest disclosure under section 3, if the Competent Authority considers, after conducting a preliminary inquiry that such disclosure—

(a) is frivolous or vexatious;

(b) is misconceived or lacking in substance;

(c) is trivial; or

(d) has already been dealt with adequately;

it shall dismiss the complaint and inform the person making the disclosure accordingly.

(2) If an issue raised in a disclosure has been determined by a court or tribunal authorized to determine the issue, after consideration of the matters raised in the disclosure, the Competent Authority shall decline to act on the disclosure to the extent that the disclosure seeks to reopen the issue.

(3) If the Competent Authority is of the opinion that the disclosure should be inquired into then it shall proceed in accordance with the provisions of section 5, to inquire into the facts and allegations contained in the disclosure.

5. Procedure of Inquiry.—(1) Where the Competent Authority proposes to conduct an inquiry under sub-section (3) of section 4, it—

(a) shall forward a copy of the disclosure along with relevant documents and material, if any, to the public servant concerned and to his superior in the official hierarchy;

(b) shall afford to the public servant concerned an opportunity to offer his comments upon the disclosure and the accompanying documents and material, if any; and

(c) may make such orders as to the safe custody of documents and material relevant to the inquiry, as it deems fit.

(2) The inquiry by the Contempt Authority shall not be open to public and the name of the public servant making the disclosure and the public servant named in the disclosure shall not be disclosed to the public.

(3) The name of the person making the disclosure shall be disclosed to the public servant:

Provided that if the person making the disclosure requests that his identity should not be disclosed to the public servant named in the disclosure, and if the Competent Authority is satisfied that such a request may be acceded to in public interest or the safety of such person, it shall make necessary directions in that behalf after recording its reasons.

(4) The Competent Authority shall be bound by the

principles of natural justice and subject to the other provisions of this Act, the Competent Authority shall have the power to regulate its own procedure including the fixing of places and times of its inquiry.

(5) If, after conducting an inquiry, the Competent Authority is of the opinion that—

(a) the facts and allegations contained in the disclosure are frivolous or vexatious or are not made in good faith, or

(b) there are no sufficient grounds for proceeding with the inquiry, it shall close the inquiry and inform the concerned persons, the reasons for its opinion.

(6) If after conducting such inquiry, the Competent Authority is of the opinion that discussible conduct is established against a public servant,—

(a) it shall, if such public servant is other than a Minister, record the appropriate findings and send its findings along with the relevant records, to the Authority competent to take disciplinary action against the public servant; and

(b) it shall, if such public servant is a Minister, record the appropriate findings and send its findings along with the relevant records, to the Prime Minister.

(7) The authorities referred to in clause (a) of sub-section (6), as the case may be, shall upon receipt of the findings under that sub-section, take appropriate action immediately against the person named in its findings.

(8) If the inquiry held by the Competent Authority discloses conduct, which constitutes an offence punishable under any law, the Competent Authority shall direct the appropriate authority or agency to initiate criminal proceedings against such public servant including a Minister in accordance with law:

Provided that where such a direction is made, any requirement of sanction or prior approval for such prosecution under any law for the time being in force, shall not be necessary to be complied with.

(9) The conduct of an inquiry under this Act in respect of any action shall not affect such action, or any power or duty of any public servant to take further action with respect to any matter subject to the inquiry, in accordance with any law for the time being in force.

6. Matters not subject to inquiry by Competent Authority.—(1) The Competent Authority shall not entertain or inquire into any disclosure—

(a) in respect of which a formal and public inquiry has been ordered under the Public Servants Inquiries Act, 1850, or

(b) in respect of a matter which has been referred for inquiry under the Commission of Inquiry Act, 1952.

(2) The Competent Authority shall not investigate,-

(a) any disclosure which is made after the expiry of twelve months from the date on which the action complained against becomes known to the complainant; and

(b) any disclosure involving an allegation, if the complaint is made after the expiry of five years from the date on which the action complained against is alleged to have place:

Provided that the Competent Authority may entertain a disclosure referred to in clause (a), if the person making it satisfies him that he had sufficient cause for not making the disclosure within the period specified in this clause.

(3) Subject to the provisions of sub-section (2) the provisions of this Act shall apply to all discussable conduct committed before the commencement of this Act.

(4) Nothing in this Act shall be construed as empowering the Competent Authority to question, in any inquiry under this Act, any administrative or statutory action taken in the exercise of a discretion except where it is satisfied that the discretion is so exercised because of the discussible conduct.

7. Powers of the Competent Authority.—(1) Without prejudice to the powers conferred on the Competent Authority under any other law for the time being in force, the Competent Authority or any person or agency authorized by it in writing, for the purpose of any inquiry (including preliminary inquiry, if any, before such inquiry) under this Act, may require any public servant or any other person who in its opinion will be able to furnish information or produce documents relevant to the inquiry, to furnish any such information or produce any such document.

(2) For the purpose of any such inquiry (including the preliminary inquiry), the Competent Authority or any person or agency authorized by it in writing shall have all the powers of a civil court while trying a suit under the Code of Civil Procedure, 1908, in respect of the following matters, namely:-

(a) summoning and enforcing the attendance of any person and examining him on oath;
(b) requiring the discovery and production of any documents;
(c) receiving evidence on affidavits;
(d) requisitioning any public record or copy thereof from any Court or office;
(e) issuing commissions for the examination of witnesses or documents; and
(f) such other matters as may be prescribed.

(3) All proceedings before the Competent Authority or any person or agency authorized by it in writing shall be deemed to be judicial proceedings within the meaning of section 193 of the Indian Penal Code.

(4) Subject to the provisions of sub-section (5), no obligation to maintain secrecy or other restriction upon the disclosure of information obtained by or furnished to Government or any public servant, whether imposed by the Official Secrets Act, 1923 or any other enactment or by any rule of law, shall be claimed by any public servant in the proceedings before the Competent Authority or any person or agency authorized by it in writing and the Government or any public servant shall not be entitled in relation to any such inquiry, to any such privilege in respect to the production of documents or the giving of evidence as in allowed by any enactment or by any rule of law in legal proceedings.

(5) No person shall be required or be authorized by virtue

of this Act to furnish any such information or answer any such question or produce so much of any document—

(a) as might prejudice the security or defence or international relations of India (including India's relations with the Government of any other country or with any international organization), or the ongoing investigation or crime; or

(b) as might involve the disclosure of proceedings of the Cabinet of the Union Government or any Committee of that Cabinet;

and for the purpose of this sub-section a certificate issued by a Secretary to the Government of India certifying that any information, answer or portion of a document is of the nature specified in clause (a) or clause (b), shall be binding and conclusive.

(6) Subject to the provisions of sub-section (4), no person shall be compelled for the purposes of inquiry under this Act to give any evidence or produce any document which he could not be compelled to give or produce in proceedings before a Court.

8. Report on disclosures.—(1) Every Competent Authority shall prepare annually a consolidated annual report of the performance of its activities in such form as may be prescribed and forward it to the President.

(2) On receipt of the annual report under sub-section (1), the President shall cause a copy thereof together with an explanatory memorandum to be laid before each House of Parliament.

9. Time limit for completion of inquiry.—(1) The Competent Authority shall hold every such inquiry as expeditiously as possible and in any case complete the inquiry within a period of six months from the date of the receipt of the complaint:

Provided that if the Competent Authority is of opinion that the inquiry cannot be completed before the said period, it may, for reasons to be recorded in writing, extend the said period and in on case the said period shall be extended beyond a period of two years from the date of receipt of the complaint.

(2) Nothing contained in sub-section (1) shall operate as a

bar against initiating or continuance of any action or proceeding under any other law for the time being in force against the public servant named in the complaint.

10. Safeguards against victimization.—(1) The Central Government shall ensure that no person who has made a disclosure under this Act is victimized by initiation of any proceedings or otherwise merely on the ground that such person had made a disclosure under this Act.

(2) If any person other than the Minister, is aggrieved by any action on the ground that he is being victimized due to the fact that he had filed a complaint under section 3, he may file an application before the Competent Authority seeking redress in the matter.

(3) On receipt of an application under sub-section (2), the Competent Authority may, after making such inquiry as it deems fit, is of opinion that allegation of victimization—

(a) is true and is relatable to the complaint or its subject matter, it may give appropriate directions as it may consider necessary, to the concerned public servant or public authority as the case may be, and

(b) is not true or is not maintainable for the reason that the alleged victimisation is not relatable to the complaint or its subject-matter, it may dismiss the application.

(4) Notwithstanding anything contained in any other law for the time being in force, the power to give directions under sub-section (3), in relation to a public servant, shall include the power to direct the restoration of the public servant making the disclosure, to the *status quo ante*.

(5) The Competent Authority issuing directions under sub-section (3), shall take such action as is necessary and reasonable to prevent the victimization continuing or occurring in the future.

(6) Every direction given by the Competent Authority shall be binding upon the public servant or the public authority against whom the allegation of victimization has been proved.

11. Transfer of Public Servant for avoiding victimization.—(1) The public servant making a disclosure may, during or at the conclusion of the inquiry, apply to the Competent

Authority for transfer from the Office or Department in which he is currently posted to another Office or Department.

(2) The Competent Authority on receipt of an application under sub-section (1) shall, if it is satisfied that the applicant has been victimized or is likely to be victimized because of the disclosure, direct the appropriate authority, even if the inquiry has not resulted in any finding against the public servant, to transfer the regard to the application to another Office or Department, if such transfer is feasible having regard to the qualification and experience of the applicant and the availability of an equivalent post.

12. Protection of witnesses and other persons.—The Competent Authority may pass such orders granting adequate protection to the witnesses and other person assisting the inquiry as may be necessary in the circumstances of the case

13. Power to pass interim orders.— During the pendency of the inquiry and at any time after the first disclosure of the discussable conduct, the Competent Authority may pass such interim orders as it may deem fit, to prevent victimization of the public servant making the disclosure or to prevent the discussible conduct continuing or occurring in the future.

14. Burden of proof in certain cases.—Where the Competent Authority conducts inquiry into an application under sub-section (3) of section 10, the burden of proving such action or proceeding which is the subject of victimization would have been taken even if no disclosure had been made by the applicant, shall be upon such public servant or public authority against whom allegation of victimization has been made.

15. Protection of action taken in good faith.—No suit, prosecution or other legal proceedings shall lie against the Competent Authority or against any officer, employee, agency or person acting on its behalf, in respect of anything which is in good faith done or intended to be done under this Act.

16. Punishment for False or Frivolous Disclosures.—Any person who makes any disclosure which was false to his knowledge or reckless or malicious, shall be punishable with imprisonment for a term which may extent up to three years and also to fine which may extend up to fifty thousand rupees.

17. Power to make rules.—(1) The President may, by notification in the Official Gazette, make rules for the purpose of carrying out the provisions of this Act.

(2) Every rule made under this Act shall be laid, as soon as may be after it is made, before each House of Parliament, while it is in session, for a total period of thirty days which may be comprised in one session or in two or more successive sessions, and if, before the expiry of the session immediately following the session or the successive sessions aforesaid, both Houses agree in making any modification in the rule, or both Houses agree that the rule should not be made, the rule shall thereafter have effect only in such modified form or be of no effect, as the case may be; so, however, that any such modification or annulment shall be without prejudice to the validity of anything previously done under that rule.

GUIDELINES ON THE RIGHT TO KNOW PROMOTING OPEN GOVERNMENT COMMONWEALTH PRINCIPLES*

I. Introduction

The Commonwealth Law Ministers at their meeting in Barbados in 1980 emphasized the "public participation in the democratic and governmental process was at its most meaningful when citizens had adequate access to official information."

Since that time a number of Commonwealth countries have enacted freedom of information legislation establishing a public right of access to government information. Their experience had demonstrated that these laws enhance the effectiveness of government. Other Commonwealth countries are preparing legislation drawing on this rich piratical experience.

During the 1990s the Commonwealth, guided by its Fundamental Political Values enshrined in the 1991 Harare Commonwealth Declaration, has sought to promote democracy, the rule of law, just and honest government and fundamental human rights. In consolidating the achievements of the past decade the Commonwealth seeks to focus its efforts on strengthening the processes of open and accountable government together with the promotion of sustainable development.

The 1990s has been a decade of democratization with a number of countries, many within the Commonwealth making the transition from one party and authoritarian regimes to elected representative governments.

The new millennium promises to be an era for transparency

and educatability on the part of government and all sectors of society concerned with public life. These trends will be further stimulated by the growth of information technology and increased globalization and inter-dependency of national economies.

II. Benefits of Freedom of Information

Freedom of information has may benefit. It facilitates public participation in public affairs by providing access to relevant information to the people who are then empowered to make informer choices and better exercise their democratic rights. It enhances the accountability of government improves decision-making, provides better information to elected representatives, enhances government credibility with its citizens, and provides powerful aid in the fight against corruption. It is also a key livelihood and development issues, especially in situations of poverty and powerlessness.

Following a review of the successful experience of Commonwealth freedom of information laws, the Expert Group on the Right to Know submits for the consideration and endorsement of Commonwealth Law Ministers, at their forthcoming meeting in Trinidad from 3-7 May, 1999, the following Principles and Guidelines on the Right to Know. The Group further recommends that the Law Ministers submit the Principles and Guidelines to the Commonwealth Heads of Governments at their submit in South Africa from 12-15 November, 1999 for their consideration and adoption.

III. Principles

- Freedom of information should be guaranteed as a legal and enforceable right permitting every individual to obtain records and information held by the executive, the legislative and the judicial arms of the state, as well as any government owned corporation and any other body carrying out public functions.
- The legislation should contain a presumption in favour of maximum public functions.
- The right of access may be subject to only such exemptions, which are narrowly drawn, permitting

government to withhold information only when disclosure would harm essential interests such as national defence and security, law enforcement, individual privacy or commercial confidentiality, provided that withholding the information is not against public interest.

- Decisions under the legislation should be subject to independent review capable of ensuring compliance.

IV. Guidelines

- Governments should enact freedom of information legislation containing appropriate administrative measures for its implementation.
- Government should permit any individual to obtain information promptly and at law or to cost.
- Legislation should provide for an independent review of decisions capable of providing an effective remedy in any case of delay or denial.
- Government should maintain and preserve records.
- Government should promote a culture of openness, publicly disseminating information related to the exercise of their functions and the information held by them.

V. The Role of Commonwealth

The Commonwealth through its various institutions should take steps to promote these principles and report periodically on their progress in this regard. The Secretariat should report to the Commonwealth Law Ministers about the progress achieved at their meting in 2002.

In particular, the Commonwealth Secretariat should facilitate and assist government in promoting these principles through technical and other assistance including measures to promote the sharing of experience between member-states and the involvement of civil society in this process.

Commonwealth associations and organizations are encouraged to consider ways in which they can contribute to this process.

ANNEXURE C

THE OFFICIAL SECRETS ACT, 1923

[19 of 1923, dt. 2-4-1923]

An Act to consolidate and amend the law relating to official secrets

WHEREAS it is expedient that the law relating to official secrets should be consolidated and amended; it is hereby enacted as follows:

1. Short title, extent and application

(1) This Act may be called the Official Secrets Act, 1923.

(2) It extends to the whole of India and applies also to servants of the Government and to citizens of India outside India.

2. Definitions

In this Act, unless there is anything repugnant in the subject or context,

(1) any reference to a place belonging to Government includes a place occupied by any department of the Government, whether the place is or is not actually vested in Government;

(2) expressions referring to communicating or receiving include any communicating or receiving, whether in whole or in part, and whether the sketch, plan, model, article, note, document, or information itself, or the substance, effect or description thereof only be communicated or received; expressions referring to obtaining or retaining any sketch, plan, model, article, note or document, include the copying or causing to be copied of the whole or any part of any sketch, plan, model, article, note or document; and expressions referring to the communication of any sketch, plan, model, article, note or document include the transfer or transmission of any sketch, plan, model, article, note or document;

(3) "document" includes part of a document;

(4) "model" includes design, pattern and specimen;

(5) "munitions of war" includes the whole or any part of any ship, submarine, aircraft, tank or similar engine, arms and ammunition, torpedo, or mine intended or adopted for use in war, and any other article, material or device, whether actual or proposed, intended for such use;

(6) "Office under Government" includes any office or employment in or under an department of the Government 2[***];

(7) "photograph" includes an undeveloped film or plate;

(8) "Prohibited place" means:

(a) any work of defence, arsenal, naval, military or air force establishment or station, mine, minefield, camp, ship or aircraft belonging to, or occupied by or on behalf of Government, any military telegraph or telephone so belonging or occupied, any wireless or signal station or office so belonging or occupied and any factory, dockyard or other place so belonging or occupied and used for the purpose of building, repairing, making or storing any munitions of war, or any sketches, plants, models or documents relating thereto, or for the purpose of getting any metals, oil or minerals of use in time of war;

(b) any place not belonging to Government where any munitions of war or any sketches, models, plans or documents relating thereto, are being made, repaired, gotten or stored under contract with, or with any person on behalf of, Government, or otherwise on behalf of Government;

(c) any place belonging to or used for the purpose of Government which is for the time being declared by the Central Government, by notification in the Official Gazette, to be a prohibited place for the purposes of this Act on the ground that information with respect thereto, or damage thereto, would be useful to an enemy, and to which a copy of the notification in respect thereof has been affixed in English and in the vernacular of the locality;

(d) any railway, road way or channel, or other means of communication by land or water (including any works or structures being part thereof or connected therewith) or any place used for gas, water or electricity works or other works for purposes of a public character, or any place where any munitions of war or any sketches, models, plans or documents relating thereto, are being made, repaired, or stored otherwise than on behalf of Government, which is for the time being declared by the Central Government, by notification in Official Gazette, to be a prohibited place for the purposes of this Act on the ground that information with respect thereto, or the destruction or obstruction thereof, or interference therewith, would be useful to an enemy, and to which a copy of the notification in respect thereof has been affixed in English and in the vernacular of the locality;

(9) "sketch" includes any photograph or other mode of representing any place of thing; and

(10) "Superintendent of Police" includes any police officer of a like or superior rank, and any person upon whom the powers of a Superintendent of Police are for the purposes of this Act conferred by the Central Government.

3. Penalties for spying

(1) If any person for any purpose prejudicial to the safety or interests of the State:

(a) approaches, inspects, passes over or is in the vicinity of, or enters, any prohibited place; or

(b) makes any sketch, plan, model, or note which is calculated to be or might be or is intended to be, directly or indirectly, useful to an enemy; or

(c) obtains, collects, records or publishes or communicates to other person any secret official code or pass word, or any sketch, plan, model, article or note or other document or information which is calculated to be or might be or is intended to be, directly or indirectly, useful to an enemy for which relates to a matter the disclosure of which is likely to affect the sovereignty and integrity of India, the security of the State or friendly relations with foreign States], he shall be punishable with imprisonment for a term which may extend, where the offence is committed in relation to any work of defence, arsenal, naval, military or air force establishment or station, mine, minefield, factory, dockyard, camp, ship or aircraft or otherwise in relation to the naval, military or air force affairs of Government or in relation to any secret official code, to fourteen years and in other cases to three years.

(2) On a prosecution for an offence punishable under this section [1][***] it shall not be necessary to show that the accused person was guilty of any particular act tending to show a purpose prejudicial to the safety or interests of the State, and, notwithstanding that no such act is proved against him, he may be convicted if, from the circumstances of the case or his conduct or his known character as proved, it appears that his purpose was a purpose prejudicial to the safety or interests of the State; and if any sketch, plan, model, article, note, document or information relating to or used in any prohibited place, or relating to anything in such a place, or any secret official code or pass word is made, obtained, collected, recorded, published or communicated by any person other than a person acting under lawful authority, and from the circumstances of the case or his conduct or his known character as proved it appears that his purpose was a purpose prejudicial to the safety or interests of the State, such sketch, plan, model, article, note, document, [2][information, code or pass word shall be presumed to have been made], obtained, collected, recorded, published or communicated for a purpose prejudicial to the safety or interests of the State.

** Substituted by the Act 24 of 1967.

*** Words "or of the Government of the United Kingdom or of any British possession" omitted by Act 24 of 1967.

BIBLIOGRAPHY

BOOKS

A.V. Diecey, Law of Constitution, 10th Ed.

Austin, J., Lectures on Jurisprudence, 5th Ed.

B. Holden, Understanding Liberal Democracy, Oxford, Philip Allan, 1988.

Dr. Madabhu Shi Sridhar, Right to Information 2006.

Fred N. Kerlinger, Foundations of Behavioral Research, 2nd Ed.

G.N. Joshi, The Constitution of India, 7th Ed, 1983

Gary, J.C., The Nature and Sources of the Law, 2nd Ed.

Good Hart, The Rule of Law and absolute sovereignty.

Holland, T.E., The Elements of Jurisprudence, 13th Ed., Oxford 1924.

Hursh Mandar and Abha Joshi, The Right to Information Movement in India (Power People to Control Corruptions) (CHRI), New Delhi, 1998.

I.P. Massey, Administrative Law, 7th Ed.

J. Michel, Freedom of official Information, Vol VI.

Jain and Jain, "Principles of Administrative Law", 4th Ed. 1993.

Karl Pearson, The Grammar of Science, Adam and Charles Black, London, 1911.

Krishna Iyer, Justice V.R., Freedom of Information Prolegomenom, EBC, 1990.

Myneni, S.R., Legal Research Methodology, Allahabad Law Agency.

Nigam, Shalu, Right to Information: Law and Practice.

Olivercrona, K., The Concept of Right according to Hrotious and Pufendorf (1969).

P.V. Kane, History of Dharmashastra, Vol. II.

Patrick Birkinshaw, "Freedom of Information and Openness", Fundamental Human Rights.

Rajeev, Dhawan, Information Law Now: Need for a New Strategy, 2000.

S.N. Jain, Official Secrecy and the Press.

S.P. Sathe, Administrative Law.

S.P. Sathe, 'Tilak's Philosophy of law' in N.R. Inamdar (ed.), Political Thought and Leadership of Lokmanya Tilak.

S.P. Sathe, The Right to Know, 1991.

Shukla, V.N., Constitution of India, EBC, 10th Ed.

Soli Sorabjee, Enforcing the Right to Know *exct juris*, 1986.

U.P.D.. Keshari, Administrative Law, 7th Ed.

Upendra Baxi, Liberty and Corruption—The Antulay Case and Beyond.

W. Keeton, George, The Elementary Principles of Jurisprudence (London, 1929).

William Wade, Administrative Law, 8th Ed.

Wortley, B.A., Jurisprudence Manchester University Press, 1967.

ARTICLES

Dr. K. Chandra Segarm and Dr. Ambedkar, Rule of Law and Right to Information, *Journal of Indian Legal Thought*, Vol. I.

Dr. Minial M. Bapat, Right to Information : Its Scope and Need.

Dr. S.R. Maheshwari, Open Government in India.

Irdell Jenkins, The Concept of Right and the Competence of Courts, 18 AJ (1973).

Justice, A.H. Saikia, The Right to Information Act, 2005: An Instrument to Strengthen Democracy,

Justice Y.K. Sabharwal, Right to Information and Good and Dr. Ambedkar Governance.

Justice R.S. Sarkaria, Right to Information, *Press Council of India Review*, 1993, Vol. 14.

Kejriwal, A., More Stories of Parivartan", *India Together*, April 2003.

Mr. Abhimanyu Ghosh, Open Government and Right to Information.

Mr. Prabha, Importance of Human Right to Information—A Key to Good Governance, In Chapter 27 of the Book, Good Governance in India.

Prashant Bhusan, "Judicial Accountability or Illusion", *EPW Commentary*, November 25, 2006.

Praveen Dalal and Shruti Gupta, Bring Transparency through Electronic Governance (2003), ACE(J).

Prithvis Chakravarti, Freedom of Information, PCIR, Vol. 19, 1889.

P.K. Tripathi, 'Free Speech in the Indian Constitution: Background and Prospect', 67, *Yale Law Journal* (1957-58).

S.N. Shukla, Need for Openness and Transparency, *IJPA*, Vol. XLIV, 1998.

Saxsena, Ambrish, Right to Information and freedom of press, Ist Ed., Good Governance: Need for Openness and Transparency, *IJPA*, Vol. XLIV, 1998.

REPORTS

1. United Nations Development Programme, *Human Development Report*, 1997.
2. *Many Voices, One World,* Report by the International Commission for the Study of Communication Problems, 1980.
3. N.H. Vohra Committee Report.
4. Report of National Commission on working of the Constitution, 2002.
5. Report of the Committee on Panchayati Raj Institution, New Delhi.
6. Law Commission of India's 179th Report.
7. CHRI Report, 2003

NEWSPAPERS/MAGAZINES

1. *Amar Ujala* (Hindi Dainik), 27 November 2009.
2. *The Hindu*, 27 December 2009.
3. *The Hindustan Times*, 3 September 2009.
4. *The Times of India*, 3 September 2009.
5. *Harijan*, 20 July 1941 and 29 January 1946.
6. *Yojana*, January 2006. (Republic Day Special)

WEBSITE/WEB PORTAL

http://www.minbzk.nl./contents/pages/00012478/public_access_government_info_10-91.pdfhttp:/www.bdpressinform.org/rti.htm. Retrieved 2008-10-29.

http://www.humanrightsinitiative.org/programs/ai/rti/india/Comparative%20Table%20-%20Indian%20RTI%20laws.htm.

http/www.tpls.org/services/kusht/contents:html
http://www.uni-wuerzburg.de/law/p100000_html
http://www.wverzvurg.de/Law/SP00000_html.
http://www.uni-wuerzburg.de/law/p100000_html
http://www.parbament.th/Files/Library/bes-b.htm
www.privacyinternational.org/countries/zimbabwe/accessinfo-amend-102
http://www.Australiaedu.au/au/legis/cth/consal act/Foia 1982222/
http://www.CFio.org.vic/Foiact2000html
http://www.ePic.org/opengov/Foia/us_Foia_act, html.
http://www.oppnas verige.gov.SC/page/1/42.html
http://imej.wfu.edu/articles/1999/1/02/demo/golossary/glossaryhtml/efficiency.html
http://www.ebc-india.com) Practicallawyer index.pnp?option =com content and task=view and id=7309
http://www.foi.gov.ky/pls/portal/docs/page/foihomedraftimplementationplan11jan08.p
http://www.UNI-wuerzvurg.de/Law/nzo1000-.html
www.Article 19.org/docimages/116 html
http://www.um.es/siu/marca/30
http://www.bdpressinform.org/rti.htm. Retrieved 2008-10-29.
http://www.ombudsmen.govt-nz/offical.html
http://www.krisdika.go.th/Law/text/lawpub/eo2092 s40/text.htm
http://www.datainspektionen.se/PBF Filer/
http://www.gov.za/gazette/acts/2000/a2-00.PdF.
http://www.dity.org.zo/govdocs/constitution/Saconst.html
www.indiatogather.org/2003
www.transparency.org

INDEX